WORLD WAR I
IN PHOTOGRAPHS

J.H.J. Andriessen

WORLD WAR I
IN PHOTOGRAPHS

REBO
PUBLISHERS

© 2002 Rebo International b.v., Lisse, Netherlands

This 3rd edition reprinted in 2008.

Text: J.H.J. Andriessen
Production: Studio Imago, Amersfoort, Netherlands
Cover design: AdAm Studio, Prague, Czech Republic
Layout: Barbara van Overhagen, Studio Imago, Amersfoort, Netherlands
Typesetting: Astron Studio, Prague, Czech Republic
Translation: Stephen Challacombe, United Kingdom
Pre-press services: Garamond Studio, Prague, Czech Republic

ISBN: 978 90 366 1871 7

CONTENTS

FOREWORD

The appalling battles that took place between 1914 and 1918, originally described as the Great War but later to be known as World War I, were more than eighty years ago and have truly become history.

Why is it that this war is still remembered even after a second and perhaps even more terrible World War II? Interest in the First World War today seems greater than ever and publications dealing with this period are increasingly sought after.

The writing of the history of World War I was dominated for a long time by British historians. Great Britain played a leading role in the conflict and almost every British family mourned the death of a father, son, or member of their family but this was even more the case for the French and the Germans who lost most of a generation on the battlefields.

Both French and German historians did pay attention to this period and many books have been published about the 1914–1918 period. It was the English language texts though that gained the widest world audience and it is entirely understandable that these views of the events of World War II bear a distinctive British stamp.

This arose because of the leading role the English language has acquired with English texts being widely read and understood while German and French has a much smaller audience. Historians consequently often turned to English language source material. This is quite logical since they could more readily understand it and thus their research was simplified. Non British sources were often included in biographies but these were generally in translation rather than the original source.

It was in the 1920s that a number of historians raised doubts about the validity of article 231 of the Treaty of Versailles that identifies Germany as solely responsible for the war. American historians were foremost in this move. Not only did the US Congress refuse to sign the treaty but historians such as Sydney Fay, Barnes, and R. Owen published impressive criticisms of the treaty.

In Germany too there was a flood of facts produced for the government of the Weimar republic and a parliamentary commission was established to examine the question of guilt. This drew on the sworn statements of the main parties involved. There were other publications by French, British, and Dutch writers that added to the revisionist thoughts. The attitude of the time though was not right and efforts to have the treaty revised were counter-productive and hence nothing came of them.

It was not until the 1960s that the topic aroused fresh interest following publication by the German historian Fritz Fischer of *Griff nach der Weltmacht* in which he lay the sole blame on Germany. This provoked a tremendous debate between those on both sides of the argument which continues to the present day.

There has been a careful adjustment of attitudes surrounding the history of World War I in recent years and progress is clearly being made. New insights, availability of new source material, and a more critical examination by a new generation of historians both within the United Kingdom and elsewhere is slowly leading to a rewriting of the history of the First World War. It will probably take a good many more years though before the views of the past can be replaced by a possibly more just vision of the roles of the countries that took part in World War I.

The author has sought to find a place for new viewpoints arising from new source material in *World War I in Photographs*, and to ignore the myths that arose during the twentieth century.

He emphasizes that these sometimes different views of events during World War I and the role of the different governments in no sense brings into question the sacrifice, verve, and bravery of the soldiers at the front of whatever nationality. Quite the contrary, the soldiers of the "Great War" often performed supreme acts of unimaginable heroism, courage, self-sacrifice, persistence, and comradeship that we find impossible to comprehend in this twenty-first century. The author therefore hopes that this collection of photographs might give some insight into the inhuman suffering and slaughter of the front line soldiers of the First World War and that this might lead to new critical interest in the how and the why of the 1914–1918 war with its around thirty million casualties, that robbed an entire generation of young men of their lives and totally changed the world.

Akersloot,
February 2002

J.H.J. Andriessen

ON THE EVE OF THE CONFLICT

The inevitable war

THE FRANCO-PRUSSIAN WAR OF 1870–1871

Misplaced pride, politics, personal ambitions, overconfidence, and an absence of reality were the causes that led to the Franco-Prussian war of 1870–1871, following French opposition to the ambitions of a Prussian prince towards the vacant Spanish throne. France did not wish to see Prussian influence in a neighboring country and demanded of the Prussian king that he should prevent the prince from pursuing his claim. The Prussian king did indeed act and the prince sulkily withdrew. This proved not to be enough for the French. France demanded a guarantee from the Prussian king that a Prussian would never accede to the Spanish throne. This was clearly an impossible demand that the Prussian king could not give into but which led to the French declaring war.

This was a disastrous step since the French army was routed, Emperor Napoleon III was captured and imprisoned, and Paris was occupied by German soldiers. To rub salt into the wounds, the German state was declared in Versailles's Hall of Mirrors and the rich province of Alsace-Lorraine that had been appropriated from Prussia by the French once again became German soil as Elzas-Lotharingen. The state of Germany had been born and it seemed the power of France had been broken for all time.

And yet the seeds of a new war were first germinated at this moment: a war that was to set Europe ablaze and become known as World War I. The French people, shocked and defeated, lost trust in their army that was greatly humiliated and kept a very low profile. It took until 1880 before the French once more took the defense of their land seriously.

The border with Germany in the years that followed was equipped with a fortified line of virtually impenetrable defenses and the military started making plans to reconquer Alsace-Lorraine.

The last meeting of the crowned heads of Europe in 1910 for the funeral of King Edward VII. Pictured (left to right): Hakon (Norway), Ferdinand (Bulgaria), Manuel (Portugal), Wilhelm II (Germany), George (Greece), Albert (Belgium), Alfons XIII (Spain), George V (Great Britain), and Christian (Denmark).

THE IMPERIALISM OF THE GREAT POWERS

FRANCE

The increasingly open desire for revenge coupled with a growing hostility towards Germany among the French was not shared by everyone. Some politicians were of the opinion that a new war with Germany could only have disastrous results. They pointed to the reality that other countries such as the USA, Great Britain, and Russia had not been idle and had amassed great colonial empires. They suggested that France should do likewise as quickly as possible before all the opportunities vanished. They suggested that the only sensible policy was one of colonization. For the time being they got their way, although the French never entirely forgot about revenge.

The people did recognize though that France first needed to attempt to extend is colonies. The opinion generally was that this would make the country more important and hence eventually increase the chances of winning back Alsace-Lorraine. Slowly but surely French foreign policy turned to the acquisition of new colonies and the eye naturally fell upon Africa where large expanses were up for grabs.

THE CONGRESS OF BERLIN REDRAWS THE MAP AGAIN

The first attempts by the French to expand their colonies in Africa was made in 1878, during the famous Congress of Berlin. A large number of countries came together there under the leadership of the German chancellor Bismarck to settle the so-called "Eastern question."

This matter resulted from the Russian-Turkish war of 1877–1878 when Russia defeated Turkey and took possession of large areas of the Turkish empire, sharing them among her friends in the Balkans. This resulted in the Russian satellite state of Greater Bulgaria that extended to the Aegean Sea.

This aroused anxiety in the British who did not wish to see Russian influence in the Mediterranean. Italy was also troubled, while the Austro-Hungarian empire viewed a significant extension of Russian influence in the Balkans with great concern. They demanded a significant change in Russian plans which Russia politely but determinedly refused. Britain and Austria-Hungary now began to rattle their sabers. Bismarck offered mediation and eventually Russia agreed to a conference to resolve the problems arising out of the redistribution of territory won over from the Turks.

Russia did not come out of the meeting with much success. Little remained of Greater Bulgaria with part of it being returned to the Turks. Serbia was also granted

A young Kaiser Wilhelm II of Germany in state uniform.

Sultan Mohammed of Turkey (1844–1918).
Ascended to the throne aged 65 after
imprisonment in his own palace for many years.
He died shortly after the collapse of the central
powers in 1918.

General Kitchener during the Boer war in South
Africa. In 1914 he became Minister of War.

part, which in one stroke doubled the size of the country, and
Romania also gained from the process. Southern Bulgaria was re-
named Rumelia as an autonomous province under the Turkish sultan
but with a Christian governor and its own army. The Austro-
Hungarian empire was charged with the protection of Bosnia-
Herzegovina to the dismay of Serbia which also had its eye on the territory in which many Serbs lived. This was to lead to great problems
in the future. Great Britain took control of Cyprus during the conference against the sultan's will but he was powerless to prevent this
"theft" of his domain as he referred to it.

This was not the final word though because Russia opposed the
fact that the conqueror had come away with virtually nothing.
Britain – generous with other people's land – offered the Russians the
Caucasus in compensation but this led to fresh demands from the
French.

The French suggested that if Britain was to take control of
Cyprus – an area the French regarded as within their sphere of
influence – then France should receive something of equal standing.
Generously, the British once more offered the French the territory of
others – namely Tunisia. The French happily accepted this offer and
hence, provided nobody kicked up a fuss, territory of others was
simply expropriated as gifts to one another and the world was carved
up anew at the Congress of Berlin.

THE FRENCH IN AFRICA EXERCISING COLONIAL POWER

Immediately after the Congress of Berlin Europe appeared to be at peace. The proponents of colonial expansion in France gained support against those in favor of revenge following the Congress of Berlin.

The ripe apple of the Turkish province of Tunisia was now ready to be plucked. The great powers had offered this province to the east of Algeria – that had been occupied by the French in 1830 – to the French on a plate!

Strangely enough though they were uncertain about claiming their prize. It was only after Bismarck – who was eager to award Tunisia to the French to keep their minds off revenge – threatened to support Italian claims to Tunisia that the French got moving. The French finally sent 30,000 soldiers to Tunis on April 28, 1881 on the pretext of supporting the Turkish governor to quickly put down a rebellion on the border, and took over the governance of the country.

The occupation of Tunis was the start of further French expansion in Africa. France would eventually become the second largest colonial power. The French politicians though wanted more and quickly turned their eyes to Egypt and the Nile delta, where they had previously trod under Napoleon. This interest in Egypt though would bring them into conflict with Great Britain which had reserved Egypt for itself.

Edward Grey, British Foreign Secretary

THE DANGEROUS DEVELOPMENT OF FASHODA

The French sent a military mission to the Upper Nile in 1898. The French government was entirely in disagreement with the British occupation of the Sudan after their subjection in 1882 of all of Egypt. The French also had great interest in that part of Africa and were angry with the British occupation of the Sudan without any discussion with the French.

The French military under Capt. Marchand arrived in the small settlement of Fashoda in 1898 and immediately raised the French flag. The British reacted immediately by sending several gunboats up the Nile. The warships arrived there on September 19 and were welcomed by Marchand in best dress uniform. This irritated the

British General Henry Wilson, the driving force behind British-French preparations for war.

Kaiser Wilhelm II (left) and von Moltke (2nd left), German commander in chief, during maneuvers.

later-to-be-famous General Kitchener who led the British expedition and he told Marchand in no uncertain terms to pack his bags and leave, not forgetting to take the French flag with him. Marchand politely but firmly refused and both returned to their lines and asked their governments for advice.

A serious conflict between the two countries now threatened and the French foreign minister, Delcassé, offered to negotiate. The British refused: there was nothing to negotiate about, the French should leave immediately, and they gave an ultimatum. There was a risk of war and the French were forced to choose to withdraw their troops from Fashoda. The relations between these two countries after this were not good but in 1902 the British sought a rapprochement and sent King Edward VIII to Paris on an official visit. This visit marked the beginning of better official relations. A friendly atmosphere was created and eventually the two countries entered into an friendship pact that dealt with trade relations. Later still the new diplomatic links resulted in a secret agreement between the two countries for military cooperation. This was with an eye to at a possible future war with Germany, of which at that time the Germans had not the faintest notion.

EXTENSION OF FRENCH COLONIALIZATION AND THE FALL OF THEIR FOREIGN MINISTER

Meanwhile, the French looked with covetous eyes at further opportunities for expansion in Africa. There was a dream of a great colonial empire stretching from the Atlantic Ocean to Tunisia, with Morocco forming a part. French diplomats now started secret discussions with Italy, Spain, and Great Britain about the extension of French interests in Africa, while they were one of the signatories, together with Germany, of the Treaty of Madrid which guaranteed that Morocco should remain as it was. Because France wanted more it negotiated with Britain, Italy, and Spain but intentionally omitted Germany because the French knew Germany would demand compensation.

Germany had commercial interests in Morocco since 1886 and three German shipping companies were established there and Germany was the third largest trading nation in Morocco. It was clear that Germany would not be prepared to merely allow these interests to be handed to the French without protest. When Germany discovered the true intentions of the French in 1904 they made it unambiguously clear that they were extremely displeased. The French position was regarded as improper and insulting.

The German government decided to give a clear signal that they would resist extension of French influence in Morocco. The German chancellor urged the Kaiser, who just happened to be cruising in the Mediterranean at the time, to pay a short visit to Tangiers. Although Wilhelm II had little interest in such a visit he was given little choice and so he landed on March 31, 1905 for

Delcassé

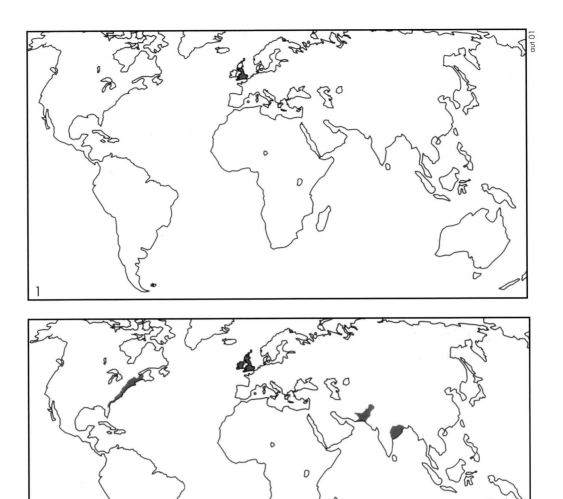

British colonial expansion. 1. England in 1600. 2. expansion by 1700. Right-hand page: 3. expansion by 1800. 4. British Empire in 1918.

a short visit to the sultan. He declared himself as protector of Moroccan integrity and hence in direct opposition to the French. This visit resulted in great disagreement between Rouvier, the French Prime Minister – who feared a serious conflict with the Germans – and his foreign minister, Delcassé who regarded Wilhelm's visit as a bluff and wished to continue with the expansion plans. He planned to send several warships to Tangiers to enforce his policy. Rouvier sought the help of the French President and after a stormy cabinet meeting Delcassé was fired and disappeared for a while from the political stage.

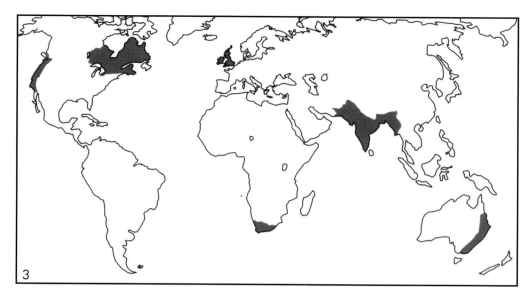

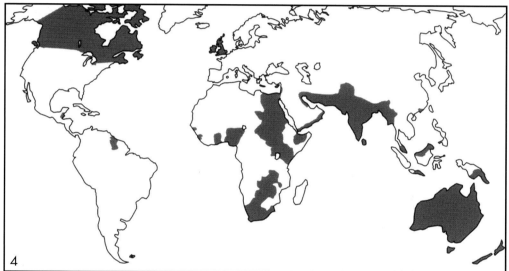

THE AGADIR CONFERENCE BLAMES GERMANY

German diplomacy appeared to have prevailed but this was not widely appreciated and that soon become readily apparent. Germany demanded an international conference to discuss the problem. The conference was held in Algeciras in April 1906 and the outcome was a treaty in which the position of France with respect to Morocco was regulated and established. The conference was a great disappointment for Germany. The French got their own way on all but a few points. It was painfully obvious to Germany that the country had few friends and was threatened with isolation. In fact almost no country supported the German viewpoint. Only the Austro-Hungarian state supported Germany but all the other

Postcard of both allies: Kaiser Wilhelm II and Emperor Franz-Joseph of Austria-Hungary.

countries, including Italy that was part of the tripartite alliance between Germany, Austria-Hungary, and Italy, abandoned the Germans.

The shock was enormous, particularly as Germany had not expected such an outcome and now realized her position as a major power was weakened.

THE SECOND MOROCCAN CRISIS, THE GERMANS DISPATCH THE WARSHIP PANTHER

A new crisis arose in 1911 when France decided to send troops to Morocco under the pretext of protecting their nationals against a rebellion that had broken out. Although the French had consulted the British, they had left the Germans out of the picture and Germany regarded the dispatch of troops as the latest attempt to thwart German interests in Morocco. The German response was to send the warship SMS Panther to Tangiers as a signal that Germany was not prepared to acquiesce to the situation or allow her interests in Morocco to be compromised.

This time too the matter blew over. Once again France dared not allow the matter to lead to war – but this was the last time. Once more Germany got no support from other states and was apparently totally isolated. The Panther action though had driven the French more firmly into the arms of the British and had been counter productive.

Germany stood alone amid a hostile world and it was clear that matters would soon lead to a major conflict. German diplomacy prevailed once more. The new German foreign minister Kidleren Wächter deemed it more prudent to withdraw from Morocco after all the problems that had arisen. He wished to exchange the German commercial interests there for compensation. Because he considered a further gathering in Morocco would solve nothing and merely drive the British and French closer together – which he expressly wished to prevent – he decided first to apply pressure to the French before making the demands for compensation and departing Morocco.

If the arrival of the Panther had created a storm then the German demand for compensation was like a bomb going off. Germany demanded the entire French Congo in exchange for its Moroccan interests and offered as sweetener the island of Togo or part of the German Cameroons. France immediately turned to the British and Russians. The British reacted with particular vehemence. The British Prime Minister Lloyd George made a speech in which he even threatened war if Germany threatened the British role on the world stage. It was at this moment that the British decided to prepare for war with Germany and their General Henry Wilson traveled to Paris to coordinate possible French-British military action.

The German Kaiser, who had not been in favor of the sending of the Panther to Tangiers, was greatly shocked at this British reaction

The German warship Panther that was sent to Tangiers in 1911 as a signal to the French that they must not ignore German interests.

President Poincaré of France (second from right) who played a major role in the outbreak of World War I.

and made it clear to his foreign minister that the Moroccan question was not worth a war and that he should not go all the way.

France too was shocked by the follow-up action to the Panther crisis. Once again the fear was of war and French politicians had little trust in the support of the Russians and British if it came to that. Consequently, they decided to negotiate with the Germans about their compensation demands. The two countries reached agreement in November 1911. Germany approved a remaining French interest in Morocco, including any French decision to send troops. In exchange Germany received around 250,000 square km (96,526 square miles) of the French Congo, which had helped to make the French a major colonial power.

The Panther action had borne fruit and Kidleren Wächter got his way. France was also satisfied that it could now do what it pleased in Morocco without German interference. Only the British kicked up a major fuss and rattled their sabers. There was a sudden easing of tension though following the Franco-German agreement and relations between the three countries were normalized and even friendlier. World peace gained a respite of a few years before the dark clouds rolled in again to cast their shadow.

GERMAN COLONIAL EXPANSION AND ECONOMIC AND POLITICAL RIVALRY

Germany was a fast-growing nation in the late nineteenth century. More than a third of its rapidly-expanding population was younger than fifteen years old. The country was turning into a highly industrialized nation that developed an ever-increasing range of new products for which it clearly needed markets. This was quite a problem, since the Germans also found it difficult to find ready markets and even the import of necessary raw materials became increasingly more difficult.

To set the scene, German imports grew by at least 244 percent between 1887 and 1912 and their exports rose by about 215 percent. This made the growth in German exports at this time greater than the growth of the USA (173%), Great Britain (113%), and France (98%). German became the largest producer of coal, iron, and steel, and the German chemical industry became the most important one in Europe. Great enterprises arose which developed at a staggering rate.

Naturally this economic growth was viewed closely by the British, especially when the German chemical industry started to win large orders that had previously gone to British companies. Once wholly British export markets were suddenly awash with cheaper and often better quality products, especially in the field of electrical engineering, textiles, and shipbuilding, with which the Germans were fiercely competitive. In some cases the Germans exported more goods to a British territory than the British themselves. Once Germany also started to build its own merchant fleet (until then the majority of German goods were shipped in British vessels) the British became truly alarmed. Germany was now regarded as a threat, not a military one but an economic threat against which the British had no immediate defense.

It was obvious to the German government that if it was to feed the

Russian Czar Nicholas II

hungry bellies of its increasing population and to find work for them then industrialization and exporting were dire necessities. In order to be assured of the necessary raw materials without constantly being dependent upon the "goodwill" of the British it was deemed essential to establish its own colonies. These strides though were not appreciated by everyone and in many respects worked counter-productively for Germany. Everywhere that they wished to expand, such as the lease in China of Kiow Chow in 1897, efforts to colonize the Solomon Islands in 1897, efforts to establish a trading post in the Philippines, attempts to establish bunkering stations or trading posts in Aden, The Yemen, along the Persian coast, and on the route to India they found Russia, Japan, or Britain opposing them. Germany found it virtually impossible to expand economically by peaceful means.

It is entirely logical that the demand for her own colonies and for a fleet capable of protecting the supply routes grew in direct proportion to the opposition from other countries. It is equally understandable in the light of those times that the British – who possessed the strongest navy in the world as a sine qua non (or

Russian troops march past the French president during a visit to St. Petersburg in July 1914.

necessity) of its status as an island state – felt this as a military threat. Although the Germans recognized this they felt there was no other choice than to continue on their chosen course. Unfortunately Germany's tactics and diplomacy were not always carefully executed, resulting in the British feeling increasingly ill at ease.

THE BRITISH EMPIRE, GREAT BRITAIN AS SUPERPOWER

The British had been busy establishing their colonies since the seventeenth century. When World War I began in 1914, Great Britain had the largest empire in the world, encompassing territories such as Australia and New Zealand, Hong Kong, Singapore, Malaya, India, South Africa, Egypt, The Sudan, Nigeria, The Gold Coast, British East Africa, Uganda, Somalia, Rhodesia, Sierra Leone, The West Indies, and Canada, but even this was not enough.

By the outbreak of war British eyes had also fallen on parts of Persia, parts of Anatolia (Asian Turkey) and Mesopotamia and Baghdad, the Bay of Haifa, Akkad in the Mediterranean, Heligoland, of course the German colonies.

British Minister of War, Haldane, who established the British Expeditionary Force that was sent to France in 1914.

The British had built up an enormous naval fleet over the centuries in order to protect their colonies and the sea routes between them. This was the world's largest navy and no nation dared challenge its supremacy. For this reason Great Britain could be regarded as the world's greatest power and the British understandably wished to maintain this position.

It was clear that anything or anyone who threatened this position was to be treated as an enemy and dealt with. The British policy was to maintain a balance of power in the world. As soon as any nation threatened to become too strong, the British allied themselves with that nation's enemies so that a double stranglehold was applied.

The British managed to maintain peace in Europe for many years by this means even though beneath this calm exterior processes were under-way that would bring an end to this peace. Germany played a key role in these processes with her economic expansion and plans to build up her navy.

A SERIES OF ALLIANCES

GERMANY AND HER ALLIES

Immediately after the Franco-Prussian war Bismarck did everything possible to isolate the French politically. He wanted to prevent France from ever again being one of a select circle of major powers since France would probably then turn against Germany and become a danger once more. Consequently, Bismarck did what he could to prevent France from gaining powerful allies. One possible ally was Russia and Bismarck sought diplomatic contact with the Russian ambassador in Berlin and offered an alliance. Earlier Bismarck had formed an alliance with the Austro-Hungarian empire and then in 1873 an alliance of three realms came into being in which the Kaiser,

Russia's minister of war, Suchomlinov, who rebuilt the Russian army after the defeat by Japan (1904–1905) but who later fell from favor.

The German deep-sea fleet, source of British agitation, here in the North Sea.

the Austro-Hungarian Emperor, and the Czar promised to cooperate with each other and adopt the same policy if their peace was threatened by another power.

This arrangement between the three countries was not ideal and almost fell apart in 1879 when the Czar protested that Germany always sided with the Austro-Hungarians in any important matters.

It was at this moment that Bismarck decided not to put all his eggs in one basket because he felt the Russians could no longer be trusted. Without informing them he entered into an extremely secret military pact with the Austro-Hungarian empire on October 7, 1879 in which both countries agreed to help one another if Russia attacked either of them. Naturally, the Russians were not privy to this and only learned of this secret pact some nine years later by accident.

In 1881 and 1884 the tripartite alliance was renewed but by 1887 relations between Germany and Russia had deteriorated to such an extent that Russia quit the alliance in protest. Bismarck immediately attempted to limit the damage and offered a separate alliance with Russia which he described as "covering his back." Bismarck promised Russia that Germany would remain neutral if that country was attacked by the Austro-Hungarian empire and he declared himself prepared to accept the Russian sphere of influence in the Balkans. Bismarck of course failed to inform Austria-Hungary of this treaty –

which was a flagrant breach of his alliance with them. It was therefore entirely to be anticipated that this would lead to problems.

Bismarck did manage through these secret accords to prevent the French from gaining new allies and kept them ideally isolated.

In 1881 Italy too was added to the alliance between Germany and Austria-Hungary making a new tripartite arrangement. Italy was concerned at the growth of French influence in North Africa where Italy also had interests. The Italians hoped to bring sufficient strength to bear by this arrangement to thwart French plans. This treaty was also kept secret but the Italian involvement leaked out of course in time. Once France learned of this it tried to prize Italy from the Triple Alliance with all manner of promises about the possible division of each others spheres of influence in Africa. Although Italy did not formally enter into these agreements a number of agreements were made in secret and in 1902 both countries agreed a very secret treaty in which Italy promised to remain neutral if France was attacked by Germany. Despite this, Italy extended its treaty with Germany soon afterwards. Italy's partners in the triple alliance distrusted her from this time and were later proven right to have done so.

When Bismarck had to step down as chancellor in 1890 he was succeeded by Count Caprivi who deemed Bismarck's secret accord with the Russians in conflict with their treaty with the Austro-Hungarian empire and hence unacceptable. He regarded it as downright treachery towards that state (which of course it was) and he advised the Kaiser not to renew the treaty when it expired. Wilhelm II followed his advice, which, however well intended, proved to be a turning point in history that enabled the French to free themselves from isolation and would have very negative consequences for Germany in the long term.

THE SECRET MILITARY CONVENTION BETWEEN FRANCE AND RUSSIA OF 1894 WHICH LED TO WORLD WAR I

It took some time, as we have seen, before the French recovered from its catastrophic defeat by the Prussian army in 1871, leaving it diplomatically isolated. It was some time before France once again sought to properly defend her borders. In about 1880 the French started to construct a chain of forts along their border with Germany with which they intended to hermetically seal their border against attack. Thoughts of revenge also began to emerge around this time and in 1887, shortly after the final fort in the defensive line was completed, the French general staff drew up their first offensive plans that were naturally designed to return Alsace-Lorraine to the France. These plans took no account of a defensive strategy and the army was transformed from a purely defensive force. The holy creed became attack and French soldiers trained to attack with all means and at any

Admiral Tirpitz (center) and Prince Heinrich of Prussia (second from left) during a private visit to the Royal Yacht Club of Queenstown in 1900.

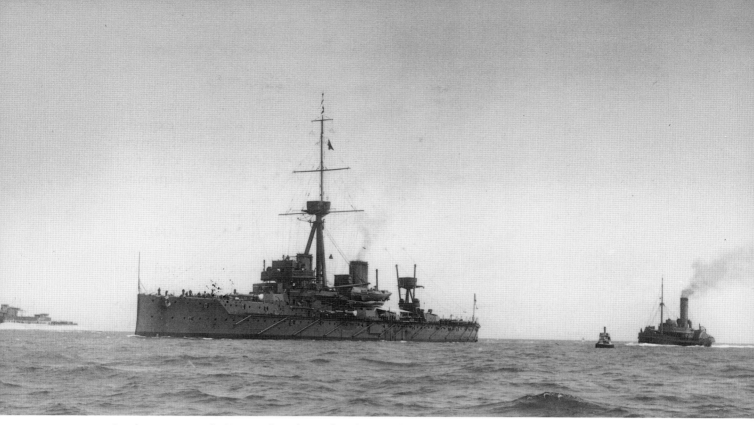

British construction of HMS Dreadnought significantly intensified the naval arms race with Germany.

cost. The word defense was removed from the French military vocabulary.

While the military prepared themselves to regain Alsace-Lorraine the diplomats were also busy. Every effort was made to break out of the diplomatic isolation that Bismarck had caused in order to make France a major power once more on the map of Europe.

The first chance for the French arose when Germany no longer wished to extend its treaty with Russia which we learned about earlier. Once the French saw this chink of light in 1890 they sent General Boisdeffre to Russia who opened discussions about a possible military cooperation between Russia and France.

Boisdeffre was received with open arms by the Russians. Their old desire for an open corridor from the Black Sea through the Dardanelles and the Bosporus to the Mediterranean was still very strong. This sea route was barred to warships following the Treaty of Paris at the end of the Crimean war in 1856 between the great powers of the age of Britain: France, Prussia, and Austria, and hence Russian warships were locked in the Black Sea.

In order to bring about a change in this the agreement of all the parties was required but up to then each party had indicated their agreement with the terms of the treaty. The Russians hoped it might now be possible with French help to make a first move towards deconstructing this treaty. The Russian problems with the British concerning Persia also made an alliance with France attractive.

French emperor Napoleon III (1808–1873).

The French made every effort to take their relationship with Russia to the highest level. In July that same year the French even sent a naval squadron to Russia on an official visit to clearly underscore the closeness between the two countries. The following year the Russian foreign minister Giers visited Paris to advance their discussions. It took until 1893 though before a definite agreement was reached. The Czar, who signed the agreement for Russia, demanded that the agreement must remain strictly secret, known only to the French president and prime minister. Hence was it that France entered into a secret military treaty with Russia without the French government or parliament being aware of it.

Thorough examination of this treaty makes it clear that in spite of the promises of peace in its introduction there can be no doubt of the aggressive intentions of both countries. France wanted to regain Alsace-Lorraine and Russia wanted free access to the Mediterranean. Both nations could only achieve these objectives by working together and thus decided to do so. France and Russia would join in conflict with Germany when their military preparations were complete and the time was ripe. Meanwhile both nations built up their armies and navies, proposed joint plans, and prepared themselves for the "great moment" that they imagined would happen around 1917.

Through careful diplomacy and deft steps France had succeeded not only in gaining Russia as a powerful ally but also in greatly weakening the Triple Alliance by holding secret talks with one of its members, Italy. That alliance was consequently weaker than it imagined itself to be. Things did not remain so either. France now directed her attentions towards Britain in an effort to establish that nation as a ally in the future war with Germany.

END OF THE VICTORIAN ERA IN GREAT BRITAIN

The British Queen Victoria died in 1901 at a great age, bringing to an end a period of great advancement and prosperity. Victoria was succeeded by Edward VII, a man with outspoken and critical views concerning Germany and the German Kaiser, who was also a true lover of the French culture and style of living.

At the end of 1905 the Conservative government fell and was replaced by the Liberals. The Foreign Secretary of the new government was Edward Grey, who was strongly anti-German and who had written in 1885 that Germany was Britain's principal enemy. Grey was a leading proponent of the entente cordiale or friendship agreement made with France in 1904 and had remarked that it would be a good thing if this was extended to other (perhaps military) areas. He also wrote that Europe remained divided into two camps: the Triple Alliance (Germany, Austria-Hungary, and Italy), and the Duple Alliance (France and Russia) but that it was now clear to everyone that Britain had joined the side of the French. He therefore heartily supported the secret military discussions that the British government had started with the French which he allowed to progress unaltered when he became Foreign Secretary in 1905.

The British people, Parliament, and most members of the British government had no knowledge of these secret Franco-British military discussions and Grey kept them secret because he knew there might well be resistant to them. Only Prime Minister Asquith, Minister of War, Haldane, and several generals and senior civil servants and diplomats were party to Grey's secret and it was this group of men that quickly came to the conclusion that Britain needed an army that could be sent to France quickly in the event of a war with Germany.

War Minister Haldane presented plans on January 10, 1906 for a British Expeditionary Force that could land in France or Belgium within fourteen days and a start was made to enlarge the army, so that it could be positioned in Belgium or France to assist the French in an anticipated war with Germany.

Meanwhile the British General Grierson attempted to hold military discussions with the Belgians. Although the Belgian government could not do so because of its strict policy of neutrality supported by treaty, the Belgian General Ducarne secretly met to discuss matters and said that if the Germans mobilized and massed troops in the area near Aachen the Belgian army would attack immediately. In this event, Grierson promised to make 100,000 British troops available to Belgium. Henry Wilson who succeeded

French General Boisdeffre, one of those who initiated the Franco-Russian convention of 1894.

Grierson increased this number to 160,000 men. When the Belgian government took tighter control of matters and banned further military discussions with the British, Wilson presented new plans and did not have qualms about telling the Belgians that if necessary the British would land in force even if that landing was opposed by Belgium. What emerges from this is that British military leadership was violating Belgian neutrality that in part was guaranteed by Great Britain because of what it considered a military imperative. This is precisely what Germany was accused of doing as a "heinous crime". The French had also developed plans to invade Belgium without permission of the Belgian government if required, if it deemed it militarily necessary, and the French general staff made such a request of their President Poincaré just before the outbreak of World War I.

The British General Henry Wilson was appointed director of military operations in 1910 and therefore became the most important driving force of Franco-British military planning as these were developed, including the cooperation between the French and British navies. By March 1911 the plans for landing around four British divisions in France and Belgium were ready in detail and Wilson signed an agreement with the French General Dubail on June 20 of that year in which this was increased to six divisions. The British parliament and most members of the cabinet remained entirely igno-

The end of an era. The body of Queen Victoria is carried in the royal yacht (center) on the River Thames to its final resting place.

rant of all these discussions and agreements and when questions were asked, Grey responded to the house by telling Parliament that there were no agreements with the French that would oblige the British to join them in a war against Germany. He was not believed for certain details had leaked out. Various ministers threatened to resign if the truth was not revealed. A written declaration was demanded of the Prime Minister that there would not be further Franco-British discussions about military cooperation without prior permission of Parliament. This declaration had to be given but Grey took little notice of it and the discussions continued as before. The following year the French

British Minister of War, Lord Kitchener who envisioned a long struggle and foresaw the need of a huge army.

and British planners discussed the role of the navies. It was decided to remove the French fleet entirely from the North Sea and to position it in the Mediterranean and consequently the British fleet almost entirely withdrew from the Mediterranean in order to be able to protect the French coast from attack by the Germans. By this means the fleets of Britain, France, and Germany were arranged as efficiently as possible and each was able to concentrate on its own territory.

Now that military relations with France were in place, albeit that Grey had not signed a single document and these oral agreements were made in strictest secrecy, Grey determined to forge closer relations with Russia. For Russia, which had been seriously weakened by the war with Japan of 1904, he envisaged an important role. He intended cooperation between France, Britain, and Russia against Germany. Such cooperation would be fatal for Germany in the event of a war. The two nations signed a treaty on August 31, 1907, in which they resolved various differences and the following year the British king visited the Czar accompanied by senior military figures. During the discussions that followed the British urged strengthening the Russian military capability so that they could play a decisive role on the world stage with France and Britain if the situation so demanded. The British made it clear that they expected a crisis to arise within seven or eight years if the Germans proceeded with the building of

The British fleet was regarded as invincible but this proved not to be the case against the German navy at the battle of Jutland in 1916.

their fleet. In such a situation Russia would be able to play a decisive role indicated the British spokesman. The Russians reacted positively and thus the British Foreign Secretary had taken one more step in the diplomatic and military isolation of Germany. That country would now be forced to fight on two fronts against three powerful enemies in any war. Germany could not win such a war and the outcome was therefore predictable for both sides. `

Therefore there were two opposing blocs in 1914: the Triple Entente of Russia, France, and Great Britain, and the Triple Alliance of Germany, Austria-Hungary, and Italy, with Italy being the weakest link and regarded as unreliable. It was clear to the Germans that within a few years the supremacy would be too great and a war would then prove fatal. Consequently the German military began to press for a preemptive war while Germany still had a chance of winning a war that was regarded as inevitable. Both the German Chancellor and Kaiser refused to grant this request.

CONSTRUCTION OF THE "DREADNOUGHTS" AND EXPANSION OF THE GERMAN FLEET

Meanwhile Germany's expansion of its navy, planned by Admiral Tirpitz in order to defend Germany from attack, had induced a certain degree of panic among the British, not the least in the Admiralty.

In early 1900 the British government began to be concerned about the rapidly growing economic power of Germany. The question was raised of where this was leading and what would happen if Germany interrupted supplies of raw materials from the empire e.g. during a war. The expansion of the German fleet increased this concern further and the British government had studies carried out to find out what might be done. The conclusion was that it would be nothing short of a disaster if Germany succeeded in severing the links between Britain and her overseas colonies. It was noted on the other hand that the same was true of Germany. It was therefore decided to blockade German ports in the event of war. By 1907 these plans were prepared and although these were in direct contradiction of maritime law established by the British themselves, in 1909 it was regarded as a "military imperative".

For Admiral Tirpitz the possibility of a British blockade was one of the strongest reasons for continuing with the fleet's expansion, for if the Germany navy was strong enough then perhaps the British would think twice about blockading them. His view was widely supported.

During this time the British had started building the Dreadnought, an entirely new type of warship that was a considerable advance on previous warships in terms of speed, armor, and armaments. British naval supremacy was guaranteed for the foreseeable future with the construction of this type of ship.

This had its consequences of course and it was obvious that the naval arms race with Germany had reached a higher tempo. To pre-

A British soldier says goodbye before leaving for the front.

vent this the British now sought a disarmament conference in The Hague in which they proposed reducing the size of all fleets, including the Royal Navy. At face value this was a positive initiative but a naïve one. After all, the British could afford to scrap a number of old ships if they were replaced by fewer but more powerful Dreadnoughts.

It is not surprising therefore that Germany resisted the British proposal, especially as the Germans had received rumors of the Russo-British treaty of 1907 that was now rightly being regarded as an entente between the two nations. The Germans began to become very concerned, particularly when the French President made a state visit to Britain in 1908 and immediately after this French newspapers began to press for conscription in the United Kingdom. Germans fears were not eased when the British king visited Russia that same year with senior military figures in his retinue. It made them suspect that a military accord between the two countries was being considered. Germany saw itself increasingly surrounded by hostile countries and this increased the German desire to further strengthen their defenses.

The British Admiralty used the concerns of the British people about the expanding German navy to win additional funds for its own plans. In January a report was published in which it was indicated that not only did Germany have its own "Dreadnought" program but that the Germans would have twenty-one of this type of ship in 1912. To stay ahead of the Germans funds were required to build an extra eight Dreadnoughts for completion by 1912.

The Admiralty ran into criticism from an unexpected quarter. Churchill, who was President of the Board of Trade at that time, considered the proposal misguided and argued it resulted from panic-ridden proposals put forward for party-political reasons as part of a fantastical, sensational, aggressive, and poorly-directed policy. This was a clear challenge that got a lot of attention in and support from the press. The Royal Navy continued to spread sensational warnings though about the increasing strength of the German navy but the falsehood of its claims were shown in 1912 when the German navy did not have twenty-one "Dreadnoughts" but just twelve. In reality the German fleet had never been a threat to the Royal Navy.

Criticism in Britain about the manner in which the naval arms race had come about was increasingly more serious. The press openly questioned why there were no thoughts of cooperation instead of increasing the differences between them. The criticism was so severe that the government had no other choice – at least for public consumption – than to make an attempt to reduce tensions between the two countries. When the Germans also proposed talks to reduce the bad relations between the two countries in 1912, the British Foreign Secretary Grey sent the Minister of War, Haldane, to Berlin under strict instructions to merely assess German intentions and not to make any kind of agreement.

To his great surprise, Haldane was warmly received in Berlin. The Kaiser put himself out to make Haldane welcome and the German Chancellor did everything possible to reach a workable solution. Both of them developed a concept accord about which Haldane later wrote that he had not gone to Berlin with instructions to reach an accord. Such a step required much greater preparation but his objective was to see if such an accord was possible. He did not know how the British government would react but regarded the talks as very successful, in a manner neither foreseen or expected.

Unfortunately, Grey, probably shocked at Haldane's success, put obstacles in the way and made a number of new demands and delayed his response. This tactic led to great frustration for the German Kaiser who feared the British were not taking the German proposals, or their readiness to come to terms, seriously. Nothing eventually came of the developments that Haldane had reported positively about. The obstinacy of Grey – who had kept the French ambassador informed about the visit and assured him that whatever the outcome he would ensure it would not change relations with France – was the principal obstacle. Britain had allowed a very good opportunity to reduce tension to slip away.

The arms race between the two countries continued undiminished and the chance of continued peace was visibly reduced with the passage of time.

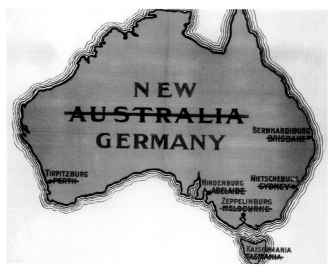

The British government warned of Germany's lust for power with this kind of strident propaganda.

The appalling assassination of King Alexander of Serbia and his queen distressed the entire world. His successor King Peter Karadjorjevic is shown in this photograph of 1903. He sought to create a Greater Serbia and allied himself with Russia.

SERBIA AS SOURCE OF TENSION AND THE ASSASSINATION OF ALEXANDER OBRENOVIC

While tension increased on the international diplomatic stage, the situation in the Balkans became increasingly unstable. After a rebellion in 1800 and 1807 during which Serbia succeeded in partially throwing off the yoke of Turkish rule, the country once more fell under Turkish control in 1812. The Russian Czar forced the Turkish sultan though to grant autonomy to the Serbs in 1829. As a result their influence naturally increased. In 1867 the ruler of Serbia of the time, King Milan Obrenovic succeeded, with the help of the Austro-Hungarians, to drive the remaining Turkish troops out of Serbia for good and the country became independent although quickly dependent economically on the Austro-Hungarian empire. In reality the Austro-Hungarians treated Serbia as a kind of protectorate, taking advantage of the weakness of King Milan Obrenovic. The dissatisfaction about this matter of dependence increased daily and there was a great deal of plotting and actions in the air. Milan was forced to abdicate in 1889 in favor of his son Alexander but it was a question of like father like son. Alexander followed the same policies as his father in respect of the Austro-Hungarian empire which did not make him popular. During a coup by army officers in June 1903 he was assassinated in a bestial fashion, together with his wife and the minister of war, which brought an end to the Obrenovic dynasty. Because the Austrians had secretly supported the coup it hoped for a new leadership that would be grateful. But they were to be disappointed. Eight days after the assassination there was a new ruler on the Serbian throne.

This was the sixty-year old Peter Karadjordjevic who had returned from exile in Geneva to be immediately recognized and supported by Russia. Peter propagated the notion of a Greater Serbia and openly declared himself in favor of Bosnia-Herzegovina being merged with the Serbian homeland. He established close ties with Russia, which was eager to help. Russian influence in Serbia now grew considerably and the position of the Austro-Hungarians crumbled away as Serbia slowly unraveled its economic links with the Austro-Hungarian empire which had meant that virtually all Serbian trade and exports were in the control of that power. The Austro-Hungarians reacted badly to these attempts at economic independence and tried everything to reestablish Serbian economic dependence and to re-assert the privileged position they had once enjoyed.

The so-called "pig war" happened in 1906, in which the Serbians succeeded in being able to export their most important commodity directly to markets in France,

King Peter and his Prime Minister Pasic (with beard) who played a major role in the causes of World War I.

Pasic and the Serbian Crown Prince Alexander, later King of Yugoslavia.

Germany, Italy, Egypt, and Bulgaria, without passing through Austro-Hungarian hands. This meant a definite end to the Austro-Hungarian monopoly position.

Once Peter had succeeded in gaining economic independence for his country from the Austro-Hungarians he also adopted policies against that nation. His weapon was Bosnia-Herzegovina. Control of this country which had previously been ruled by the Turks passed to Austria-Hungary at the Congress of Berlin. Large numbers of Slavs lived in that country and Peter now began to sow discord and to press for the country to be united with Serbia, calling for all Slavs to be housed in a single state. Quickly the Serb army, government, and the population were eager to adopt this idea. Russia was also keen to see Serbian aspirations come to fruition and supported them eagerly.

The situation in the Balkans had therefore changed to the detriment of Austria-Hungary following the accession of King Peter Kardjordjevic. They had also lost an ally in Serbia while Russian influence in the Balkans had increased significantly.

The grounds for a future conflict were now in place and the Austro-Hungarian empire began to have concerns for the integrity of its borders – not, as we shall see, without good cause.

Close ties were now forged between Russia and Serbia which held inherent danger for the continued existence of the Austro-Hungarian empire and even for European peace.

The smallest scale conflict in the Balkans could have the most serious consequences as a result of a series of alliances. Serbia had great ambitions of forming an enlarged Serbian homeland in which all the Slavs could be united. The province of Bosnia-Herzegovina was under the control of Austria-Hungary but had several million Slavs within its borders who were increasingly influenced by continuous Serbian propaganda and agitation. Russia, which wanted to maintain its own position, was happy to allow Serbia to meddle since this caused a constant source of unrest that was detrimental to the position of Austria-Hungary, which also wanted to be the major power in the Balkans. All the conditions for major conflict were present and the tension ensured a continued silent threat.

Russia clearly held all the cards. It merely had to support Serbia's ambitions for a Greater Serbia to cause the spark that would ignite a conflict. A conflict between Serbia and the Austro-Hungarian empire would also involve Germany, through the alliance that obliged them to come to their support. France, and perhaps Britain, would join with Russia if that country should join in a conflict with Austria-Hungary over Serbia. All Europe would be in flames in a very short time.

Putnik, Serbian commander and chief in 1914.

King Nicholas of Montenegro who joined Russia and Serbia in war.

This was precisely what various statesmen in France and Russia envisaged when they made their alliance and sought to involve the British too: a European war in which Germany would simultaneously be confronted by three enemies. Given the supremacy over Germany, that country would be sure to lose such a war and France could regain Alsace-Lorraine, Russia would gain access to the Mediterranean and remain as a continuing influence in the Balkans, and the British would be rid of a competitor which threatened to become stronger than them both economically and politically. The motives of the countries of the entente were plain enough to see.

Of course such a war should only break out when the allies were prepared for it. Only then could the great pay off be achieved. This would take several years they estimated, probably in 1917 and

Sergeant Flora Sands was a remarkable woman – especially for her time. She fought with the Serbian army and was wounded several times and was awarded the Cross of the Order of Kara George.

meanwhile it was necessary to calm the unrest in the Balkans as much as possible and to prepare for war.

It was entirely in keeping with the era that a new radical party was established in Serbia with Russian money and support that among other things provided support to revolutionary movements in Austria-Hungary and Bosnia-Herzegovina. Other associations and organizations in addition to this party were also founded with the purpose of propagating the notion of a Greater Serbia among the Slavs. These included the Narodne Odbrana and the Ujedindenje Ili

Smrt or "Black Hand". This latter group, led by the head of army intelligence, Colonel Dimitrijevic, was the most dangerous with terrorism as its principal weapon. Its members swore an oath of allegiance and secrecy on pain of death. It was this organization in particular that directed itself to the "liberation" of Bosnia-Herzegovina and within a few years had infiltrated every area of public life. Its members were found at the highest level and eventually they succeeded in occupying virtually every post in the army, police, and government.

Serbia now openly directed itself with all its strength towards aggression, agitation, and terrorism against the Austro-Hungarian empire, secretly supported by Russia. The number of attacks and terrorist acts in Bosnia-Herzegovina reached unprecedented heights and Serbia gradually became a veritable threat to that throne. The situation had become extremely explosive.

In 1908 the Austro-Hungarian foreign minister, Aehrenthal (1906–1912) decided to do something about it. He sought out his Russian counterpart Iswolski and informed him that Austria-Hungary had decided to annex Bosnia-Herzogovina so that their army could restore order. In exchange for Russian cooperation he offered support

The view of the world was to change drastically.

for Russia's aims to gain permission from the great powers for the Dardanelles and the Bosporus to be opened to Russian warships.

Iswolski jumped at the proposal but considered there should first be an international conference to discuss matters. He had only just given his response when Aehrenthal announced the annexation and Austro-Hungarian troops entered the province. Because none of the other great powers had any interest in such a conference, Iswolski was powerless to act and hence a clear break came with Austria-Hungary.

In Serbia they saw their ambitions for a Greater Serbia suddenly vanish. They were furiously enraged and even threatened war. Only the involvement of the great powers prevented conflict and Serbia was forced to acquiesce in the annexation. As a consequence of this, Russia and Serbia now worked even more closely with each other and antipathy towards the Austro-Hungarians became more pronounced. In the two Balkan wars that followed of 1912 and 1913 the political situation in the Balkans changed again. A Slavic bloc formed that enabled Serbia to further expand and Romania allied itself (but not yet openly) with Russia and Serbia, while the weakened Bulgaria gratefully accepted the proffered hand of Austria-Hungary and took its side.

THE CRISIS OF 1914

Tension rises, Europe mobilizes

THE STANCE OF THE AUSTRO-HUNGARIAN EMPIRE AND RUSSIA

As we have seen the position of the Austro-Hungarian empire had been weakened following the Balkan wars. That nation now found itself placed in opposition to a hostile Slavic bloc under Russian leadership and the Russians doing everything to awaken Serbian nationalism and increase tension in the Balkans. Serbian agitation had caused an explosive situation in Bosnia-Herzegovina. Attacks and assassinations followed each other with clockwork regularity and the Bosnian government declared that only the most severe of measures could now save the country from catastrophe. The position of the Austro-Hungarian empire as a great power and of the Emperor too were now also in play and the government began to think of measures, with the commander in chief, General Conrad von Hötzendorff, applying increasing pressure for mobilization and an incursion into Serbia in order to put an end to the terror regime there. His view was that Serbia could only be "corrected" by force of arms. Waiting merely increased the chance that Russia would involve itself in open support of Serbia. He said they should attack now, particularly as Russia was not yet ready for war.

His analysis of the situation shows that things were indeed very serious. He said that the Austro-Hungarian empire was threatened both from within and without. Internal opposition resulted from the ethnic groups in Bosnia: the Serbs who wanted to join Serbia, the Czechs who wanted an independent state, the Muslims who wanted to be part of Turkey, and the Christians who wanted to remain part of the Austro-Hungarian empire. There was also unrest in the Hungarian part of that province.

The external threats came from:
1. Russia's efforts for influence in Constantinople, a leading role in the Balkans, and to counter Germany's plans in Asia.
2. Italy wanted to seize parts of Austro-Hungarian territory on the Italian borders and to form a hegemony in the Adriatic.
3. Serbia's efforts to form a Greater Serbian realm which used agitation among the Serbs of Bosnia-Herzegovina to achieve this.

Archduke Franz-Ferdinand of Austria-Hungary with his family. He was assassinated during a visit to Bosnia in 1914.

Unique photograph of the Archduke during maneuvers in Bosnia on June 27, 1914, several days before his assassination.

4. Romania wished to take possession of Romanian-speaking Austro-Hungarian territory.
5. Increased open hostility of France towards their ally Germany.

Von Hötzendorff clearly painted a picture of great concern for Austria-Hungary that cannot be described as rosy. Problems were piled high and only very wise statesmen could find a solution. It is a question whether the Austro-Hungarians had such a statesman.

In the meantime Russia was fully aware of the problems confronting the Austro-Hungarians for these were a direct consequence of the policies they had pursued towards their neighbor.

After the annexation of Bosnia-Herzegovina by Austria-Hungary the attitude of the Russian foreign minister Iswolski changed completely. He felt personally betrayed by the "treachery", as he called it, of Aehrenthal and he now did everything he could to minimize the damage. In 1909 he opened discussions with Bulgaria and entered into a military accord with them. In article five of that treaty we read: "In view of the fact that the realization of the holy ideal of the Slavic peoples in the Balkan countries, which is so close to the heart of Russia, can only be brought about by a positive outcome of a war with Germany and Austria-Hungary..." This is a clear indicator of the Russian's future plans.

In October of that year Iswolski decided to enter a further secret accord with Italy in which both countries recognized each other's spheres of influence, thus further weakening the Triple Alliance. Iswolski could be satisfied with himself. He had laid the foundations for further weakening of the Triple Alliance and strengthened the Russian position in the Balkans. For him the future European war, or "his war" as he described it when it did happen, could not come soon enough. He departed for Paris where as Russian ambassador he pursued his efforts to bring the war about.

Iswolski was followed as Russian foreign minister by Sazonov who largely pursued the same policies. He tried to bring about the formation of a Balkan

The Austro-Hungarian commander in chief, Field-Marshal Conrad von Hötzendorff (1852–1925). He continually urged for a war against Italy and Serbia. When war did break out in 1914 his army appeared not to be prepared and mobilization had to be delayed.

League under Russian leadership and managed to strengthen the ties between Serbia and Bulgaria. He was also behind the alliance between Serbia and Montenegro which strengthened the Balkan League. The Balkan wars disturbed this though when Serbia and Bulgaria opposed each other and the Bulgarians unexpectedly invaded Serbia. Its troops were ignominiously defeated and a weakened Bulgaria turned its back on Russia and gratefully accepted the offered hand of the Austro-Hungarians. But Austria-Hungary did not achieve much through this since Bulgaria was so completely weakened as to be out of the struggle. Sazonov did succeed though in prizing the Romanians – who helped the Serbs against the Bulgarians – free from the Triple Alliance. Romania had secretly entered into a military and political treaty with Austria-Hungary in 1883. When war broke out in 1914 Romania declared itself neutral but later joined the entente.

Sazonov was also busy with respect to naval matters. In addition to the existing army treaty Russia now entered into a naval treaty with the French on June 16, 1912, which included an agreement for the re-deployment of both fleets. France was to move its entire fleet to the

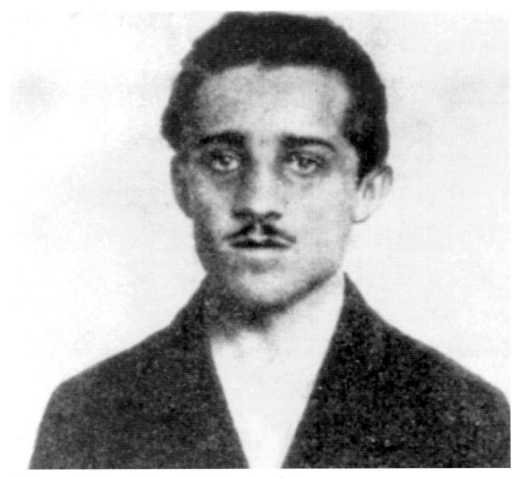

Princip, assassin of Franz-Ferdinand. He died in prison of TB.

Mediterranean and Russia would reinforce the Black Sea fleet. It was agreed with the British that they would move their Mediterranean fleet to the North Sea, with the British Navy promising to defend the French coast should Germany attack. Earlier in 1907, Russia, France, and Britain made a treaty with each other in which they resolved their differences regarding Persia, Afghanistan, and Tibet. Furthermore discussions were held about a naval treaty in which the British were also asked to defend the Baltic coast. Discussions about this were still underway when war did break out in August 1914 and Britain's involvement was a fact. Finally, Sazonov also made a secret accord in July 1912 with Russia's arch-rival, Japan, so that Russia did not risk danger from that direction if it should become embroiled in a war with Austria-Hungary and Germany.

Two of the conspirators, Cabrinovic and Grabez, who planned the assassination of Franz-Ferdinand.

Meanwhile agitation within Bosnia-Herzegovina had broken out extensively once more and the Bosnian government declared that a catastrophe could now only be avoided through direct military intervention. It was against this background that the heir to the Austro-Hungarian throne, Archduke Franz-Ferdinand and his wife Sophie made an official visit lasting several days to Bosnia-Herzegovina on June 25, 1914, in order to be present at annual maneuvers. This visit was to light the fuse that caused the Balkan powder keg to explode. The war that was to cost the lives of thirty million people was about to break out.

THE ASSASSINATION IN SARAJEVO WITH DRAMATIC CONSEQUENCES FOR WORLD PEACE

Archduke Franz-Ferdinand, the heir to the Austro-Hungarian throne, and his wife Sophie, were assassinated during a carriage ride through Sarajevo on June 28, 1914. Who were the assassins and what was their motivation?

This drama, that directly led to the First World War, began in the village of Sabac on the Sava river. Three young Bosnian students,

Princip, Grabez, and Cabrinovic arrived in the harbor of this small place by boat from Belgrade in the morning of May 28, 1914 where they made contact with one Popovic, member of the secret Serbian brotherhood of "The Black Hand", the terrorist organization that sought the union of Bosnia-Herzegovina with Serbia. The Black Hand was the main source behind terror acts and rebellion in Bosnia and its members swore a strict oath of silence on pain of death. The organization was deeply rooted with members in the highest political and military circles. They were led by the Serbian Colonel Dimitrijevic of the intelligence service who had earlier been complicit in the assassination of the Serbian royal couple.

The three students had been in trouble as a result of their anarchist and anti Austro-Hungarian activities and fled to Serbia to avoid arrest. Despite their illegal entry they met little by way of difficulties in Serbia. They quickly were once more in anarchist circles and when news of the archduke's visit became known in Belgrade they saw this as a magnificent opportunity to prove their service to their fatherland and strike against the hated Austro-Hungarian empire. The plan to assassinate Franz-Ferdinand was born and work started to bring the plan to fruition.

Contact was quickly made with a certain Major Jankovic, right-hand-man of Colonel Dimitrijevic, who provided them with weapons and ammunition and ensured they were trained in their use. He arranged for them to cross the border into Bosnia without difficulties and put them in touch with Popovic, who was ordered to help them.

In his turn, Popovic gave them a letter of recommendation to the head of customs, a certain Prvanovic, and also a member of the Black Hand, at the nearest border point of Loznica who helped them cross the border with Bosnia via Tuzla. The three students reached Sarajevo on June 6, where they stayed with their families. Princip met his friend Ilic, also a revolutionary and revealed the plan to assassinate the archduke to him. During the following weeks the co-conspirators discussed the assassination, considering a series of different scenarios. The program for the visit was only published in the newspapers on June 27, the day before the archduke's arrival. The team was meanwhile expanded by

Emperor Franz-Joseph of Austria-Hungary (1830–1916) ruled continuously for 68 years. He was opposed to war with Serbia and only grudgingly gave the order to mobilize.

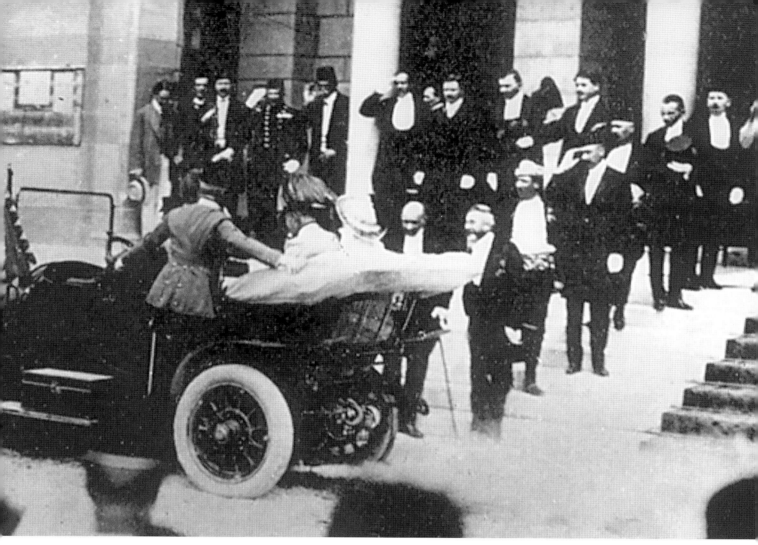

Archduke Franz-Ferdinand and his wife Sophie arriving at the town hall in Sarajevo.

a further three men who they had met at various places. Once the program became known they decided to stake out the route and take the opportunity as it presented itself to use their weapons.

The following day, Sunday June 28, 1914 came and Franz-Ferdinand arrived in Sarajevo in the morning by train and was taken by car to the town hall for a reception. The public thronged the route and among them at some distance from each other were the six conspirators. In addition to their weapons they each had a flask of potassium cyanide in case the assassination attempt failed and they were arrested.

The procession passed Cabrinovic who removed the pin from a grenade without hesitation and threw it in the direction of Franz-Ferdinand. The grenade landed on the folded-down hood and rolled off before exploding in the street. The driver of Franz-Ferdinand's car immediately increased his speed while Cabrinovic attempted to swallow the cyanide but he dropped the bottle and its contents were lost. He ran away and jumped in the river where he was subsequently captured and arrested.

Franz-Ferdinand looked behind and saw that the car following him had stopped and its occupants were wounded but his driver immediately sped away, passing Princip and then Grabez but these were too far away to be effective. The attempt had failed and Franz-Ferdinand decided to continue with his program as before. After a short visit to the town hall he and his wife got back into the car to head to the military hospital to visit the wounded. His car then passed the spot where Princip was still in position. Princip drew his pistol and fired several shots in the direction of the archduke and his wife. The shots were on target and Sophie died almost instantaneously, Franz-Ferdinand a little later. All the conspirators were arrested but the deed had been done. The assassination of Franz-Ferdinand set the world ablaze, empires and kingdoms disappeared, and millions were to lose their lives in a struggle lasting four years but which was to give

Archduke Franz-Ferdinand and his wife leaving the town hall to start their final journey.

rise to a new and even greater conflict that was to become known as World War II.

REACTION OF THE GREAT POWERS, MOBILIZATION OF THE AUSTRO-HUNGARIAN ARMY POSTPONED

The assassination of the heir to the Austro-Hungarian throne caused a great shock throughout the world and if they had invaded Serbia at that moment none of the major powers would have opposed them but there was no attack by the Austro-Hungarian army.

It appears that their troops were far from ready for combat. There had been talk of a preemptive war for some years but when that moment arrived they were not in a position to respond immediately. Austria-Hungary failed completely and allowed a unique opportunity to achieve their objectives with respect to Serbia to pass without taking advantage. Instead a process began of endless discussions, political consultations and ministerial meetings. In short, a plethora of activity that stood in the way of a quick solution.

This delay gave the world time to recover from the initial shock and old antipathy towards the Austro-Hungarians re-emerged and the initiative passed to their opponents. The day after the assassination, General von Hötzendorff requested a general mobilization but his emperor turned down the request and von Hötzendorff noted in his diary that the necessary political will did not exist for the only just action in either his own country or in Germany. The minister of foreign affairs, Berchtold, also wanted immediate action but found the Hungarian Prime Minister Tisza opposing him. He first wanted to see proof of any Serbian government complicity in the assassination. He also deemed the timing for a war with Serbia as quite unsuitable because he feared that Italy and Romania would not hold to their treaty obligations and the alliance with Bulgaria was not yet officially in place. Furthermore he argued that it was essential first to ascertain if Germany would support them in action against Serbia.

Foreign minister Berchtold concluded that the careful foreign policy he had pursued was counterproductive rather than helpful. He had consistently opposed the commander in chief when he had called for a preemptive war. During both Balkan wars Berchtold had remained un-

Princip, who fired the fatal shot.

involved, allowing the Serbs and Russians freedom to make many changes with the result that nobody took Austria-Hungary seriously any more and no longer believed it could continue as a major power. Berchtold feared that now that Turkey had more or less disappeared from Europe, his nation would be next on the list. This concern was reinforced following the assassination of the heir to the Austro-Hungarian throne and he now came to the conclusion that it was essential to remove the Serbian regime as the prime cause of the intrigues against Austria-Hungary.

Berchtold was not alone in this view. Even the old peace-loving Emperor Franz-Joseph had come to the same conclusion, although he still urged the utmost caution. The emperor wrote to his ally, German Kaiser Wilhelm II, expressing the view that the situation had become untenable. He accused the Serbians of activities in their efforts to unite all Serbs that must inevitably lead to conflict with his country and that Serbia had also become a continuing source of threat to the monarchy. He finished with a formal request for Germany's help in the coming war and sent a mission to Berlin, headed by Count Hoyos, to reinforce the request.

GERMANY'S "BLANK CHECK"

Count Hoyos was received by Kaiser Wilhelm II on July 5 and told by him that Germany would not desert her ally and directed him to talks with the German Chancellor. He pressed for rapid action because the world was appalled by the horrific assassination and was therefore sympathetic towards the Austro-Hungarian state. He also said he was certain Russia would not intervene because that nation was far from ready for war. The German chancellor confirmed in a letter of July 6 that Germany was convinced of the danger that its ally faced and was fully behind them. The chancellor also urged rapid action. This letter was later described as a "blank check" from Germany to the Austro-Hungarians.

In Vienna they regarded the mission to Germany as a great success and Berchtold informed a cabinet meeting on July 7 of Germany's support. He proposed that they should now enter Serbia, accepting that this ran a risk of Russian intervention. "But," he maintained, "Russia did everything it could to unite the Balkans in order to later use this against the dual Austro-Hungarian throne." War was inevitable, he maintained, and things could only get worse. The Hungarian prime minister was once again opposed to this and

The funeral procession of the royal couple in Trieste in August 1914.

The Austro-Hungarian Prime Minister, Berchtold.
He took the decision to declare war on Serbia
even if it should result in a wider war.

demanded an undertaking that if it did come to war that no Serbia territory would be annexed. The meeting ended without a firm decision.

Berchtold now urged the emperor to issue an ultimatum to the Serbian government but the emperor refused because he considered the diplomatic means had not yet been exhausted, neither was there any definitive proof to Serbian government involvement. Berchtold did not give up though and determined to issue the ultimatum himself. He informed the German ambassador by word of mouth of the demands he proposed to make to Serbia and he also sent a senior diplomat to Serbia to ascertain matters and to seek evidence of Serbian complicity.

Meanwhile the tension within Austria-Hungary grew rapidly. The press in particular got itself particularly worked up. They published an interview with the Russian ambassador in Belgrade with a Bulgarian journalist in which the ambassador declared himself certain that if Serbia was to get its hands on Bosnia-Herzegovina, Bulgaria would be able to acquire Macedonia. This article had a great influence upon Tisza, who together with the mounting pressure upon him, slowly but surely began to desert his fixed position.

Berchtold called a further cabinet meeting on July 14 and this time Tisza agreed to a declaration of war against Serbia under certain preconditions. He did though maintain his demand that there should be no annexation of Serbian territory in order to remove any excuse for Russia to intervene.

THE VIENNESE ULTIMATUM

The meeting now unanimously decided to present Serbia with an ultimatum. Tisza's agreement was decisive. Until then he had done everything possible to prevent a war. That he finally agreed after being opposed for so long in spite of the pressure applied to him rules out any suggestion that Austria-Hungary decided on the dangerous course of war with Serbia in a cavalier manner, or without due consideration. Both the emperor and Tisza changed their minds at the last moment but not before they were both convinced of the necessity

An elderly Emperor Franz-Joseph at a reception in Vienna.

of such a decision. For them the choice was between their dual realm or war but the choice was difficult for them.

The final text of the Austro-Hungarian ultimatum to Serbia was ready on July 19. The demands made in the text were so severe that all expected Serbia to reject them. One of the demands was that the Austro-Hungarian state reserved the right to carry out its own investigation on Serbian soil. Such a demand could not be accepted by any self-respecting nation. There was no trust however in Serbian promises and the ultimatum was drawn up to make war inevitable. The note containing the ultimatum was finally handed to the Serbs at 6 p.m. on July 23, 1914. As anticipated the ultimatum was rejected and Emperor Franz-Joseph signed the order for a limited mobilization on July 25, followed by declaration of war against Serbia on July 28. The first action happened very quickly. A small flotilla of gunboats fired on the Serbian capital of Belgrade, causing considerable damage. But these were also the first shots in the Great War that lasted for four years and cost millions of lives.

The Austro-Hungarian ambassador eventually handed over the fatal ultimatum in Belgrade that led to the Great War on July 23, 1914.

An enthusiastic crowd gathered at the outbreak of war on the "Unter den Linden".

THE GREAT POWERS MOBILIZE
GERMANY MOBILIZES

Once the German ambassador had learned of the text of the ultimatum to Serbia he immediately passed it on to Berlin. The German minister of foreign affairs, Jagow, described the ultimatum as "reichlich scharf" (rather harsh) and complained that it was now far too late "dazu Stellung zu nehmen" (to express an opinion about it). He also declared that Vienna had burnt its bridges with this ultimatum but he did not distance himself from them. On July 27 he even sent a telegram to Berchtold to warn him that there were likely to be mediation proposals sent through from Berlin in the coming days but that he should not concern himself about them because Germany was sending them on merely to avoid conflict with Great Britain at this stage. On July 28 though he advised Berchtold to have direct talks with Russia. Berchtold ignored this and invoked the rage of the German chancellor the following day who declared that Germany stood ready of course to support its ally but that he did not want to become involved in a war if the Austro-Hungarians were so cavalier about it and would not listen to his advice.

Shocked, Berchtold instructed his ambassador to hold discussions with the Russian foreign minister but it turned out to be too late. The German commander in chief, von Moltke wrote to his opposite number General Conrad von Hötzendorff that same day urging him not to delay mobilization as this was Austria-Hungary's only chance of survival. Germany would take part in the war without any reservations, he promised. Emperor Franz-Joseph signed the general mobilization order on July 31 at 12:33, in other words including war against Russia, but not in effect until August 4. Russia had meanwhile already announced a general mobilization on July 30, which removed the option for the announcement of a restricted Austro-Hungarian mobilization just against Serbia. The Russian mobilization therefore preceded that of Austria-Hungary and caused Germany to announce the "imminent threat of war" and to issue an ultimatum to Russia to call a halt to its mobilization within twelve hours or war would result according to the conventions of the time. It was therefore the Russian mobilization that turned a local conflict between Austria-Hungary and Serbia into a global war in which France, Great Britain, and

A send-off for German troops heading for the front from their families and a military band.

Russian cavalry on its way to the front.

Germany also participated as a result of the alliances in place between the parties.

RUSSIA MOBILIZES

Although the general Russian mobilization turned a local conflict into a World War it cannot be denied that the Russian foreign minister had warned the Austro-Hungarian government on July 22 not to take action against Serbia or the consequences would be serious.

The French President, Poincaré, who had been on a state visit, departed Russian waters on his way home on July 23. Several hours after his departure the Austro-Hungarian ultimatum was handed over in Belgrade. So as we have seen the timing was chosen to prevent it from becoming a matter of discussion between the French president and the Russians. This remained an idle hope. President Poincaré had also given the Russian a "blank check" with a firm assurance that he would support Russia and meet his treaty obligations.

News of the ultimatum to Serbia became known throughout the world on July 24. Sazonov is said to have called out that this meant "the European war" when he learned. He immediately called a meeting of the cabinet and instructed the finance minister to remove Russian state deposits from banks in Germany. The cabinet decided initially on a partial mobilization in four regions because the Czar was opposed to a general mobilization. During the following

Men reacted enthusiastically in Britain too. An army recruiting office is shown in the photograph. Around one million men volunteered for service.

days great pressure was applied to the Czar and he finally succumbed. The general mobilization now came into force on July 30. This was a decision that set its seal on the fate of the world. This measure forced both Germany and Austria-Hungary to follow suit. Both the Franco-Russo treaty and the conventions of the time meant that a general mobilization was tantamount to a declaration of war and hence this too happened.

ONE MILLION VOLUNTEER IN GREAT BRITAIN

Edward Grey, the British Foreign Secretary, gave his famous speech regarding the declaration of war in the House of Commons on August 3, 1914 following the German invasion of Belgium. Grey insisted that the British were obliged by treaty to come to Belgium's aid and could not allow Germany to wipe this "small and courageous" nation off the map.

The claim that Britain was duty-bound by this treaty to assist Belgium was not actually correct. Such an obligation did not exist under the treaty. The signatories had each individually promised not to usurp Belgium's neutrality but did not call for force of arms in the event that the neutrality was violated. Lord Loreburn, former Lord Chancellor, insisted that for the historical record he should inform the upper house that Britain was not obliged to intervene, either by the terms of the 1839 treaty or any other treaty because Great Britain, Austria, Russia, and the Netherlands had simply made an agreement to always regard Belgium as a neutral state. Britain had obliged itself along with the others not to violate Belgium's neutrality but had not agreed to defend Belgium if another state withdrew from this agreement. Grey carried on though as if such an obligation did exist and used this as an argument to the British people that the country was both morally and legally justified in going to war. He represented it as if Britain's failure to live up to its (non existent) treaty obligations would be reprehensible and that it was a righteous and

The first British troops depart their barracks for embarkation to France. First Battalion Irish Guards, August, 1914.

justifiable war to save a small and defenseless country and a war that threatened the entire civilized standards of Europe. It was this argument above all others that stirred the British people most and brought them to a man behind their leaders. Grey's honesty was never questioned. After all, he had done everything possible to maintain the peace when the situation in Europe quickly deteriorated and had made a number of proposals for talks that had all been rejected by Germany. Many historians still hold this viewpoint but what is clear is that most of Grey's offers of talks were made after July 25, the day on which Russia decided to mobilize. Grey was aware that in those days mobilization meant war. It was that same day that his top civil servants in the Foreign Office advised him in a memorandum that it was too late to attempt to exercise pressure on Russia by means of the French to moderate their stance with respect to the conflict between Serbia and the Austro-Hungarians because it was apparent that both Russia and France had decided to accept the risk of a wider conflict. That memorandum indicated that it would be risky for Britain to attempt to change that decision and that British interests were best served by choosing specifically the side of Russia and France in the coming war.

Further consideration raises questions about Grey's proposals for talks. In all probability Grey was playing for time just as France and Russia were also doing. The reality is that neither the British parliament or the people were eager for war. When news had leaked in 1912 that Grey had permitted secret military talks with France for some years without the knowledge of parliament or most of the cabinet this had led to considerable opposition towards the Foreign

The British War cabinet.

The German warship Goeben accompanied by the Breslau enters the Bosporus and anchors off Istanbul.

Secretary. Several ministers threatened their resignations if he did not conduct matters openly and he was forced to inform the French that the talks already held remained without obligation on the part of Britain. After this Grey was more careful and signed not one agreement and kept no written records of such matters although the talks continued unabated and morally bound Great Britain to the French course of action. In his book, *The Origins of the War of 1914*, the famous historian Albertini wrote that Grey must have realized without any doubts that with the British-French talks and also indirectly through the British-Russian talks that he had maneuvered Great Britain into a dubious position. He also raised a question about whether it could really be said that Grey had done everything within his power to prevent the fatal step that led to war. He answered the question negatively and said on these grounds Grey could not be exonerated.

Immediately after Grey's speech to the lower house the British began to mobilize and within fourteen days dispatched troops to the continent where everything was in place to move them to their designated places. Meanwhile the newly appointed Minister of War, Lord Kitchener, mounted an enormous campaign to recruit volunteers because unlike few others he envisaged a year-long war with many casualties. He wanted to strengthen the armed forces to one million men. The enthusiasm among the populace was so great that one million recruits were soon in uniform. Many of these would die in the Battle of the Somme and Great Britain was then forced to introduce conscription to achieve its necessary manpower.

The pro-German Turkish war minister, Enver Pasha and the Turkish commander in chief (3rd from left).

FRANCE MOBILIZES

The role of the French president, Poincaré, in the outbreak of the First World War is a crucial one. This is apparent from sources such as a letter sent by the Russian ambassador in Paris to his foreign minister after Poincaré had been chosen as the French president. The letter indicates that the ambassador had just had a discussion with Poincaré who advised him that now he was president he would be able to fully influence French foreign policy and would therefore make good use of his seven year term to further cooperation with Russia. The ambassador said that the President saw it as very important for the French government to sufficiently influence public opinion that they would be prepared to go to war over the issue of the Balkans. He then stressed the need for Russia to avoid any action on its part that would lead to war before discussing it with the French.

Poincaré and his foreign minister, Viviani, returned to Paris on July 29, 1914 after a state visit to Russia lasting several days and was informed of developments that had taken place. French officers had been recalled from furlough on the twenty-fifth – the day of the Russian mobilization – and plans had been made to ship colonial troops to France. The Russian government sent a telegram to the French advising them that Russia was to reject the German ultimatum that they halt their mobilization and asked the French to use its influence to press the British to ally themselves with Russia and France. To prevent the possibility of France being seen as the aggressor – which would make a British alliance impossible – Poincaré ordered French troops to be withdrawn 10 km (6.2 miles) from the French-German border, despite protests from his commander in chief. The French president signed the order for limited mobilization on July 31. The Russian military attaché reported the news to St. Petersburg that the French minister of war had informed him in an exuberant manner that France had definitely chosen war and had asked him to inform his masters that the French general staff hoped that Russian efforts would be directed against Germany. Action against the Austro-Hungarians was to be considered of a lower priority.

A telegram was sent from Italy informing its allies that the Italian government no longer considered itself to be bound by the treaty with Germany and Austria-Hungary. Only Great Britain did not yet declare itself. On August 1 at 4 p.m. the French commander in chief was given permission to move to a general mobilization which was fully under way the following day. France went to war with enthusiasm.

The head of the German military mission in Turkey, General Limon von Sanders (2nd left) prior to the outbreak of war.

THE POSITION OF TURKEY AND ITALY

ITALY

Italy had sought permission to join the alliance between Germany and Austria-Hungary in 1881. That nation sought allies because it felt threatened by the French urge for expansion. Italy's membership was strange not least because its relations with Austria-Hungary were far from ideal. Italy laid claim to certain territories of the Austro-Hungarian empire which did not please Austria-Hungary. The Austro-Hungarian commander in chief regarded Italy as much more likely to be a foe than an ally and events were later to prove his judgment to be sound. When Italy's Abyssinian adventure in 1896 ended in defeat at Adowa, it laid the blame partially at Germany's door for its failure to give them military support. Disappointed and perhaps filled with rancor but also with a hint of opportunism, the Italians then showed themselves open to French approaches. After it had renewed its treaty with Germany and Austria-Hungary, the Italians entered into a secret military treaty with the French in 1902 in which they promised to remain neutral if France was to engage in war with Germany, even if the French themselves were to take the initiative. This secret treaty was clearly a flagrant violation of Italy's treaty of alliance, more so since

Kaiser Wilhelm II during a visit to the Turkish Sultan in October 1917. General Limon von Sanders (2nd right) played a major role in the Turkish defeat of the British at Gallipoli by commanding the Turkish Fifth Army.

The Italian royal family before the outbreak of war.

Italy had just renewed that treaty. In order to cover all the angles, Italy once more signed an extension and also entered into a secret naval accord with Austria-Hungary in 1913 while also holding talks concerning closer ties with its other allies. During these talks Italy suggested that if Germany and Austria-Hungary should go to war with France and attack the French Mediterranean fleet, Italy would invade France and establish an Italian army in the western Alps and also send two army corps to Germany to support German troops. These talks had not been completed when war broke out. The unfaithfulness of Italy as an ally quickly became apparent because Italy demanded compensation for any extension of Austro-Hungarian territory. When the Austrians refused the Italian government declared itself not to support the ultimatum to Serbia and therefore to be neutral in the conflict. Contact was made quickly with the opposing allies who were prepared to offer to compensate Italy with part of the Austro-Hungarian territory. Hence Italy declared war on its Austro-Hungarian ally in May 1915 and against Germany in August 1916. This decision did gain Italy new territory after the war, including Istria but at the cost of 465,000 dead and 900,000 wounded. Italy's involvement in the war certainly had an influence on its outcome and was a major blow for the Triple Alliance.

TURKEY

British influence in Turkey had always been considerable and Britain had come to the aid of the Turks against the Russians during the Crimean War. A British naval mission had been busy in Turkey before the outbreak of war in 1914 and a British admiral headed the Turkish fleet. Germany went to great lengths to acquire Turkey as its ally though and their ambassador, Baron von Bieberstien succeeded in gaining great influence with the Turkish government and its army. The barbaric treatment of the Turks towards certain ethnic minorities led to severe criticism of Turkey in the British press and antagonism towards that country among the British people. When Great Britain and Russia entered into a treaty in 1907 to agree on their

different areas of influence it was apparent to the Turkish government that their closeness with Britain was at an end. This quickly manifested itself when Britain and France refused to grant a loan to Turkey. Germany quickly filled the breach in making the money available and thereby tightened the ties to them. Germany offered military training to Turkish officers who were being trained in Britain and France but were no longer wanted there and happily agreed to help in the reorganization of the Turkish army. The Germans sent General Liman von Sanders to Istanbul where he was appointed commander of their First Army Corps. There was quickly a conflict with Russia which felt threatened by a German general leading the Turkish army in what they regarded as their sphere of influence. The Russian minister of foreign affairs, Sazonov, protested vehemently and threatened measures. Germany backed down as it was not yet ready for outright conflict. They asked the Turks to appoint von Sanders to Field Marshal, too senior a rank to command an army corps in the field, and the tension was reduced and the whole matter blew over.

A group of "Young Turks" gained power in 1913. One of these, Enver Pasha, had been trained in Germany and he was very pro-German. As the new minister of war his power was considerable and the new German ambassador, Wangenheim, who pursued the same policies as his predecessor, succeeded in fully gaining his trust. Both men got on well with each other and British influence perceptibly diminished. When the First World War did break out Turkey was officially still neutral. Once again the British – who totally

War is reality and British troops arrive at Le Havre to take up their pre-ordained positions.

underestimated the importance of Turkey and the role it could play in the approaching conflict – made a fatal error by impounding two warships being built in Britain for the Turkish navy. The off-hand manner in which this was done, without discussion or any offer of compensation, was the straw that broke the camel's back. When Germany immediately reacted by offering the German warships Goeben and Breslau that just happened to be in the Mediterranean and now steamed rapidly to the Dardanelles to show the flag, the Turkish government accepted their offer and allowed both ships to enter Istanbul. By this act Turkey had officially sided with Germany in the world conflict at great expense to the British as we shall later see.

WAR BREAKS OUT

The offensive is prepared

THE MILITARY PLANS

The outbreak of World War I was not entirely unexpected. In fact this war appears to have been foreseen for some time by the principal nations participating with detailed military planning. Immediately after the Franco-Prussian War of 1870–1871, Bismarck recognized that their annexation of Alsace-Lorraine would lead to a new conflict with France. His policy was directed towards the isolation of France to prevent the French from becoming a threat to the new German nation. To this end he entered into a number of secret accords with Austria-Hungary and Russia and others and pursued policies to make Germany a permanent political and military power. Bismarck's successor did not pursue the same policy and did not renew the treaty with Russia, enabling France to escape its isolation in 1894 by forming a secret alliance with Russia that would eventually prove to be directed against Germany.

From that moment the French and Russian military staffs jointly developed their plans for victory if a war with Germany should happen. From 1904 on the French also had talks with the British about military cooperation in the event of a war with Germany. Fresh impetus was given to these talks by the Foreign Secretary, Grey, when the new Liberal government was formed in 1906. From this time on the French and British military staffs were in close but secret contact with one another and the British decided to form a British Expeditionary Force (BEF) for the

Germany encircled by hostile nations, 1914.

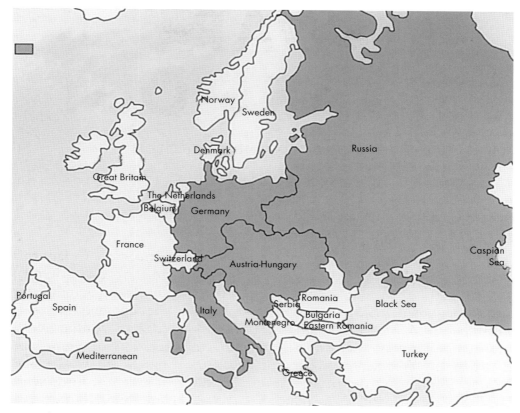

Bismarck's Europe in 1890.

purpose of these troops being sent to France to support the French army in the event of a war with Germany. In 1908 the British also had talks with Russia. Edward VII made official visits to both countries and the Czar and both nations talked about cooperation between their navies. These talks were still under way when war did break out in 1914.

THE MOTIVES

Why was everybody so convinced that the coming war was inevitable? That conviction must rest in the fact that all the major participants had a motive that led to war.

The French motive was Alsace-Lorraine which had been seized from the French by the Prussians in 1871 and French pride made it imperative that this wrong be righted. The French credo was for the return of Alsace-Lorraine to France but the French government knew this objective could never be achieved without outside help. The Franco-Russo treaty of 1894 was a first step towards possible execution of French plans to regain their lost territory.

The Russian motive could be found in the Dardanelles and the Bosporus. Since the Crimean War these seaways had been closed to warships. The Russian Black Sea was therefore closed off and the Russian Black Sea fleet was trapped and ineffective much like during the Russian-Japanese war of 1904. It was an essential point of Russian foreign policy to be able to gain free access to the Mediterranean by being able to pass through the Dardanelles and the Bosporus. This desire could not be realized though without the agreement of the great powers. By working closely with France, Russia aspired to French support for its wish for passage from the Black Sea. At the same time Russia also counted on support in a future war against its greatest rival in the Balkans, the Austro-Hungarian empire. Since that nation was an ally of Germany, war with them would bring Germany in conflict too which Russia could not afford to allow to happen. The military treaty with France though significantly changed Russia's position.

Field-Marshal Alfred von Schlieffen head of the German general staff from 1891–1905 who developed the plans for the German offensive. He anticipated a war on two fronts and planned a rapid victory against France before Russia could fully mobilize.

The danger of having to fight on two fronts simultaneously – against France and Russia – had been foreseen for many years in Germany and the Germans knew they could not win such a war. When both France and Russia extensively expanded their armed forces the German high command pressed for a preemptive war to prevent this fear being realized. Kaiser Wilhelm refused to give in to their pressure but the German military position became increasingly more difficult and when a conflict eventually arose over the Balkans for Germany's Austro-Hungarian allies, Germany decided to support them even if it meant world-wide war because it considered it was strong enough at that time to win.

For Great Britain matters were entirely the other way around. The enormous increase in the economic power of Germany was a great concern to that nation. The Germans also had colonial ambitions that the British feared would harm its own empire. The enlargement of the German navy was a further reason to choose the side of France and Russia in a future conflict. The British Foreign Secretary, Grey, uttered the view following the visit of the British king to the Czar that the cooperation with France and Russia would enable him to keep the increase in German power under control and hence he chose to side with Russia and France. The motives of these countries were clear enough and eventually led to war. It is surely certain that none of the nations involved had any notion that such a war would last four years and claim more than thirty million victims and change the world to such an extent.

THE VON SCHLIEFFEN PLAN

The German commander in chief Field Marshal von Moltke realized immediately after the victory against France in 1871 that the seeds had been sown for a future war and that the territory gained would have to be defended. He also anticipated that France would count on Russia's support. Von Moltke developed a plan that made it possible to consider fighting a war on two fronts. He based his plan on as strong a defense of the French-German border as possible. After all this was where the French according to the latest information had built an extremely strong defensive line that would be extremely difficult to penetrate. An attack on that front would probably turn out badly for the Germans, not least because it also had to defend itself against the Russian bear to the east. Consequently he planned to assemble half his army on the French border in defense and to use the other half for a preemptive strike against Russia in order to first defeat that nation before using his full strength against the French. In this way he hoped to avoid a battle on two fronts and to emerge victorious.

Field Marshal von Schlieffen, who succeeded von Moltke as head of the general staff in 1891 rejected the von Moltke plan as too risky. He too regarded Russia as the greatest threat for Germany while recognizing that the thirst for revenge that manifested itself increasingly more openly in France could well lead to a new war. He maintained quite clinically that Germany would lose such a war because of limitations of men and materials which did not permit a long drawn-out war and certainly not on two fronts. Von Schlieffen was of the opinion that is would be disastrous for the Germans to invade the vast expanses of Russia, particularly if half the army was tied up defending the border with France.

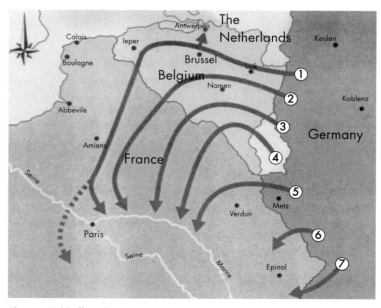

The von Schlieffen plan.

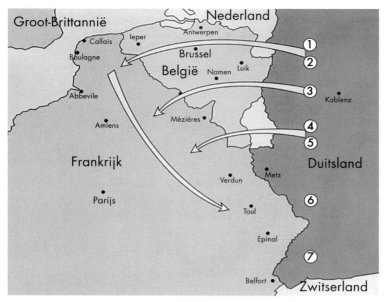

The moves of the von Schlieffen plan. Troops slipped through to the west of Paris, leaving the German border open to attack.

He therefore developed an entirely new plan based on rapid movement and modern modes of transport that was diametrical-ly the opposite of the von Moltke plan. It called for an immediate attack against France and a more defensive stance towards Russia.

The principal element of his plan was that no attempt should be made to attack the French border itself but for lightning speed deployment through The Netherlands and Belgium into northern France for a counter-clockwise offensive with Metz as its central pivot. The thrust would drive along the French coast to the west of Paris before turning back towards the east in order to attack the French border fortifications from the rear. The plan called for a very strong right flank utilizing about ninety percent of the German army for the march through France. The remainder were to be set up defensively near Metz and along the eastern border. Von Schlieffen counted on the French taking advantage of the relatively weak German defenses on the border in order to mount an attack to retake Alsace-Lorraine. His plan called for not too much by way of initial opposition to the French. By temporarily yielding German territory, French troops would be kept away from the battle in the north and west thus enabling a rapid German advance. Speed was of the essence to take advantage of the different amounts of time needed to mobilize the French and Russian armies. Intelligence reports suggested that the French could mobilize within two weeks while the Russians needed at least six weeks. The nub of von Schlieffen's plan was to defeat the French before the Russians were ready so that the majority of the German troops could be moved from a defeated France to the eastern front.

In this way von Schlieffen hoped to avoid a war on two fronts. It is obvious that timing was the greatest element of risk in his plan. After all, if the Germans failed to reach their objectives within the time allowed or even worse, the Russians managed to mobilize more quickly then precisely the very dangerous situation would arise that von Schlieffen sought to avoid at any cost. Apparently the matter concerned him greatly and he continued as an advisor to the general staff after his retirement. In 1912 he sent a memoranda calling among other things for reinforcement of the right flank.

THE FRENCH PLAN NO. 17

Documents make it apparent that the French knew the contents of the von Schlieffen plan at an early stage. General Dubail traveled to St. Petersburg in 1911 and got the agreement of Russians to significantly reduce their mobilization time and that they would enter East Prussia before completion of the general mobilization. This was a crucial decision for it went to the very heart of the von Schliessen plan that depended on four weeks difference between the French and Russian mobilizations and negated it. In 1912 further agreements were made that the number of Russian troops to take part in the early invasion of East Prussia was to be 800,000 and their mobilization was reduced to fourteen days.

The French too of course had a plan of war. After many amendments they eventually settled on the now renowned Plan no. 17. This was a somewhat obscure plan that left much to circumstance. At its core lay the notion that the French soldier was always to retain the initiative and that the holy creed was to attack.

Plan 17 was so obscure because it was apparently never committed to paper. When General Joffre was questioned about it after the war by a parliamentary commission he pleaded poor memory. Plan 17, he insisted, had never been written down and he could no longer recall which staff officers he had discussed the outbreak of war with. His temporary chief of staff, General de Castelnau, told the same commission that he had never seen the operational plan, which sounded quite unfeasible but was not denied by Joffre. In other words there was something wrong with the French plan. Unless it served as cover for the true French plan. A reconstruction of the plan would be along the following lines.

Count Berchtold, Austrian foreign minister, who decided to attack Serbia, even if it caused a world-wide conflict.

The Sultan of Turkey, 1914.

Using their knowledge of the von Schlieffen plan the French intended to arrange matters as follows:

1. Immediately after the outbreak of hostilities French troops attack and enter Alsace-Lorraine where it will find little opposition because of the von Schlieffen plan. To press home this advantage the French forces are to be as strong as possible. This attack though is to follow Germany's invasion of Belgium because only then can the British become active. The German invasion is therefore an imperative condition and France must avoid being regarded as the aggressor. Therefore most of their troops will be drawn back from the border to prevent misunderstandings.

2. British troops to land in Belgium and France and delay the German advance as much as possible. This will tie the Germans down in this sector so that troops will not be available to support either the eastern front or Austria-Hungary, which the French deem essential because:

3. The Russians will quickly (within fourteen days) after mobilization invade East Prussia with 800,000 men and establish a second front. This will mean that Germany, with almost its entire army in Belgium, will be caught in a two pronged pincer movement.

4. France to take advantage of the von Schlieffen plan that envisages the temporary invasion of French troops into Alsace but the French intend to make this occupation permanent.

5. France hands over the initial defense of its country almost entirely to the British with the intention that most of the war will take place in Belgium.

Elements of this reconstruction can be found in the minutes of the annual meetings between the French and Russian military staffs in which both nations closely developed and discussed their offensive plans. We now know that matters in reality were very different. The Russians did attack earlier but were quickly humiliatingly defeated. The British did land in Belgium as agreed but were so hard pressed by the Germans initially that they had to retreat, and the rest of the French plan largely failed to work out either. The situation only changed somewhat after the battle of the Marne.

THE BRITISH BATTLE PLAN

Soon after the creation of the entente in 1904, French and British military chiefs had discussions about cooperation if France should become involved in a war with Germany. These talks were under the auspices of the respective ministers of war and hence were politically covered. Britain's General Wilson, then head of military operations, made an agreement with the French on June 20, 1911 in which he promised to send 150,000 men and 67,000 horses to Boulogne and Le Havre to protect the French left flank from encirclement. It is striking that this is precisely the point at which the German's main force was anticipated and it was the intention that the British were expected at least to delay if not hold the German advance. This would give the French the ability to establish a superior force on their eastern border and hence to cut-off the German right flank from the rest of their army. In September 1912 the British also promised the support of their navy to protect the French west coast in the event of war, and the fleets were reassigned. The British moved most of their navy from the Mediterranean while the French moved its entire fleet to this sea.

British military plans were prepared in detail and in March 1914 an Anglo-French logistical exercise was conducted on French soil to practice the deployment of British troops from their port of entry and check transport, positions, and departure and arrival times.

Enver Pasha, the Turkish minister of war.

The German warship Goeben that with the Breslau was sold to Turkey and fired on Russian Black Sea ports.

THE AUSTRO-HUNGARIAN BATTLE PLAN

This nation had also prepared itself for war. Surprisingly though the Austro-Hungarians believed that any conflict could be kept purely restricted to a war against Serbia.

The Austro-Hungarian military plans were therefore prepared in this vein. Should Russia intervene, as not expected, then it was believed this could be accommodated by halting the war against Serbia. There were two plans: the "Balkan war plan" and the "Russian war plan." The latter plan was solely for the eventuality of Russian intervention. No consideration was given to fighting a war on two fronts simultaneously. The explanation for this is that the commander in chief of the Austro-Hungarian army, General Conrad von Hötzendorff, also anticipated a long period for Russia to mobilize and considered they would have defeated Serbia before the Russians could intervene. The Balkan plan made allowance for reversing troop movements up to five days after mobilization against Serbia. After the sixth day this was no longer possible and any Russian attack from then on would could only be met with the help of the ally, Germany.

Subsequent studies show that the Austro-Hungarian plan and particularly the entire movement planning had many serious flaws which meant that the march against Serbia was a fiasco from the very start and help was needed at once from their German ally. When Italy withdrew from the alliance at the last moment and Romania also failed to honor agreements, Austria-Hungary faced great difficulties and became entirely dependent on German assistance.

RUSSIAN WAR PLANS

Russia's plans for war were primarily drawn up in cooperation with and approval of France. The Russian task was to open a second front by an early invasion of East Prussia in order to tie down and if possible defeat German troops there. The Russian army's top brass had devoted their efforts to this end and expected to be ready to do so by 1917. Under the leadership of the minister of war, Suchomlinov, the Russian army was rebuilt from bottom to top and modernized following their defeat against Japan. If his plans had been fully implemented, Russia would have had the biggest and most powerful army in the world. However, the modernization of the Russian military was far from complete when politics took over from military planning in 1914. The time was ripe for Russia, France, and Great Britain to finish Germany as a great power and to achieve Russia's own ambitions for the Balkans and the destruction of the Austro-Hungarian empire. But the operational plans were not completed and the armaments, supplies, equipment etc. were wholly inadequate. Russia therefore entered the war technically unready for battle. The country was far from prepared for war and that quickly became apparent as we shall see later.

The Russian commander in chief, Grand Duke Nicholas.

THE MOVING WAR

The first skirmishes break out

THE GERMANS INVADE BELGIUM AND LUXEMBOURG

The German Kaiser signed the order to mobilize at five o'clock in the afternoon of August 1 and that evening, Lichnowski, the German ambassador in London, sent a telegram in which he informed his superiors that the British Foreign Secretary, Edward Grey, had informed him that Great Britain was prepared to guarantee the neutrality of France if Germany would undertake not to attack that country.

General von Moltke, who was on his way to carry out the mobilization order, was immediately recalled. The German chancellor, Bethmann Hollweg, who had constantly striven to maintain good relations with Britain and had hoped to the last moment that this nation would not enter the war greeted him excitedly. "The British are staying out of the conflict," he declared triumphantly, passing the telegram to von Moltke. "Now we only have to fight Russia. Let our armed forces turn around and march to the eastern front," added the

Kaiser Wilhelm II of Germany

General von Moltke, the German commander in chief at the outbreak of war. He was quickly removed following the debacle of the battle of the Marne.

King Albert of Belgium in his headquarters.

voice of the Kaiser. The world fell apart for von Moltke. Turning an entire army around was impossible and could have catastrophic consequences. He also knew that the order for general mobilization had also been given in France. The British telegram simply could not be true.

General von Kluck, commander of the German First Army.

Von Moltke told the Kaiser this and that if he must turn his armies around the German border would be wholly undefended and open to her enemies. Wilhelm II refused to listen though. "Your uncle would have given me a different answer," the emperor added, meaning the elder von Moltke who had ensured victory for the Germans during the Franco-Prussian war of 1870–1871. Bethmann Hollweg also got involved and turned on von Moltke who fought for his conviction with his back to the wall and refused to accept responsibility for such a far-reaching decision. "The German plan of battle," he declared, "is based on our strongly attacking French units

German troops in cover on the edge of "no man's land" immediately before entering Luxembourg in August 1914.

German field guns in action near the town of Liege.

German infantry advances across open terrain.

while only lightly armed defensive units are in the order of battle against Russia. Sudden and unconsidered changes to this plan will therefore be catastrophic." Von Moltke finally persuaded the Kaiser after a long discussion that the mobilization plans must be carried through and only then should any thought be given to sending more powerful units to the east.

The discussion with the Kaiser and Chancellor had exhausted von Moltke. The tensions of the previous days prior to the outbreak of war had taken too much out of him and he later declared that this broke him and that he never recovered. The principal cause of this was Bethmann Hollweg's demand in any event to delay the occupation of Luxembourg. This put the entire German plan of attack at risk because the capture of the extremely important railway junction there was an essential part of the

Belgian militiamen.

Belgian soldiers take a rest behind the front line.

German battle plan. Bethmann Hollweg though was of the opinion that this occupation was a direct threat to France whereupon the British offer of neutrality would certainly be withdrawn. The Kaiser called for his adjutant and without consulting von Moltke dictated an order for the Sixteenth Division to halt its march on Luxembourg.

Despite strong protests from von Moltke, Wilhelm II stuck to his decision and dismissed von Moltke. When he returned to his headquarters the order already lay their awaiting him but von Moltke stuck to his guns and refused to countersign the order. Several hours later at 11 p.m. he once more received an order to report to the Kaiser. The emperor received him in his bedroom and handed him a telegram from the British King that stated that Lichnowski's statement had been based on a misunderstanding and their was no question of the British guaranteeing French neutrality. The Kaiser was in a very bad mood and told von Moltke: *"Nun können Sie machen, was Sie wollen"* (now you can do what you like), at which von Moltke could take his leave.

Right: Shared Belgian/British water station at the farthest point on the Belgian front line.

The fatal moment had arrived and the appalling drama that was first to become known as "The Great War" and later as World War I was about to break out. Von Moltke now sent the Sixteenth Division an order to enter Luxembourg without delay and to seize the railway junction.

THE BATTLE COMMENCES

Eight German armies now set about the execution of the von Schlieffen plan. Seven were destined for the western front and one for the east.

The German First Army under General von Kluck, the Second under von Bülow, and the Third, commanded by von Hausen were to enter Belgium. The Fourth Army under Duke Albrecht was destined for Luxembourg. The Fifth, led by the German crown prince, and the Sixth, under crown prince Rupprecht von Beieren, and the Seventh commanded by General von Heeringen were drawn up in readiness between Saarbrücken and Basle.

In the early morning of August 2, 1914, the Germans entered Luxembourg. Just before this the Luxembourg government received a telegram advising it that Germany had learned from reliable sources that a force of French troops was en route to Luxembourg and that Germany, unfortunately, was forced to defend itself by taking control of the railway junction there. The Luxembourg government protested strongly but did not have the means to defend its country which quickly fell to German hands.

The huge troop movements could now begin. Between August 2–14 more than 2,200 troop trains passed through Cologne alone heading west. The objectives were known. The First and Second Armies were headed for Brussels. The Third Army was required to cross the Meuse (Maas) at Namur and Dinant and the Fourth Army was expected to take control from there to the southernmost tip of Belgium at its border with Luxembourg. The Fifth Army of the crown prince finally was required to take up posts around Metz while the other two armies were to engage with the French on the left flank.

On Sunday August 2, the German ambassador handed an ultimatum to the Belgian government demanding free passage through Belgium for the German army. If this request was acceded to Germany promised to compensate Belgium after the conflict for any damage and need to vacate land. It pleaded with the Belgian government to offer no resistance in order to avoid unnecessary bloodshed and went to some

The destroyed bridge and church of Our Lady at Dinant.

German General von Emich, who commanded the attack on Liege.

lengths to insist that the German state was merely defending itself and had no intention of occupying Belgian territory. Finally, the ultimatum required an answer within twelve hours. The Belgian government naturally rejected the ultimatum and the following day, August 3, German troops entered Belgium on their way to France.

THE BATTLE OF LIEGE

Liege was the German's first objective. The town itself was defended by several strong forts that protected the entire area of eastern Belgium and its capture at any cost was essential to the Germans to prevent delays to the German right flank that would put the von Schlieffen plan in jeopardy. Speed was of the essence and the German general staff had developed a separate plan for the capture of the town at the outset of the war. Around 34,000 men and some 125 pieces of field artillery, including some of the heaviest caliber, approached the ring of forts surrounding the town on August 4. The Belgian 3rd Division, numbering about 23,000

German troops in the field.

German ordnance officer receives instructions for the troops attacking Liege.

men was deployed between the forts that were about 4 km (2.5 miles) apart. The entire defense, including the fort garrisons, was commanded by General Leman.

The Germans had thoroughly appraised the situation before the war and noted that there were few defense obstacles between the forts. Their plan was for a nighttime advance at various points between the forts. The defenders must be overwhelmed in order to gain access within the ring to reach Liege. The forts would then have little option but to surrender. The special force assembled for this daring feat was commanded by General von Emmich who was supported by an officer from the general staff, Erich Ludendorff, who was later to play the most important role in the history of World War I.

Nothing could apparently withstand the heavy German artillery. Remains of Fort Loucin near Liege.

On the night of August 5–6 a start was made to carry out the plan with attacks on three fronts between the forts. Units of the German Fourteenth Brigade succeeded in penetrating between the Fléron and Evegne forts. Because of the darkness they were not noticed so there was no artillery fire. They did encounter soldiers of the Belgian Third division who offered stiff resistance but did not manage to halt the Germans. When the German commander died in the action, Ludendorff assumed command and urged the men forward to the hills to the east of La Chartreuse where they had command over the bridges crossing the Meuse (Maas). Ludendorff gave orders to seize the bridges which was miraculously accomplished without a shot fired.

On the morning of August 7 Ludendorff ordered his troops to enter Liege. He personally led troops directly to the Citadel which appeared to be hermetically sealed. He knocked on the door several times and to his surprise the door was opened. He told the guards to surrender and then entered and had himself taken to the commander who surrendered the garrison to the Germans. This feat of dash was the start of a glittering career. Much more was to be heard of Ludendorff.

The town of Liege was now in German hands and Belgian defense fell back to join other Belgian forces at Louvain.

Remarkably the forts around Liege remained in Belgian hands and their artillery was a considerable threat for the continued German advance. There was a significant artillery barrage with heavy pieces such as the 305 mm (12 inches) Austrian siege mortar and even heavier 420 mm (16½ inches) Krupp guns known as "Fat Bertha" in order to destroy the forts which eventually proved to be not strong enough. One by one they were reduced to rubble and their garrison were killed or surrendered. One of the last to fall was Fort Loncin that succumbed on August 15 following a direct hit on its magazine. The resulting explosion killed most of the occupants. The Belgian commander, General Leman, who was in the fort, survived. He was pulled out unconscious from the rubble. His first words when he came round were: "I have not surrendered," and when he was taken prisoner he requested that the German officer who came to fetch him should include this in his report. The final two forts fell to the Germans on August 16 which put an end to the threat to the further German advance to the open flat country of Belgium.

Belgian infantry retreating to Antwerp, August 20, 1914.

Belgian soldiers preparing defensive positions near Antwerp.

THE BATTLE OF NAMUR

After the Belgian Third Division regrouped around Louvain, the battle moved towards the west. The Belgians had built a defensive line by the small river Gete before the war following the line of Namur, Dinant, and Givet. The Belgian Fourth Division reinforced the Namur garrison and made every effort for a well-ordered defense. A specially assigned German force under General von Gallwitz though immediately reduced the forts surrounding Namur to rubble with their very heavy artillery that included six batteries of 420 mm (16 ½ inches) guns and four batteries of Austrian 305 mm (12 inches) Skoda guns.

At the same time the Germans succeeded in crossing the Sambre and Meuse so that Namur was threatened with being surrounded. On August 22 the Belgian Fourth Division began to withdraw towards Mariembourg where about half the originally 30,000 men arrived. A week later they retreated towards Antwerp where they joined the rest

One of the Antwerp forts before it was destroyed by German heavy artillery fire.

The inhabitants of Antwerp flee as German troops approach.

French cycle-mounted troops rush to help Belgium.

Right: The British also send troops to help that are enthusiastically greeted.

of the Belgian army on September 2. Dinant also fell to the Germans with units of the German Third Army encircling the town which they entered early on the morning of August 22.

Meanwhile around half a million men of the German First Army under General von Kluck and Second Army commanded by von Bülow pressed forward into Belgium to the north of the Meuse. Here too there was fierce Belgian resistance. The Belgian 22nd Regiment of the line lost more than half its men at St. Margriete. The overwhelming numbers of Germans were too great and on August 18 the Belgian King decided his troops must withdraw behind the little river Dijle to create a new defensive line in the direction of Antwerp. As soon as August 20 the Belgian army had to fall back further to within the fortifications of Antwerp. On this same day the German Fourth Corps under General Sixt von Arnim reached Brussels and occupied the city while the German First, Second, and Third Armies penetrated deeper into Belgium. Meanwhile both the French and British came to the aid of Belgium. The French Fifth Army under General Lanrezac took up positions to block the German advance on the right bank of the Meuse. The British Expeditionary Force under General Sir John French had now also arrived on the continent and took up positions linking up with those of the French Fifth Army. On August 21 the French troops counter-attacked but

British prisoners of war wait for transport by the town hall at Menen.

A German light mortar battery parades past Admiral Schroeder as they enter Brussels.

found themselves greatly outnumbered. They had ill-prepared their offensive and quickly had to retreat with considerable loss of territory. By August 23 their position was no longer tenable and General Lanrezac gave an order for a general retreat. Meanwhile, the British had established a front of 35 km (22 miles), roughly along the line of Harmignies, Condé, and Binche. They were soon threatened by the German Second, Fourth, and Ninth Corps and the British front line quickly yielded on the morning of August 23. Somewhat later that day the British had to abandon Mons and when General French learned that evening that the French were also forced to retreat he was worried they could become surrounded and gave orders for a retreat towards Le Cateau. This was reached on the evening of August 24 with stalwart rearguard action that cost about 3,800 men. Here they were attacked early on the morning of the 26th by units of von Kluck's army. The battle that lasted all day, with the British Second Corps under General Smith Dorrien being hardest hit, forced the British to retreat once more. The British lost about

German Admiral Schroeder who commanded the German navy in Flanders.

8,000 men and thirty-six guns in this battle and narrowly avoided becoming surrounded.

The situation for the Allied forces was not good. General French saw a somber outcome when he signaled London on the 31st with his plan to withdraw to a line behind the Seine to the west of Paris because he no longer believed in a French victory and was frightened his entire army might fall into German hands.

THE BATTLE OF ANTWERP (ANVERS)

The Germans now wanted to reach the Belgian coast as quickly as possible before the allies did. They advanced rapidly towards Antwerp (Anvers) where the Belgian army had established itself behind fortifications. Preparations had been underway from the moment the Germans entered Belgium to strengthen the fortifications around Antwerp. Several forts had been reinforced with concrete to provide defense against German heavy artillery and munitions and supplies were laid in to prepare for resistance to a long siege. Troops gained confidence when they saw the tremendous fortifications and felt

German troops march into the city of Lille.

certain the Germans would not succeed in conquering the Antwerp defenses.

The German attack on Antwerp began on September 27. That same day German forces led by General von Besseler took the town of Mechelen. The following day the German heavy artillery opened fire and the forts fell one by one to 420 mm (16 ½ inches) and 305 mm (12 inches) shells. On September 29 the German troops reached the first bridges into Antwerp where they came under fire from Fort Wealhem. German artillery returned fire and a shell landed in the magazine causing an enormous explosion that killed and injured many. Fort Wavre-St.Catherine, that had withstood thirty hours continuous shelling, also

Generals Hindenburg and Ludendorff during a visit to Brussels.

Kaiser Wilhelm II during his visit to the German submarine base at Zeebrugge.

received a direct hit to its munitions store and the occupants were forced to evacuate the fort. Germany artillery also fired mercilessly on the other forts and their surroundings so that gradually they were each in turn put out of action and destroyed. The Belgians still hoped for help from the allies but on the evening of the 29th things appeared hopeless with the allies still some distance from Antwerp and unlikely to reach the city in time. By October 2 it was quite clear that the Belgian army could no longer hold Antwerp and King Albert gave orders for preparations to be made for the army to withdraw to form a new defensive line near Ostend. Belgian resistance was once again fierce against overwhelming German forces. Fort after fort was destroyed but the Belgians fought like

Commander of the British troops in France, General Sir John French, constantly retreated with his troops until Field Marshal Lord Kitchener ordered him to stand.

devils rather than surrender to the Germans. They even launched counter-attacks and conquered several supply points but were then driven back by superior numbers. The exploits of the Belgian army rank highly among the valor of World War I.

Help finally arrived on October 3. British troops arrived in Ostend and marched to link up with the Belgian army. More British troops arrived in the following two days, totaling around 6,000, chiefly consisting of Royal Marines, and their arrival was greeted with tremendous enthusiasm by the people of Antwerp. Churchill himself managed to visit the city to encourage the people of Antwerp but it was all too late. The German advance could no longer be halted and on October 6 the British were forced to retreat. On the night of October 6, the Belgian army vacated the fortifications of Antwerp under cover of darkness and crossed the River Schelde.

On the morning of October 7 the Belgian government and the diplomatic corps based in the city also departed for Ostend. Their departure caused great panic among the citizens who tried to leave the city en masse. Antwerp surrendered to the Germans on Friday October 9. German troops did not enter the city until the next day when they paraded triumphantly past the new military governor of Antwerp,

Admiral von Schroeder. The city of Antwerp was to remain in German hands for the next four years.

GERMAN ATROCITIES IN BELGIUM: THE DEATH OF CAPT. FRYATT AND EDITH CAVELL

Quickly after the invasion of German troops into Belgium there were reports of gruesome deeds perpetrated against the civilian population. These reports became stronger and reached the international press who frequently grossly exaggerated them. It is certainly true that in many cases the Germans were quite brutal towards the civilian population and often terrorized them without good reason. The Germans imagined themselves surrounded everywhere by *francs tireurs*. If a bridge was blown up somewhere then the local civilians were blamed and punished. Sometimes the German's suspicions were founded but frequently they were not.

General Haig who succeeded French as commander of the BEF in France.

German sentry guards a building in Lille.

The British merchant marine captain, Charles Fryatt, who attempted to follow Churchill's orders and ram a German U-boat. He was arrested and executed as a *franc tireur*.

N° 29

Bekanntmachung	Bekendmaking	AVIS
Der englische Handelsschiffs-kapitän	De Engelsche handelsscheeps-kapitein	Le capitaine anglais de la marine marchande
Charles Fryatt aus Southampton	**Charles Fryatt** van Southampton	**Charles Fryatt** de Southampton

Proclamation of the execution of Charles Fryatt.

But the Germans were not really interested who the culprits were. They endeavored by intimidation and brutal response to crush any form of civilian resistance and this frequently led to scandalous and outright criminal acts. One example is when occupying the village of Andenne the Germans found the bridge destroyed. The village was immediately set on fire and about three hundred villagers were shot dead on the spot. About three hundred houses were destroyed and in the following days the village was plundered and then destroyed by the Germans. The Germans were brutal too after the fall of Namur and Dinant. They plundered houses, entered churches during mass and shot all the men. More than eighty men were executed in the market square as a public warning and then the city was set on fire and almost entirely destroyed. The famous library in the town of Louvain was set on fire so that centuries of culture were lost without any effort being made to save these treasures. Throughout the German advance through Belgium there was murder and looting. Notorious among these acts were the executions of the British merchant marine captain Charles Fryatt and the British nurse Edith Cavell. Their deaths disturbed world opinion and did great harm to the name of Germany. The Germans attempted later to defend their actions and to put them into context and it is certainly true that allied propaganda often significantly exaggerated them but the reality is that the German advance through Belgium was in itself inexcusable and nothing can justify the atrocities they committed. It made the Germans greatly hated by the people and played right into the hands of enemy propaganda.

British propaganda poster after the death of Edith Cavell.

Propaganda poster designed to strengthen the British population's will to fight.

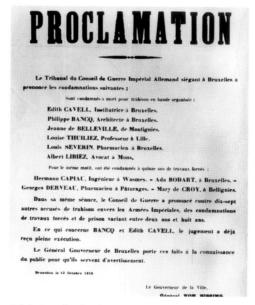

The British nurse, Edith Cavell, offered help and refuge for wounded British soldiers and was accused of espionage and treachery and executed.

Edith Cavell's death caused widespread concern and harmed Germany. The proclamation in Brussels of October 1915.

German soldiers in their trenches in Flanders.

THE BATTLE OF THE MARNE

THE TURNING POINT

The French commander in chief was forced to order his armies to retreat by the rapid advance of the German forces. He ordered a new defensive line to be created along the line of Verdun – Laon – Amiens and ordered the formation of a new Sixth Army to rapidly take position around Amiens and surroundings that lay entirely open for German advances. Through the British defeat at Le Cateau the six divisions of this new army immediately ran into difficulties and had to retreat towards Paris.

The French government decided that special measures were now required to ensure Paris was safeguarded and gave orders for three Corps to be dispatched there. The elderly General Gallieni, who had already retired, was asked to take command of these troops and to defend the city at any cost. The new Sixth Army that had meanwhile arrived near Paris was reinforced with Moroccan and Algerian units commanded by General Manoury who ordered his troops to deploy and dig in to the north of Paris. The city prepared itself for the coming battle with the population waiting anxiously for unfolding events.

German pressure grew relentlessly and the allies were forced to retreat throughout the line but this rapid German advance gave them increasing problems. The lines of communication became increasingly longer between the German units and their commander in chief. In fact, von Moltke no longer had a thorough overview of the front and did not know precisely what was happening. His thoughts for the events on the western front were further diverted by the entirely unexpected Russian advance in the east.

Cries of alarm from that front caused von Moltke to pull two corps from the western front and quickly move them to halt the Russian advance. It is clear that von Moltke panicked. The von Schlieffen plan envisaged a flexible defense on the eastern border that took account of possible short-term occupation of German territory in Prussia by the Russians.

French recruiting poster

Von Moltke had also noticed that his troops were quickly winning a lot of the enemy's territory but that they were not taking large numbers of prisoners of war or capturing booty. The French and the British constantly retreated but their armies did not surrender and remained combat ready. Von Moltke wanted to see results and although he did not change the objectives he agreed to a request from von Bülow commanding the Second Army to pursue the French Fifth Army and to chop it to bits when it retreated from east of Paris towards the southeast. This meant that the essential element of the von Schlieffen plan was ignored. German troops now pressed further west of Paris, ignoring the city, intent on — they thought — a quick and easy victory over the French Fifth Army.

This decision of von Moltke to grant the request from von Bülow had far-reaching consequences, cost him victory in the battle for France, and hence eventually lost Germany the war. The German First Army under von Kluck did not want von Bülow to keep the booty from the trapped French Fifth Army all to himself. Without permission he departed from the route recommended to him, crossed the Oise and reached the rearguard of the still retreating French. Only at this point did he inform von Moltke that he had deviated from his original route. Von Moltke did not intervene but now ordered the First Army to protect the flank of the Second Army to protect it against attacks from the west. This meant that von Kluck had to advance more slowly to keep pace with von Bülow's forces but von Kluck took absolutely no notice of it. Eventually

Colonial troops are advised about the course of the battle of the Marne by their French officer.

though, he was unable to maintain his rapid advance and had to give up the pursuit of the French because of shortage of supplies. The Second Army, not surprisingly, had not been able to match the rapid advances of von Kluck and his troops and now urgently needed rest. Thus, an increasingly large gap opened up between the two armies.

Once the elderly General Gallieni realized on September 3 that the Germans were apparently going to by-pass Paris and were exposing their flank to him he ordered the newly-formed Sixth Army to assemble. He advised Joffre that the Germans were apparently no longer planning to attack Paris but would pass to the east and that a large gap had opened between the two Germany Armies. He asked Joffre's permission to attack. The closeness of the Germans to Paris had meanwhile caused great panic in that city and the government had evacuated to Bordeaux.

Panic broke out also in the German headquarters. Von Moltke saw the great danger posed by the increasing distance between the First and Second Armies. He sent one of his staff officers, Lieutenant-Colonel Hentsch to both generals with strict orders to immediately get rid of the gap between them. Hentsch had some difficulty convincing the generals of this necessity. The French Fifth Army was in full retreat and was ripe for the plucking as it were. On September 6 German reconnaissance reported that there was dangerous troop movements from the direction of the Paris defense lines and that French troops appeared to be preparing for an attack on the German flank. The report was barely received before a battle broke out along the Marne. Von Kluck now fought for his life near Paris. His flank lay exposed to the French Sixth Army but his troops withstood these attacks and he was optimistic of defeating the French. Things were different for von Bülow's Second Army. After four days of severe battle with attack after attack by the French, von Bülow was forced to retreat on September 9 so von Kluck was also forced to disengage and retreat. Now it was von Bülow's troops who moved more rapidly and instead of the gap between the two armies closing, it became wider, growing to around 19 miles. General Joffre requested that the British Expeditionary Force insert themselves into this gap to isolate the two German forces from each other but the British response was somewhat tepid. They did advance but so slowly that the chances of success were lost.

Battle of the Marne (September 6–12, 1914). The ruins of the village of Sermaize-les-Bains after German artillery fire.

The River IJzer where Belgian and French forces held the Germans.

During this time the French had formed a new Ninth Army under General Foch that was now sent to reinforce the Fifth Army. It immediately came in contact with the German Third Army and several corps of von Bülow's Second Army, which succeeded in driving the French back several kilometers on September 8. Foch ordered a counter-attack but he did not succeed in breaking through.

Foch's initiative did have results though. The stiff opposition had the consequence that von Moltke gave the order to disengage and to restore the link with von Kluck's First Army. On September 11 von Moltke made his first visit to the front and came to the conclusion that the positions of the First and Second Armies were still at risk of becoming surrounded. He now gave the order for a coordinated withdrawal to new positions on the Aisne and the Vesne near Reims. The other German armies also withdrew so that a new line was formed from Reims to Verdun following the battle of the Marne.

The disobedience of von Kluck and the fact that von Moltke did not immediately punish this, together with the jealousy between von Kluck and von Bülow, was the eventual cause of the failure of the von Schlieffen plan. The chances of a quick end to the war were now over.

THE RACE TO THE SEA, THE BATTLE OF IJZER AND YPRES

VON MOLTKE DISMISSED AND FALKENHAYN APPOINTED

The retreat of the German armies after the battle of the Marne resulted in General von Moltke being relieved of his command and replaced by the minister of war, Lieutenant-General Erich von Falkenhayn.

Falkenhayn went back to basics. He was convinced that Germany had a longer war ahead for which the reserves of manpower, materials, and food were possibly not sufficient. He gave orders for German industry to switch over wholly to war production and to make the production of consumer goods of lower priority. He also introduced a much stricter policy regarding those excused from conscription so that far more men could be armed. Then he ordered his troops to reach the Belgian coast as rapidly as possible and proposed to encircle the French and British troops and cut them off from the sea. The front line at this time ran from

British recruitment poster after the first recruits had been expended on the battlefield.

French positions on the IJzer.

German headquarters on the banks of a canal at Ypres.

Soissons northwards through Péronne, Arras, Loos, to the east of Ypres (Ieper), Langemark, Lille, Diksmuide, to the Belgian coast. The French had considerably reinforced the salient between this line and the coast and attempted to push the Germans east through heavy attacks. Between the 21st and 30th of September there were furious efforts to halt the German advance on the Oise in the south and to push them back. At the same time the French Second Army under General de Castelnau to the north of the Oise tried the same ploy, while the British forces under General French were deployed between Loos and Ypres to defend against German attacks. The battle around Ypres was particularly fierce because the Germans attempted a breakthrough with a very strong force. The final salient to the north of the British line, along the River IJzer to the coast was held by Belgian and French troops. The Belgians opened the sluices at Nieuwendamme to flood the surrounding land, but not enough to halt the Germans. Once again the Belgians fought with great determination and courage.

French troops assembling on the River IJzer.

An area of "no-man's-land" by a destroyed bridge over the IJzer.

Belgian soldiers on the IJzer front.

The important railway at Boezinge linking the IJzer front.

Left: the Belgians flood the land near Raamskapelle to slow the rapid German advance.

Australian troops waiting for the order to attack at Ypres.

Four new German corps comprising 165,000 men broke through on October 16 to reach the IJzer. The first battle of the IJzer was about to begin.

THE BATTLE OF IJZER, HEROIC STRUGGLE BY THE BELGIAN ARMY

The 48,000 Belgian soldiers that had been fighting continuously for two and a half months faced 100,000 German troops with 350 artillery pieces across the IJzer. The Belgians were required to hold out for at least forty-eight hours until reinforcements could reach them. The ground had turned to thick mud following heavy rain, making fighting conditions extremely onerous. The Belgians deployed in positions at Diksmuide and Nieuwpoort to the north and south of the IJzer from where they controlled the possible crossing point for the Germans. In order to delay the German advance positions were also held on the other side of the river with a second line of defense created immediately behind the banks of the river. French troops were also deployed to keep communications open with Ostend and France.

British infantry on the front line.

German artillery fires on British positions just before an infantry attack at Ypres.

Damaged buildings on the bank of the River Lys.

Germany artillery fired on this bridge at Warmeton without success.

French troops also passed through Ypres on their way to the front. French soldiers on the Grote Markt at Ypres, October, 1914.

British troops enter Ypres on October 13, 1914 after the Germans had left the town.

British infantry in their trenches.

A British officer and his soldiers are taken prisoner at Ypres, 1915.

The center of the German attack was towards Diksmuide. This was the point at which the Germans hoped to break through, cutting the Belgians off from their allies before driving them into the sea or routing them. On the afternoon of the sixteenth a reconnaissance group approached Diksmuide but did not succeed in reaching the town. The following day German artillery opened fire upon the small settlement of Rattevanger and set it on fire. On the 18th fierce fighting began along the Belgian front defensive line in front of the IJzer. While the battle was raging a flotilla of the British Royal Navy opened fire on the flank of the German attackers so that the offensive faltered and then stopped.

The Germans had more success at Manneskesvere to the south of Nieuwpoort and reached this place. Their artillery succeeded in driving the Belgians from their first line of defense. That night the Belgians mounted a counter-attack and regained the positions they had lost. On October 19 Belgian units succeeded in once more occupying the outlying parts of Manneskesvere but were driven from these positions several hours later. Diksmuide also came under heavy shell fire from the Germans while most of the Belgian line fell into German hands. To the north they crossed the Passchendaele canal and took Lombardzyde.

British rail-mounted heavy artillery piece just after going into action.

Infantry leave their trenches and storm the enemy lines at Ypres, 1917.

A wounded German soldier taken behind the lines as POW.

Simultaneously Diksmuide was attacked. After a heavy barrage enemy infantry appeared from several directions at ten in the morning but they did not succeed in overcoming the Belgians. There was now heavy fighting along the whole of the IJzer. Diksmuide and Nieuwpoort were in flames and the fire spread remarkably rapidly. The Germans mounted another heavy offensive against Tervate on the night of the 22nd, managing to seize a small footbridge over the river and creating a bridgehead on the left bank of the IJzer. A Belgian counter-offensive failed and on the twenty-third the Germans managed to extend and reinforce their toe-hold on the left bank so that they now threatened the Belgian's second line of defense.

Hill 60 at Ypres. Heavy fighting saw heavy losses on both sides here.

A German artillery regiment loads horses and equipment for transport to the front.

German infantry attacking near Ypres, 1917.

A Medieval war with modern means: German cavalry with gas mask and lance.

A fearsome weapon. The enemy is hit
in their trenches with flame-throwers.

A German artillery sighting balloon at Ypres, 1917.

German infantry prepare to attack near Ypres in 1917. Note the stick grenade on the left of the picture.

A shell crater caused by German artillery in the British positions at Ypres.

Shells rain down on British infantry during the Battle of Ypres, 1917.

German machine-gun post near Ypres, 1917.

French help was called for and 6,000 French marines of Admiral Romarch helped the Belgians to defend the area until November 10 but it was really too late. Despite the fierce resistance German troops slowly but inexorably overcame the Belgian line and on the evening of the 25th the leading German units reached Diksmuide. The second Belgian line of defense fell on the 26th with Diksmuide falling on the 29th and the German Fifth reserve division taking Ramskapelle on the 30th so that the Belgian line was cut in two. The Belgians and French now mounted a fierce counter-attack. They reached the outer parts of Ramskapelle and drove the Germans from their new positions with bitter hand-to-hand fighting. The Germans were not able to advance further for the Belgians had flooded the area between the IJzer and the Diksmuide–Nieuwpoort rail line, forcing the Germans to evacuate the west bank of the IJzer. The Battle of the IJzer was over and the German attempt to break through had failed. Their losses were estimated at 40,000 men. The Belgians had lost 25,000 but their heroic defense had prevented the Germans from breaking through to the English Channel to occupy the coast. This had been a tremendous achievement.

The respite was short-lived. German troops move off for a fresh assault at Ypres.

A German cavalry patrol approaches a château at Houtrust near Ypres in 1917.

Excavations beneath enemy positions to place explosive mines.

German soldiers take a rest in their trenches at the front.

Impassable ground in the battlefield...

...as far as the eye can see.

Water-filled shell holes near Ypres.

German machine-gun post near Ypres. Note the body armor to protect against bullets and shrapnel.

British troops attack at Ypres. The ground conditions were appalling. Heavy rain and continuous shelling turned the battlefield into a great mud bath.

A life and death struggle took place over this terrain. Many died in rain-filled shell holes near Ypres.

Horses and equipment sank in the mud and it became impossible to move artillery.

Trenches filled with water with sticky and slimy mud.

Soldiers sometimes stood for days on end up to their knees in water often leading to a rotting disease of the foot known as trench foot.

Sometimes the front line could only be reached by duck-boards.

Transport regularly became stuck in the mud delaying food and munitions.

Efforts to rescue horses after a wagon has sunk into the mud.

British work squad given the impossible task of keeping the trenches free of mud. Tomorrow they would do it all again.

THE FIRST BATTLE OF YPRES (IEPER)

The Germans also tried to break through to the sea at other places. In early October the German Fourth Army was ordered to attack the British and French line at Ypres (Ieper) and then to advance towards Abbeville in France. Such a move would deliver them the important ports and the coast. When the Battle of the IJzer failed Ypres became the next major objective for their offensive. On October 21, 1914 the first Battle of Ypres was begun by the German 26th and 27th reserve corps which included

British officers help one another to reach their command post.

A wounded Canadian soldier gives a wounded German a light while they wait for transport out of the mud.

Belgian infantry at Zillebeke, where heavy fighting took place.

British Royal Artillery dig out an eighteen pounder field gun stuck in the mud at Ypres.

The battlefield at Passchendaele.

A huge mine crater at Wijtschaeten.

British Pioneer Corps soldiers create a defensive position on Passchendaele Ridge under the watchful eye of the Virgin Mary.

The battlefield at Zonnebeke.

Zonnebeke after the battle.

German reserves are brought in by narrow gauge railway at Menen.

Dead Scottish soldiers at Zonnebeke.

several thousand young students. They had volunteered and been sent to the front after a short period of training. They now wanted to show what they were made of and they fell upon their enemy towards Langemark with a certain élan. After four days of hard battle the struggle had to be abandoned. Around 3,000 students died for their emperor and fatherland at Langemark, where their graves can be seen still.

The impassable terrain at Ypres.

Delville Wood after a German artillery barrage.

British wounded on their way to a field hospital German POWs are acting as stretcher bearers.

An underground first aid post by the Menen Road.

The Menen Road. Adolf Hitler served here as an orderly.

Polygoon Wood near Ypres.

The remnants of Ypres.

Canadian cavalry pass through the destroyed town of Ypres.

Left: Wounded soldiers in the open awaiting transport to a field
hospital for first aid.

Hellfire Corner at Ypres. An ammunition wagon hit by a shell.

The infamous Hill 60 with German soldiers in their shelter.

German soldiers expecting an attack.

One of the many farmhouses destroyed near Ypres.

On October 29 a second German attempt to break through was made at Geluveld. Here too the battle was broken off after three days of heavy fighting. It was at Geluveld that the 16th Bavarian Reserves infantry regiment – in which Adolf Hitler served – suffered heavy losses with

Looking for a comrade.

Ice broken by shell fire at Beaumont-Hamel.

An icy wind blows across the battlefield. Many froze to death in their trenches.

Men tried to prepare something hot in their trenches against the bitter cold.

Conditions were even worse in the winter. British Hussars in their trenches at Zillebeke.

Wounded soldiers quickly became chilled and could often not be saved.

British Prime Minister Lloyd George during a visit to the front. He was not in favor of General Haig, who he accused of incompetent leadership because of the enormous losses of men at the front.

around half of Hitler's comrades being lost. On November 1 the Germans succeeded in taking the Menen ridge which gave them a good view across the town of Ypres and surrounding area. They prepared themselves now for a fresh attack that was launched on November 11 with 18,000 men along the Menen road towards the town of Ypres. Despite being heavily outnumbered (the British troops numbered just 8,000 men) this attack failed against stiff British resistance and hence ended the "First Battle of Ypres" – as it became known. The Germans made several more attacks but on November 22 the high command decided to call a halt to the Ypres offensive which brought to an end for the time being any breakthrough to the sea.

Indian troops of the British Empire on their way to the front at Ypres.

Gas mask inspection.

French colonial marines from Annam in Indochina near Ypres in 1916.

The French employed many Annamese troops at Ypres.

These colonial troops were renowned for their aggression and were feared for their ferocious fighting spirit against the enemy.

Annamese resting on their way to the front.

In addition to their colonial troops the British also had Chinese coolies who worked at the front.

Death was all around and not a stranger. Soldiers wash their hands in a water-filled shell hole that has unearthed new graves.

Wounded soldiers help one another to a first aid post.

Grave yards were not spared by artillery. Bodies were exposed and shattered and buried once more.

The German soldiers have been killed by shell fire.

THE SECOND BATTLE AND GAS ATTACK

The second Battle of Ypres took place between April 22 and May 25 in 1915. The Germans were more successful this time. For the first time the Germans used chlorine gas in their attack which wholly surprised the French colonial troops between Poelkapelle and St. Juliaan who suffered tremendous losses as they tried to escape. When the Canadian troops on their flank got orders to fill the gap they too were enveloped in clouds of gas and 2,000 of the 18,000 men were killed. The gas attack had caused a breach about four miles wide in the allied lines and

British medical orderlies take a severely-wounded man to a field hospital with the ground conditions making their task extremely onerous. Victims often could not be found or sank into the mud and drowned.

Dismembered bodies and human remains everywhere. Recovering the body of a soldier drowned in the mud.

A wounded Canadian soldier is taken through the mud to a field hospital.

A dead German soldier following a British attack on his trench.

Missing in action but later found...

Another victim of an attack.

Help came too late for many. They died of loss of blood, exhaustion, or lack of water.

A severely-wounded British soldier is given first aid. He died later of his wounds.

First aid in a Trench near Ypres.

The narrow trenches often made it difficult to render first aid.

A German command post hit by shell fire.

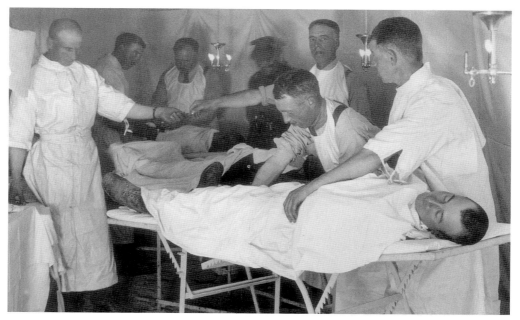

Operation at British Third Field Ambulance Regiment field hospital at Ypres.

was so deep that the Germans could certainly have broken through if they had had the reserves available. This was not the case and the allies managed temporarily to close the gap. On April 24 there was a further gas attack and the Germans once more gained significant territorial gains but the allies again managed to retake their positions and to hold the Germans. The German attacks ceased on May 25. The total losses in dead and injured during the second Battle of Ypres was 105,000, mainly young men, ground down or mutilated in the mud of Flanders. The Canadian military doctor John McCrae wrote the famous poem *In Flanders Fields* on May 2, 1915, inspired by the death of his friend that day who was found amid the millions of poppies growing there. The poem was published by *Punch* that same year in the issue of December 8 and has been recited annually since at remembrance gatherings.

The battlefield was strewn with decaying corpses and the stench was often unbearable.

Dead German soldiers alongside their bunker.

German stretcher bears bring a comrade to a first aid post just behind the front.

Dead German soldiers after a British attack on their position.

Gas alarm during the first gas attack by the Germans at Ypres. Note the primitive gas mask.

In Flanders Fields

In Flanders Fields the poppies blow
Between the crosses row on row
That mark our place; and in the sky
The larks, still bravely singing, fly
scare heard amid the guns below

We are the dead, short days ago
we lived, felt dawn. Saw sunset glow,
loved and were loved, and now we lie
In Flanders Fields

Take up our quarrel with the foe
To you from failing hands we throw
the torch. Be yours to hold it high
If ye break faith with us who die
we shall not sleep, though poppies grow
In Flanders Fields.

Gassed British soldiers on their way to a first aid post. Many were blinded and died a slow death after much suffering.

German soldiers of the 27th infantry regiment with early gas masks.

THE THIRD BATTLE

The third battle of Ypres took place between July and November in 1917 and is also known as the Battle of Passchendaele. This too was a bloody affair. The Germans used a new form of gas, the infamous mustard gas.

This third battle began on July 31 preceded by fighting at Messines on June 7 where the British significantly pushed back the Germans. The British attack began with the explosion of nineteen mines which had been placed beneath the German positions by teams of British miners digging long tunnels for several months. These were sited beneath such positions as Hill 60 and High Crater.

Once again the losses were appalling. It is estimated that the British lost 340,000 men and the Germans about 250,000. British territorial gains amounted to about five miles in the north and to about one and a quarter miles in the south. The conditions in which the battle was fought are impossible to convey. The combination of heavy artillery

A good ending for him. He is wounded but happily on his way home.

Many soldiers did not gain a decent burial. British troops bear a comrade to his grave.

bombardments and torrential rain made the ground virtually impassable with mud and many drowned or suffocated in the pools of mud through which the battle was fought.

THE FINAL FOURTH BATTLE OF YPRES

The "fourth" Battle of Ypres does not appear as such in most history books although the actions certainly did take place and are recorded elsewhere. The Germans opened a new (and their final) offensive on the western front in March 1918 in an effort to breakthrough before the American troops who had now joined the war became too strong. The Germans had prepared for this offensive for many months and transferred troops from the eastern front to the west. The German strength increased while British forces were significantly reduced. The attack that is also sometimes called the Battle of Hazebroeck, took place from April 9 to 30 and was intended to drive the British into the sea. The Germans succeeded in gaining back territory they had lost to the British but once again failed in the decisive breakthrough.

APPALLING CASUALTIES AND LOSSES

The British lost half a million men killed, wounded, or missing in action, defending the Ypres salient between 1914 and 1918. About 42,000 of these have no known grave. The Germans lost a similar number of men. The battles for the salient cost around one million casualties without any appreciable gain in territory for either side. At the outset the British

The Russian commander in chief, Archduke Nicholas reviews his troops on their way to the front.

Russian infantry headed for the German border, August 1914.

General Smith Dorrien had recommended straightening out the line but his advice was ignored. Four years later he was to be proved right but only at the cost of one million men's lives: that is an almost an entire generation that was sacrificed in the prime of their lives.

THE EASTERN FRONT, THE RUSSIANS ATTACK

The Germans expected a Russian assault against East Prussia to the east of the River Weichsel, and allowed for it in the von Schlieffen plan. The intention was to defend this territory but it was envisaged that Russian forces would outnumber the defenders and therefore occupy East Prussia for a time. The loss would be temporary because the German Armies fighting in the west would quickly be switched to the eastern front en masse once the French had been defeated. A series of fortifications had been constructed to slow any Russian advance towards the Weichsel along the line of Thorn, Kulm, Graudenz, Marienberg, and Danzig (Gdansk).

East Prussia shares a border with Russia along both its eastern and southern borders so preparations had to be made for simultaneous attacks from two directions. It was therefore important to prevent the two Russian armies penetrating deep into East Prussia and uniting. The Masurian Lakes played an important role in this because the German forces from the east and south would need to part at the lakes so that the German forces could attack them individually and perhaps defeat them.

The defense of East Prussia was left to the German Eighth Army commanded by General von Prittwitz und Gaffon who was ordered to hold the Russian invaders as long as possible and to use his own initiative to decide when to counter-attack.

The German forces comprised the Tenth Corps commanded by the infantry general, von Francois; the Seventeenth Corps under the cavalryman, General von Mackensen; the Twentieth Corps under the leadership of the artillery general, von Scholtz; the First Reserve Corps led by Lieutenant-General von Melow, and a number of national guard and garrison units totaling sixteen divisions. These divisions included six divisions of infantry, three reserve divisions, three and a half national guard divisions, one cavalry division, and two and a half divisions of garrison troops. The Germans also had a total of 846 artillery pieces.

To confront the German Eighth Army there were two Russian armies: the First commanded by General von Rennenkampf and the Second under the cavalry general, Samsonov, which approached the German border from the south. The Russians had eighteen divisions of infantry, three reserve divisions, and ten divisions of cavalry to set against Prussia and these took 178 artillery batteries with 1,284 guns with them.

Immediately following the outbreak of war General Prittwitz had ordered his troops into position and this was completed by August 10 without any confrontation with Russian troops. Prittwitz wanted to attack the Russians as quickly as possible and chose the First Army because it would be within his range first. He gave orders to General Francois to take up positions along the Angerapp river. This did not suit General Francois. Another example of a German general ignoring an

Russian troops take a rest on their way to the front.

Soldiers of the Russian First Army during their march to the front.

Soldiers of General Samsonov's Russian Second Army immediately at Usdau before hostilities began in the Battle of Tannenberg. General Samsonov committed suicide when it became apparent he had lost the battle.

order just as in the case of the Battle of the Marne. Von Francois pressed twenty-five miles into Russian territory to Schillehen, where he intended to surprise the Russians. Just at that moment on August 16 the Russian offensive began and a battle ensued along a line between Schillehen and Suwalki.

General Prittwitz did not discover until the following morning that Francois had disobeyed his order and that his troops were therefore not where they were supposed to be. An order was issued immediately to disengage the enemy and to return to the original line. Once again Francois ignored the order because he correctly deemed it irresponsible at that moment to disengage. His troops not only succeeded in holding

Russian infantry awaiting the order to attack.

the Russians but in driving them back over the border with heavy losses for the Russians in casualties and prisoners. In the center though the German line was pushed back during the Battle of Gumbinnen (August 20) with heavy losses. Prittwitz was compelled to retreat behind the defensive positions along the Angerapp but he was surprised that von Rennenkampf's troops did not pursue him. They too had suffered heavy casualties and for a time imagined they had lost the battle.

The high-handed action of General Francois had put Prittwitz's overall plan in jeopardy not least because he had delayed the German advance and the chances were now minimal of attacking the First Army before the Second Army could link up with it. General Prittwitz was dismayed. He expected a large-scale Russian offensive by both Russian armies together and he advised headquarters that he wanted to withdraw behind the Wiechsel to avoid becoming surrounded. He added his thoughts that he could not guarantee that he might not be forced to retreat further. The following day with no Russian attack things looked better than he had thought. One of his staff officers, Lieutenant-Colonel Hoffman, proposed ignoring von Rennenkampf's army and moving Francois' First Corps by train to the south to join the Eighth Army there in order to defeat the Russian Second Army. It was a risky plan with everything depending upon the speed with which the Russian army of von Rennenkampf attacked the German flank.

Prittwitz accepted the Hoffmann plan but it was too late. Before even the orders could be given General Hindenburg relieved Prittwitz of his command and replaced him with General Ludendorff.

Hindenburg and Ludendorff who carried out the plan after General Prittwitz's dismissal.

THE BATTLE OF TANNENBERG AND HEROIC ROLES FOR HINDENBURG AND LUDENDORFF

When Hindenburg relieved Prittwitz of his command he quickly saw that the two Russian armies were indeed well separated from one another, giving ample time to defeat them separately. All he needed to do was to give his formal approval to the plan drawn up by Colonel Hoffmann to attack the Russian Second Army commanded by General Samsonov.

Meanwhile the commander of the Russian First Army, General von Rennenkampf realized the German forces had withdrawn and that positions on the Angerapp line were no longer occupied. Instead of advancing rapidly he took his time. The other Russian army now crossed the German border and encountered the German 23rd Corps on August 23. The German forces were initially pushed back and had to vacate Lahna and Orlau. Ludendorff now gave orders for the line to be held at any cost until the arrival of

The German brain behind the Battle of Tannenberg: Colonel Hoffman.

German artillery on its way to the front.

The poor roads often caused problems in moving heavy materials.

Hindenburg inspects his troops after the Battle of Hindenburg.

Francois' First Corps that was now on its way by train to reinforce the southern defense.

General Samsonov wanted to cut off the retreating Germans and pressed forwards towards Allenstein–Osterode to prevent them from withdrawing behind the Weichsel. He too deployed his troops extremely slowly, in part because of their tiredness and a failure in supplies. The Germans managed to intercept Russian communications – that were frequently not encoded – and hence were fully in the picture regarding the plans of the Russian Second Army. They were also aware that the Russian First Army of Rennenkampf was in the area around Koningsbergen and consequently did not pose any threat for the time being for German operations against Samsonov.

The German Second Corps of General Francois arrived by train and took up its new positions on August 26, going immediately onto the offensive about six miles from Usdau. Heavy fighting now ensued with the Samsonov's forces slowly but surely becoming surrounded. Through a misunderstanding of orders the Russian right flank became exposed. At that moment the Germans launched a surprise attack that caused panic among the Russians, causing them to flee. They succeeded in

Right: Russian prisoners of war are searched for weapons before being taken away.

A group of Russian officers taken prisoner of war after the Battle of Tannenberg.

The German's captured large amounts of Russian field artillery.

occupying Allenstein but were soon forced to abandon it.

The Russians were now in forced into a general retreat. There was heavy fighting around the important road junction of Neidenburg. Samsonov personally took command on the ground to lead his troops from the front. He quickly realized that the situation was hopeless and on August 30, after saying farewell to his staff, he committed suicide in the woods to the southwest of Willenberg because of his shame at the defeat.

The Battle of Tannenberg was over by August 31. The Russians lost 120,000 men, killed, injured, or taken prisoner and Hindenburg and Ludendorff were national heroes. Of course this was quickly followed by criticism. The battle was not the success of Hindenburg-Ludendorff but of Colonel Hoffmann. Others maintained that Tannenberg was no victory. The elderly general himself later admitted: "I have no idea who won the Battle of Tannenberg but one thing is clear – if we had lost, I would have been to blame."

Field-Marshal von Hindenburg

THE BATTLE OF THE MAZURIAN LAKES

THE GERMAN ATTACK

Once Samsonov's army had been defeated the German forces turned again to deal with von Rennkampf's army. This Russian commander

German troops cross a bridge during their advance in Galicia, May 1915.

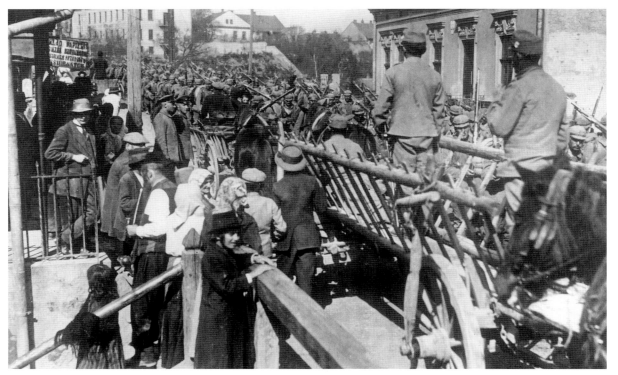

...and continue towards the front.

Russian cavalry retreats across the Weichsel.

IWM q61048

The Battle of Przemysl in 1915. German officers beside dead Russian soldiers.

The Russians surrendered themselves and their artillery when Przemysl was taken by the Germans.

Austrian troops in pursuit of the Russians in 1915.

The Austro-Hungarian emperor Charles during a visit to the front.

Russian Cossacks at the front in Galicia in 1917.

Right: The Germans broke through the Russian front line in Galicia in July 1917. The German Kaiser chose this occasion to visit the front.

The Germans quickly brought in reserves to consolidate their breakthrough in Galicia.

German troops assemble to pursue the retreating Russian in 1917.

A Russian howitzer destroyed by shellfire.

had followed events during the Battle of Tannenberg carefully but had not answered Samsonov's pleas for him to reinforce the southern army. There were many suggestions that both Generals had animosity towards each other and that personal motives were behind Rennenkampf's failure to act but the general has always denied this. He claimed himself unaware of the situation in which Samsonov's

German infantry pauses on the banks of the Weichsel during their advance in May 1915.

Russian prisoners of war are collected and checked during the German counter-offensive in Galicia, July 24, 1917.

Vanquished Russian trenches at Tarnopol.

German supply transport headed for Tarnopol which had just been captured, July 24, 1917.

Kaiser Wilhelm visits his victorious troops after the conquest of Tarnopol.

Kaiser Wilhelm inspects the Turkish 15th Corps in Eastern Galicia in 1917.

German soldiers search defeated Russian trenches near Tarnopol.

Second Army found itself and had not pursued the German forces in order to enable Samsonov to encircle them. Rennkampf eventually received direct orders from headquarters on August 29 to relieve Samsonov and was threatened with a court martial if he did not act decisively. It was too late though and the order was rescinded the following day because there was no longer any point in carrying it out.

…which the Russians vacated in great haste, leaving their weapons behind.

Germans with a captured Russian gun.

Captured Russian observation and command post.

Meanwhile von Rennkampf's troops had deployed in defensive positions between the Mazurian lakes and the Koerische Haf where they continued to pose a threat to the German forces which were now ordered to do all in their power to destroy the Russian First Army. Remnants of the Second Russian Army had withdrawn to the north of the Mazurian lakes where they had dug in to form defensive positions. The north of the Russian line extended to the Koerische Haf and the curved southern flank was protected by the Mauer lake. This was a well-chosen position that virtually eliminated a frontal attack while encircling movements towards the north flank would be hampered by difficult terrain, making an attack on the southern flank the only potential route to success.

On September 5 the Germans were ready and Hindenburg gave the order to attack. The Germans attempted to isolate the Russian First Army but Rennkamf prevented this by quickly withdrawing. During the rearguard actions that ensued he lost about a quarter of his force but he succeeded in withdrawing back across the Russian border to safety.

Through the Battle of Tannenberg the outnumbered German forces had managed to separately defeat the two Russian armies. Much was demanded of the soldiers on both sides. Long field marches of up to 30 or more each day often preceded the murderous fighting. The Battle of Tannenberg was internationally recognized as a striking and great

Cossacks from the Ukraine who fought in Galicia.

German victory won by the leadership of Hindenburg and Ludendorff. It therefore became indelibly linked with their names, making them the most famous of their age.

FIGHTING IN GALICIA

Concerning reports were received from the Austro-Hungarians while the Germans were fighting at Tannenberg and the Mazurian lakes. The Austro-Hungarian commander in chief, General Conrad von Hötzendorff, pressed for a German offensive towards the Narev. His Third Army that was defending Lemberg was unable to hold its own against heavy Russian attacks and was forced to retreat in disarray on August 29 leaving the flank of his Fourth Army threatened. Lemberg fell on September 3 and von Hötzendorff called for the German's help with urgent reinforcements of at least two German corps. This help was initially refused but once the armies of Samsonov and von Rennenkampf were beaten by mid-September and the numerically superior Russian troops drove back the Austro-Hungarian troops in Galicia it was obvious that help was urgently needed. The fear was that the Russians might reach Vienna which would lead to the collapse of Germany's only ally. It was also deemed politically necessary to help the Austro-Hungarians. Italy was just waiting for the right moment to attack its former ally and a weakening of the Austro-Hungarian army would suit that country perfectly.

The German commander in chief, General von Falkenhayn, decided to send his new Ninth Army to the aid of the Austro-Hungarians. This new army comprised four corps commanded by Hindenburg who was also responsible for all operations on the eastern front. It would be some time though before the German troops were in place.

After the fall of Lemberg the Austro-Hungarians launched a major offensive that initially yielded great results but had to be halted on September 11 because of exhaustion among the troops. Von Hötzendorff was therefore forced to concentrate his men around and to the north of Przemysl for rest and recuperation but the Russians continued to fight and crossed a bend in the San river on September 15. The Austro-Hungarian resistance crumbled at the end of September so that they were forced back to a line approximately running from the Polish border through Duklapas, Stryl, Stanislav, to Czernovitz in the south. After the fall of Czernovitz to the Russians von Hötzendorff's forces had to retire further behind the Biala and Dunajec rivers for safety. The losses were enormous, amounting to around 400,000 men and 300 artillery pieces. The Russian casualties were also heavy with 250,000 dead, wounded, or

Russian soldiers who escaped from Austro-Hungarian captivity.

Archduke Joseph, Austro-Hungarian commander on the Romanian front, visits the front line
on September 12, 1917.

taken prisoner. Von Hötzendorff's only hope now was for the German
Ninth Army which had just been assembled to come to his aid and this
army went on the offensive on September 25. The Ninth army reached
the Weichsel by October 6 and this gave the Austro-Hungarians fresh
courage and they managed to reach the San river once more and retook
Przemysl on October 11. The offensive ground to a halt after this and on
October 27 the Austro-Hungarians were once more forced to retreat.
Several days later the Russians had retaken all the territory just lost and
were even pushing towards the Carpathians and Silesia. The German
Ninth Army was also forced to retreat to prevent being surrounded and
abandoned large areas of territory it had just won. The Russian offensive
could not be pressed home though because of the ever longer supply
lines. Supplies started to run out and the offensive had to be halted. On
November 11 the Germans mounted a surprise counter attack from the
direction of Thorn after the entire army made a spectacular dash by train
to deploy at Thorn. The Austro-Hungarian Second Army was tasked to
defend Prussian Silesia. The attack started at the same time as the Russians
re-opened their offensive against East Prussia. An attack from the

Right: German troops pursuing the Russians through the Carpathians where
the Russians suffered a great defeat.

direction of Thorn was entirely unexpected and the Germans initially had great success but the Russian attack on East Prussia was unhindered and they penetrated deep into East Prussia until halted at the Angerapp. The German Ninth Army lost 100,000 men during the offensive as casualties or through exhaustion. The Russians were also unable to continue fighting due to lack of food and ammunition. Things were little better with the Austro-Hungarians where disease broke out and morale got worse by the day. There was no further heavy fighting. The battle on the Eastern Front was over for the time being.

THE GREAT BATTLES OF 1915 AND 1916

Senseless slaughter takes appalling form on both sides

GALLIPOLI

THE START OF THE BATTLE

It had been uncertain at the outbreak of war whether Turkey would enter and if so on which side. The German influence was quite pronounced with the German ambassador and German military mission to the country very active but the country was still officially neutral and free to make its own choice.

The British submarine *B11* entered the Straits on December 13, 1914 and torpedoed the Turkish warship *Medusha* that lay at anchor. The ship sink almost immediately with the loss of 400 lives.

The wreck of the *Medusha* with around 400 men in her hull.

Churchill's decision to seize two Turkish warships being built in British shipyards for the Royal Navy evoked a strong reaction from the Turks. The manner in which this act was done without any discussion or offer of compensation caused bad blood. Turkey protested and threw the British naval attaché out. The Germans reacted swiftly by offering to replace the two ships with their German warships *Goeben* and *Breslau*. The British made a second bad psychological move on September 29 by halting a Turkish torpedo boat that wished to pass through the Dardanelles and ordered it to return without reason. This closed the door and at the insistence of the German ambassador the Turks closed the Bosporus and Dardanelles to all shipping, thereby shutting off the supply route for the Allies to their Russian ally.

At the same time the Turks permitted the two German warships to enter the straits and to anchor off Istanbul where they were placed under the Turkish flag even though their German crews and their Rear Admiral, Souchon, remained on board. Through this act Turkey *de facto* relinquished its neutrality and chose the side of the Central Powers but without a declaration of war. On October 28 though Souchon took his ships into the Black Sea and fired on several Russian ports and an oil refinery which immediately led to a Russian declaration of war on Turkey.

German commander of the Turkish Black Sea corps, Colonel Freiherr von der Goltz, during the Battle of Gallipoli.

The German Admiral Souchon who entered the straits with the *Breslau* and *Goeben* which later fired on Russian Black Sea ports flying the Turkish flag.

The British bombarded the forts guarding the entrance to the Dardanelles of Sedd el Bahr shown here and Kum Kale on November 3, 1914.

Now that the British knew how things stood they reacted quickly. On November 3 ships of the Royal Navy entered the straits of the Dardanelles and fired on the fortifications of Sedd el Bahr and Kum Kale causing considerable damage. On December 13 a British submarine, the *B-11*, entered the straits and torpedoed the Turkish warship *Medusha* that sank within minutes causing the loss of life of many of her crew. These actions gave the British Royal Navy the impression that it would be relatively simple to force passage through these waterways. This was to prove a costly error.

Meanwhile the Russians requested the British to open a new front against the Turks to relieve the Turkish threat in the Caucasus. The British government's reaction was positive and Churchill proposed sending the Royal Navy to the Dardanelles. First ships would use their long range guns to put the forts out of action. Minesweepers would then clear the straits of mines so that the fleet could approach Istanbul where it would destroy the *Breslau* and *Goeben*. This would also reinstate the essential supply route to Russia. The government was enthusiastic about the proposal and decided to commence the action in February.

On January 15 the commander of the British fleet in the Aegean, Admiral Garden, was told of the plans and the French also agreed to make ships available. The Royal Navy decided to reinforce the fleet

HMS Albion also saw action in the fighting at Gallipoli.

The British commander General Hamilton was ordered to take the Gallipoli peninsula on March 11, 1915.

HMS Amethyst came under heavy enemy fire when she attempted to force her way into the straits taking serious damage and with the loss of 20 killed and 28 wounded.

The ancient fort of Sedd el Bahr. The town was conquered by the British on April 26, 1915.

The elderly Russian cruiser *Askold* was also present during the first attempt on the straits.

The British assemble an enormous fleet in the harbor of Mudros for the invasion of Gallipoli.

The French also joined the attack at Gallipoli. As usual they took good care of the inner man: a French wine store at Mudros.

The Turks saw a great armada of warships heading towards them on the morning of March 18. Here the *HMS Inflexible* leads the way into the Dardanelles.

with the ultra-modern *HMS Queen Elizabeth* even though advised that her guns were not yet ready for action. He was ordered to commence action on February 15.

One of the original authors of the British plan, Admiral Jack Fisher, began to have doubts and turned against the plan but it was too late. His remark: "*Damn the Dardanelles, they will be our graves,*" was to come true sooner than perhaps he had expected.

Fisher's resistance did have the consequence that London now decided to land troops at the Gallipoli peninsula to occupy the land. The Twenty-Ninth Division was chosen that had been ear-marked for action in Greece. The division was reinforced with two battalions of Royal Marines and troops from Australia and New Zealand. All these 50,000 troops were to assemble at the Greek island of Lemnos but

when the first 5,000 arrived it was clear the small island was not suitable because there was no accommodation and the men were forced to remain on board relatively small ships. A contingent of Marines had to be sent elsewhere because the harbor at Lemnos was full.

Meanwhile the naval action was delayed for several days because of the landings but Admiral Garden entered the Dardanelles on February 19 and opened fire on the Turkish forts but without result. Communication problems led to the action being broken off. Garden repeated his efforts on February 25 and succeeded in putting one of the outer forts out of action. Three ships entered the Dardanelles but were fired upon by well-hidden field howitzers. Marines landed on the coast and succeeded in putting about fifty Turkish guns out of action between February 27 and March 3. The reaction in London was one of enthusiasm. People forgot that the action had warned the Turks that Gallipoli was the British objective so that a surprise attack was no longer possible. Kitchener was very positive and suggested that the mere presence of the Royal Navy in the Dardanelles was enough to put the Turks to flight and a British landing would not be necessary. The British Foreign Secretary Grey thought it possible to take the

HMS Lord Nelson enters the straits alongside *HMS Inflexible*.

Left: The heavy guns of HMS Inflexible. The ship soon hit a mine and immediately started to list.

HMS Prince George was one of the first 18 British warships in the attack.

The *Suffren* took part in the second attack wave and miraculously avoided the defeat.

Dardanelles followed by a possible *coup d'etat*. Kitchener drew up plans to annex Alexandrette and Aleppo while the Royal Navy suggested the entire Euphrates valley. The colonial minister wanted the port of Marmarica included. The territory not yet conquered was eagerly divided up before the battle had even begun. Unfortunately for the planners, events were to take a different turn.

Turkish resistance was so great that the Marines had to withdraw and the landings ended on March 4. Further attempts to enter the Dardanelles were not successful and on March 12 the government decided on secret talks with the Turks. A British emissary offered the Turks five million pounds sterling to withdraw from the war and

HMS Irresistible also hit a mine and her crew were forced to abandon ship.

The French warship turned to starboard and there was an enormous explosion. She sank within one minute with the loss of around 60 men.

HMS Ocean came to the aid of the Irresistible and also hit a mine. Her crew was also forced to abandon ship.

The French warship Gaulois also took part in the attack.

The *Charlemagne* sails close to the *Bouvet* when that ship hit a mine but without damage.

HMS Cornwallis enters the Dardanelles to be greeted by a hail of Turkish shellfire.

HMS Canopus took part in the second attack wave. Here it departs Mudros.

Admiral De Robeck who replaced the sick Admiral Garden. He had a realistic view of the disaster that was befalling the Royal Navy.

further sums if they handed over the *Goeben* and *Breslau*. The Turkish government though demanded assurance that Istanbul would not be taken. The British could not promise this because they had already promised the city to the Russians and hence the secret talks stumbled and failed. The naval actions were then restarted with efforts to clear Turkish mines from the waters. These efforts failed and one ship after another came under heavy fire from Turkish field howitzers which caused considerable damage and killed many sailors. One of the escorting cruisers, *HMS Amethyst*, also came under fire and had twenty killed and twenty-eight wounded with damage to her steering gear.

The naval actions up to this point had not been successful. General Hamilton was appointed commander of the expeditionary

A counsel of war was held aboard *HMS Queen Elizabeth* on March 22, 1915. From left to right: Rear Admiral Boue de Lapeyrere commanding the French Mediterranean fleet, General Hamilton, Rear Admiral De Robeck, and the French General Baillard.

forces intended for Gallipoli on March 11, 1915. His force has now grown to about 70,000 men and consisted of the Twenty-Ninth Division, the Anzac Corps, and division of Marines, and a French corps. Action in Gallipoli from henceforth would be controlled by joint land and sea operations.

BADLY EXECUTED COMBINED LAND AND SEA OPERATIONS

British preparations for combined operations by land and sea forces to conquer Gallipoli were made in an extraordinarily casual and extremely amateurish manner. Hamilton's knowledge of the terrain to be fought over was virtually nil. For information he used some tourist guides and maps and a handbook about the Turkish armed forces. He was only given a few days to appoint his staff and create his

The German General, Liman von Sanders, commander in chief of the Turkish forces at Gallipoli.

Lieutenant Otto Hersing who commanded the *U-21* that sank the British ships *HMS Pathfinder* and *HMS Triumph* on September 5.

organization. There was absolutely no plan for communications between the army and navy. Information that was available in London regarding the position of Turkish artillery and Turkish troop positions on the peninsula was not made available to him. The required provisions were to be locally acquired and there was no coordinated approach so that it is certain that never was an operation of such magnitude undertaken in such a sloppy and unprofessional manner as this one. No care was paid to keeping the operation secret. As a result, Turkish and German intelligence were well aware of what the British were intending.

The wreck of *HMS Triumph* sunk by the *U-21*.

General Liman von Sanders rapidly reinforced the peninsula following the failed Allied attack.

A great amphibious landing at Gallipoli took place on the morning of March 23.

Allied troops landed in the wrong place at "Z" beach and came under murderous fire from the Turks.

Troops attempt to assemble after landing on "Z" beach.

Anzac infantry charges Turkish positions, December 17, 1915.

British General Birdwood sought permission to evacuate "Z" beach but this was refused.

The order to carry out the Gallipoli landings was given on March 18. It was to be a thoroughly disastrous day for the Royal Navy. The Turkish defenders saw an armada of warships heading towards them that morning. There were eighteen gigantic battleships, many cruisers and destroyers, and swarms of minesweepers navigating the entrance to the Dardanelles at great speed. The ships were arranged in two waves. The largest and most powerful ships led the way with *HMS Inflexible* to starboard with the *Lord Nelson* and *Agememnon* alongside and *HMS Queen Elizabeth* to port. They simultaneously opened fire on the forts

A drama in its own right on "V" beach where the *River Clyde* attempted to land 2,000 men of whom about half were killed.

The *River Clyde* at Sedd el Bahr. About 2,000 men were embarked in this ship for the landing on "V" beach.

View of "V" beach from the sea.

Landings were made by the Allies at several places on Cape Helles.

Turkish troops await the landings and cut the attackers to shreds.

Allied landing on "V" beach in April 1915.

Turkish troops counter attack on "V" beach.

and shortly afterwards the following ships – *HMS Prince George* and *Triumph* also engaged the forts with the thunderous power of their guns. Immediately behind them came the second wave under French command with the *Suffren, Bouvet, Charlemagne, Gaulois, HMS Canopus,* and *HMS Cornwallis.* They passed the first attack wave and opened fire at closer range. These ships were met with a rain of shellfire and around 12.30 the *Gaulois* was hit and had to withdraw. Several other ships were also hit and damaged but the Allied fire was generally effective and the Turkish artillery became noticeably reduced. This was the sign for the admiral commanding the operation to pull the second wave ships back to make room for the minesweepers. A disaster was about to happen.

The French *Bouvet* turned to starboard behind the *Suffren* and followed her into the Erén Keui Bay which because it lay to the right

Harbor at "W" beach improvised by sinking old freighters.

Men of the Essex Regiment land on "W" beach and suffer great losses without gaining a foothold.

Allied landing at "W" beach. Almost half the 1,000 attackers died in the first hours.

The Allies quickly dug in after the landings.

Turkish reinforcements arrived rapidly. A Turkish field gun on its way to "W" beach.

"A" beach was one of many landing sites.

"B" beach at Suvla Bay. The British commander failed to take the Tekke Tepe heights with dire consequences.

After the Allies failed to take the Tekke Tepe heights the Turks quickly occupied them and pinned down the Allies on the beach.

of the channel was thought to be free of mines. Suddenly an enormous explosion was heard and the astonished watchers saw the huge ship disappear to the bottom of the channel within a minute, with around 600 men on board. It is possible the explosion was from a hit by a shell on her magazine at the same moment that she hit a mine. Few of her crew survived.

The minesweepers that were now preparing to start clearing mines were raked with shellfire and one after another they left the line to seek safety out of range. Around 16:00 hours there was another explosion. *HMS Inflexible* hit a mine and immediately started to list.

The same fate overcame *HMS Irresistible* a few minutes later. *HMS Ocean* rushed to their aid but also hit a mine and her crew were forced to abandon ship. The crew of the *Irresistible* also abandoned ship. The action was halted and the order was given for the ships to withdraw and to regroup. The action had cost the Allies around 700 men and the loss of one third of their ships: three large warships sunk, three damaged and also casualties among a number of minesweepers. Only four Turkish guns had been put out of action. The Turkish casualties were forty dead and seventy wounded. The minefields still existed and the waterway to Istanbul was still closed to Allied ships.

It is obvious that the operation was a complete failure but Commodore Roger Keyers, chief of staff to Admiral Garden, who had

Allied landing on "Y" beach.

Scottish troops land at Suvla Bay and are shelled by Turkish six inch guns with heavy casualties.

The hostile coast of Cape Helles on which five landings were made.

Suvla, August 7, 1915. Around 2,000 Anzacs landed at Suvla but poor leadership and coordination made their landing a failure.

A British torpedo boat carries troops to "Z-beach".

The southern tip of Cape Helles with an Allied shipwreck in the foreground.

meanwhile been taken ill, had no problems in informing London that the enemy was defeated and the operation had been a "brilliant success" with the only task remaining being to clear the minefields. His immediate superior and successor to Admiral Garden was Admiral De Robeck who was much more realistic and called the attack the "disaster" it had really been.

The Admiralty was so thoroughly disillusioned that they gave up all thoughts of repeating the operation.

A meeting was organized by General Hamilton on board *HMS Queen Elizabeth* on March 22 to decide on joint action at which De Robeck decided he would not risk his ships in those waters again until the army had taken the Gallipoli peninsula but he "forgot" to inform Hamilton of this. It was agreed to go ahead with landings on April 14 and to prepare for them thoroughly. Those who were well prepared were the Turks who were now given time to repair their damage and to build new positions. The German Field Marshal Liman von Sanders was appointed to command the Turkish Fifth Army consisting of 50,000 men tasked with defending the peninsula and General Colman Freiherr von der Goltz was placed in charge of the Turkish Black Sea Corps. Liman von Sanders made good use of the respite given him by the British and had new defensive positions created at an astonishing pace. Once more the British had missed an opportunity in view of its initial poor defense. It would probably have fallen fairly easily but now the Turks were able to significantly improve their defenses.

Preparations on the Allied side were less smooth and rapid. Supplies for the landing forces were chaotic and nothing was right. Artillery pieces arrived without or with the wrong munitions leading to a dearth of shells. There were no landing craft and the Allies were forced to acquire them locally and this obviously caused great problems. It is no exaggeration to describe the preparations for the landings as extremely casual with a serious underestimation of the difficulties faced. But there was no way out. Both Churchill and the minister of war, Lord Kitchener had their reputations riding on them and did everything to ensure they went ahead.

General Hunter Weston during the landings on Cape Helles.

Heavily laden French troops land at Cape Helles.

Allied trenches at one of the landing places.

THE LANDINGS

The task eventually fell to the 29th Division to land at Helles while the Anzacs landed at Caba Tebe in the north. The Marines of the Royal Naval Division were to be put ashore at Bulais with a French unit making a diversion at Kum Kale and Basika Bay and a British battalion going ashore at Morto Bay. At the last moment it was decided also to send 2000 men to the west of Krithia. The expectation was for the landings to achieve results within forty-eight hours with only light resistance being met. It was even thought that once a bridgehead had been established that the defense would wither to nothing. On the morning of April 23 the day finally came. The fleet which had assembled at the island of Lemnos and the port of Mudra slowly got under way. One ship after another of the approximately 200 ships set a course for their pre-ordained destinations in the Dardanelles which they reached during the night of April 24–25. The invasion began at 03:00 hours in the morning with about 70,000 men being transferred to boats to take them in many cases to their final resting place. One of the greatest dramas in British military history was about to unfold.

Marines attack at Bulair.

French troops en route to positions at Sedd el Bahr.

On April 25 troops landed at various places, including Cape Helles at the southern tip of the peninsula and also to the north opposite Maidos. The intention was to place the enemy between cross fire. The 12,000 Anzacs in forty-eight boats were to put ashore on "Z" beach in the north but were landed at the wrong place with very difficult terrain where they were met with murderous fire from the Turks. General Birdwood sought permission to withdraw but this was refused. The Anzacs vainly attempted to climb the heights of Sari Blair that was defended by units of the Turkish Nineteenth Division. The fighting that continued until May 4 cost the Anzacs about 10,000 men. Both sides dug in after this and the battle ceased for a time.

Meanwhile landings were made at five different places at Cape Helles code-named "S", "V", "W", "X", and "Y" beaches. Another drama of its own took place on "V" beach where the British had beached the *River Clyde*, and old freighter that had been converted for the landing with a removable hull section and carried 2,000 soldiers. A number of steel sheets were placed as landing ramps for the men and those on board got the impression that the landing was unopposed because there had been no firing while all these preparations were being made but at the moment that the section was removed for the men to go ashore the Turkish machine-guns opened fire cutting down half of the attackers.

There were many casualties too on "W" beach. Of the 1,000 men landed almost three quarters of them were killed and 283 were seriously wounded and put out of action. The resistance on the other beaches was much less and by the evening of April 26 the Allies had landed around 30,000 men. The French got off lightly, landing and taking the fort and town of Kum Kale with little resistance. On April 26 the Allies took the town of Sedd el Bahr and pushed towards Krithia which they attacked two days later but were repelled by the Turks. They tried again in vain on May 6 but were forced to abandon the attempt on May 8 even though Indian troops had been rushed from Egypt as reinforcements. The troops here also were forced to dig in and did not gain another yard of ground.

More reinforcements were now sent by the Allies to Gallipoli and it was decided to make a new landing at Suvla on August 17 with these fresh troops. Initially the landing was successful and a bridgehead was quickly established but the Turks succeeded in holding the attackers and isolating the bridgehead. While all this was going on the Turks had also been busy and significantly reinforced their troops on the Gallipoli peninsula. Fourteen Turkish divisions now faced a similar number of British and French divisions so that the Allies chances of victory became smaller and smaller.

The role of the Royal Navy during these actions is fairly unclear. Mindful of Admiral De Robeck's desire to limit the use of his ships

Turkish dead after the fighting at Sedd el Bahr.

Infantry of the 6th Manchester Regiment attacking.

Lord Kitchener was so concerned about the situation that he decided to see things for himself. He arrived on November 12, 1915 and was shocked at the reality at Gallipoli.

Commander in chief, Lord Kitchener in the trenches at Cape Helles.

until the army had taken the peninsula it became apparent that the Navy's role was restricted to transporting men. Witnesses claim that the warships hardly fired a shot against the Turkish defenders.

END OF THE ESCAPADE: HAMILTON IS RECALLED

The medical situation at Gallipoli was also of great concern and resembled the drama surrounding medical care during the Crimean War. Once again absolutely no adequate provision had been made for thousands of dead and injured. Many lay unattended in the open air and died horrible deaths without their wounds being attended to and the transport of the many thousands of injured soldiers was also entirely inadequate. Despite this, Hamilton sent a telegram to his superiors on April 27 in which he reported that

General Monroe who succeeded Hamilton had the courage to advise ending the misguided action and abandonment of Gallipoli.

Troops assemble for evacuation after destroying their supplies.

everything was going to plan but he also requested reinforcements. These reinforcements were sent but were also offered up in pointless offensives in which each failed leading to death and decay among the Allied forces.

It became clear to London by May 14 that something had to be done. It was decided to send further reinforcements to maintain the pressure on the Turks. This is quite absurd because the Turks were not under any pressure, it was them pressing the Allies.

Action continued in the months that followed with Turkish attacks being halted but no advances being made and without any end to the suffering of the ordinary soldier that resulted not just from the enemy but also through misguided policy and incompetent leadership.

Finally on October 14 what ought to have occurred much sooner took place and General Hamilton was relieved of his command and replaced by General Monroe.

Monroe was charged with advising what should be done to put an end to the situation. He indicated that he would need at least 400,000 men to be certain of victory. London could not spare these men so he recommended an immediate halt to action and to abandon the peninsula to the Turks. This news was received with very mixed feelings in London and Lord Kitchener decided to see things in Gallipoli for himself. What he encountered shocked him, leaving a deep impression of the hopelessness of the situation. On November

15 he sent a telegram to Prime Minister Asquith to inform him that it was impossible to take Gallipoli.

The battle that was to have been decided in forty-eight hours lasted in reality eight and a half months and cost the British 205,000 men wounded, killed in action, or through disease. French losses were also high at around 47,000 men. The Turks also suffered heavily and lost 251,000 men wounded, killed, or from death through disease but they at least had successfully defended their country and seen off the invader. The Battle of Gallipoli remains a dark page in British military history and an outstanding example of failure of policy and leadership despite the heroism of British and colonial troops and also of the French who did their utmost duty.

It is remarkable that a number of historians later put some gloss on this fiasco by suggesting that the operation had served a valuable role in spite of the heavy casualties in destroying the "flower of the Turkish army". The Gallipoli campaign, they argue, held fourteen of the thirty-six Turkish divisions on the peninsula so that the Suez Canal could be held and led to the eventual defeat of the Turks. This is both untrue and misguided. It can equally be argued that fourteen Turkish divisions held an equal number of Allied divisions for eight and a half months away from the Western Front and other theaters of war where they and the quarter of a million casualties could have played

The bloody adventure is done. British troops peacefully evacuate Suvla bay.

Many Allied soldiers were killed in the Battle for Gallipoli.

a decisive role and were sorely missed. Another historian remarked that Gallipoli showed that a British officer knew how to fight and how to die. In his book, *Damn the Dardanelles*, author John Laffin appositely remarks that it might have been better if British officers had learned how to fight and to stay alive. This, he suggests, requires no less courage but greater skill!

THE BATTLE OF VERDUN

OPERATION "GERICHT" TO BLEED THE FRENCH ARMY TO DEATH

1915 was a bad year for the Allies on both the Western and Eastern Fronts. The Russian armies were pushed back to Poland by the Central Powers with heavy losses. By September that year the Germans had taken about 750,000 prisoners of war. The British and French had got into a position with no end in sight in Gallipoli and in the meantime

They never left. An Anzac cemetery at Gallipoli.

Left: A high price was paid.

Serbia had been defeated by the Central Powers and was being occupied.

On top of this the proud British Royal Navy was unable to prevent German submarines from attacking merchant shipping. Ship after ship was being torpedoed without the Royal Navy being able to stop them. In Africa the British fought a small German force under the legendary General von Lettow Vorbeck. This forced them to keep a sizable force there that was urgently needed elsewhere.

Germany's commander in chief and minister of war Falkenhayn (left) who had the idea for "Operation Gericht." Falkenhayn is shown here in his new role on the front in the Ukraine after his dismissal.

The German General Lettow Vorbeck who kept British troops busy in action in Africa.

German Crown Prince Wilhelm regularly visited his men.

Some 1,200 guns of every caliber opened fire on French positions on February 21, 1916.

One of the heavy artillery pieces that were used on February 21.

A 175 mm (7 inches) mortar of 1916.

A 245 mm (10 inches) mortar of 1916 used at Verdun.

This trench mortar was very useful for attacking enemy lines.

The French suffered badly too. By the end of 1915 the majority of French officers who had started in 1914 had been killed or injured and other losses were also heavy. It is no surprise therefore that the Allies held a conference in December to draw up plans to put an end to this disturbing situation in 1916.

It is clear the Germans also contemplated the immediate future. In a report to the Kaiser the commander in chief General von Falkenhayn wrote that: "a final effort, given the current favorable situation, would

German troops leave their trenches to attack.

German troops immediately before the attack.

tip the balance in Germany's favor." The British naval blockade meant that Germany had great shortages of materials and this could become much worse over time. Falkenhayn also wrote that he expected the Allies to attempt a breakthrough in 1916 in order to push Germany onto the defensive. "This must to be prevented," he added.

Falkenhayn now proposed to beat the French first and if this succeeded there would be no point in the British continuing with the war. He recommended choosing a location in France that the French would defend at any cost. "Such a place," he suggested, " is Verdun."

By defending Verdun he argued the French would bleed to death but if they were on the contrary to retreat then they would suffer such a blow to their morale that the necessary breakthrough would be possible.

Falkenhayn wanted an end to senseless man to man fighting that merely led to heavy casualties, instead planning the use of a massive force of artillery against a limited front so that the enemy's infantry in their trenches would be destroyed but their own losses could remain limited. After such an overwhelming artillery barrage the German infantry would be able to take the enemy positions effortlessly and

Left: German infantry attacks near the village of Douaumont that was defended by the 1st and 3rd battalions of the French 95th Regiment, reinforced with Algerian tirailleurs or skirmishers and a battalion of Zouaves. About 4,000 French and German soldiers died in the attack.

One of the countless shell holes on the battlefield near Mort-Homme and hill 304.

Field Marshal von Hindenburg and General Ludendorff took over command of the Verdun offensive following the sacking of General von Falkenhayn.

then the barrage could be moved forward. In this way Falkenhayn proposed to roll up the French positions a bit at a time. At first sight this was a good plan but Falkenhayn made several important mistakes. First of all he wanted to limit the attack to the right bank of the Meuse which was later to prove fatal. Secondly he made too little allowance for the often unfavorable weather and ground conditions around Verdun which was an equally serious error.

The Kaiser approved the plan though and preparations began in January 1916 in strict secrecy. These preparations were of gigantic proportions. Around 50,000 men were engaged just in the laying of the necessary railway lines to bring in men and supplies. New roads, ten new rail links, twenty-four stations, accommodation, and huge munitions depots were built. Responsibility for the Verdun offensive was given to the Fifth Army commanded by the crown prince with his chief-of-staff, General von Knobelsdorf. Six well-equipped divisions amounting to 90,000 men were readied for the battle while troops

French General Mangin who was nicknamed "The Butcher" by his men because of the relentless way he waged war.

German machine-gun team in action on the left bank of the Meuse during fighting for the infamous hill 304 at Verdun.

Right: The grim reality of Verdun in 1916.

The result of German artillery fire was dreadful.

Kaiser Wilhelm visited the front at Verdun in April 1917. Here the Kaiser inspects a Guards regiment on its way to the front.

Western corner of the courtyard of Fort Douaumont.

The ground around Fort Douaumont quickly became entirely impassable.

German soldiers climb over the fence surrounding Fort Douaumont and find it virtually abandoned, February 25, 1916.

were held in reserve on both the east bank and to the west of the Meuse. To ensure the secrecy of this operation most officers were not informed of the intended objective of this enormous effort and the plans even ran to the evacuation of several villages in the area.

Once the rail links were ready some 1,250 guns, including the famous "Fat Berthas" were deployed to bring a front of a little under ten miles under fire. Twelve wagons were needed to move one of these "Fat Berthas" and it took twenty hours to ready the gun for action. Finally 213 munitions trains brought in 2.5 million shells – the supply for six days.

Operation "Gericht", as the Germans named the Verdun offensive, was to start on February 12 but when the troops moved into position on the night of February 11 the weather worsened. Hail, snow, and rain lashed the area and the trenches and accommoda-

German *Oberleutenant* von Brandis (seated), hero of Douaumont claimed the fort as the first to enter. Shown with his two brothers who were both wounded on the Western Front.

tion filled with water so that the men could not stay there. Visibility was also so poor that artillery sighting was rendered impossible. The offensive had to be postponed. The weather remained bad for the entire week that followed and it was not until the 20th that any improvement took place with the 21st being chosen as the new date.

Eventually the greatest artillery barrage of all time commenced at 7.45 on the morning of February 21 targeting the French positions at Verdun. Tens of thousands of shells rained down continuously for nine hours changing the terrain into a lunar landscape in which it seemed impossible for any living creature to survive. There was a sudden end to the barrage at five that evening. Now Operation "Gericht", that was planned to bleed the French to death, could start. Around 90,000 German soldiers waited in their trenches certain of victory and ready to storm the enemy positions. The "mincing machine of Verdun" as the battle later was described could now claim its first victims.

Left: French storage room in Fort Douamont.

The village of Fleury near Douaumont where fierce fighting took place changed hands seventeen times. Not a single brick was left standing by the end.

The battlefield at Froidterre.

March 1916. The village of Ornes also vanished from the face of the earth and became a desert.

German orderlies use an improvised stretcher to carry a wounded soldier.

A French machine-gun post after the fall of Fort Douaumont in November 1916. French losses were very severe.

FIGHTING IN THE BOIS DES CAURES DELAYS THE GERMAN ADVANCE

The French had not regarded the Verdun sector as particularly important up to that point and did not expect a German offensive there, although the local commander, Lieutenant-Colonel Driant, who was right in the line of fire, had warned several times that the defensive works were totally inadequate. By the time anybody listened to him it was too late for the attack had exploded into reality.

During the initial barrage about 80,000 shells fell on an area just 800 metres wide and three kilometers deep of the Bois de Caures according to later estimates by General Pétain. At every instant shells were lobbed high by unseen hands, disintegrated and then came crashing down. The ground was opened up and turned over while

Father and son: Kaiser Wilhelm II and the crown prince during a troop inspection immediately before the attack on Fort Vaux.

Fort Vaux where heavy fighting took place for several months.

hissing and screaming shrapnel flew everywhere, destroying everything in its path. The German Verdun offensive had begun.

After about nine hours the area appeared to have been totally destroyed with no sign of life discernible. German infantry left their trenches as it started snowing again and carefully pressed forward towards the enemy lines. The high command did not expect any resistance but several patrols were first sent forward which surprisingly ran into fierce resistance. By evening they were even forced to pull back to their own jumping off points. The high command now ordered a repeat the following morning of the artillery barrage which they thought would mop up the last vestiges of resistance.

The guns stopped firing around noon and infantry stormed the Bois de Caures en masse. The area was defended by just two now very battered battalions of skirmishers commanded by Lieutenant-Colonel Driant. It was not to be an easy push-over for the Germans. The battle lasted three days during which every inch of ground was fought over. Colonel Driant was hit in the head by a bullet during the battle and died on the spot. Reserves were sent in and the French recovered some of the wood but the numerical supremacy forced them to yield on February 23 and it returned to German hands. Only five officers and sixty other men returned from the 56th Battalion of Chasseurs and just three officers and forty-five men survived from the 59th. The Germans also suffered heavy and wholly unexpected casualties and were held for twenty-four hours, which gave the French time to bring in reserves to continue the struggle.

German troops assembled in their trenches before the first attack on Fort Vaux.

German infantry soldiers take cover in a shell hole...

...and attack.

Killed for his country. One of about 5,000 killed at Fort Vaux.

The battlefield was strewn with bodies and limbs. The stench took the breath away.

A French machine-gun in Fort Vaux fires on the attackers.

French machine-gun section near Biquele, October 20, 1916.

Left: French soldiers operate a grenade launcher in a trench at Mort-Homme.

Germans attack with a flame-thrower at Fort Vaux.

A German infantryman during the attack on Fort Vaux alongside a dead French soldier.

THE FALL OF FORT DOUAUMONT, A FORTUNATE TURN OF EVENTS

After the fall of the Bois des Caures it was not until the evening of the 24th that the Germans pressed forward again. They forced a deep breach in the French defensive line between Bezonvaux and hill 378

Fort Vaux finally falls on June 7, 1916. The defenders were exhausted, having held out for months.

Lack of water was the chief cause of their failing resistance. Some even drank their own urine.

The Germans evacuate Fort Vaux 5,000 dead and five months later for tactical reasons and the French reoccupy it without a shot fired.

The *Voie Sacrée* or "Holy Way" was the only supply route to Verdun along which French men and materials could be brought to the front at Verdun.

and took positions in the village of Beaumont which directly threatened the allegedly unassailable armored Fort Douaumont. Panic broke out among the French and General Herr commanding French troops in the Verdun region deemed the French positions on the right bank of the Meuse to be beyond defending and he wished to withdraw but the commander in chief General Joffre did not permit this. Herr was relieved of his command and replaced by General Pétain who was instructed to defend Verdun to the last man.

French field artillery on its way to the front.

The French quickly brought in reinforcements following the fighting in the Bois des Caures.
A French munitions convoy on its way to Mort-Homme.

A French 220 mm (9 inches) mortar has just been fired.

French 320 mm (12 ½ inches) rail-mounted gun at Verdun.

French field gun in position.

Hill 304 after the battle. Thousands of French and German soldiers died fighting for this hill.

Left: a French heavy rail-mounted gun.

In the meantime the Germans planned an attack on the fort without knowing that the French were busily removing its armament following orders from French headquarters in August 1915. The order was given because the fall of the Belgian forts around Liege had shown they were not been able to withstand German heavy 400 mm (16 inches) artillery. It was considered more sensible to remove the artillery from the French forts and position elsewhere and Fort Douaumont was included in these orders. On February 25 the fort's garrison had left but a troop of engineers and artillerymen were busy making preparations to disarm the fort. No one in the fort had any idea of the coming attack and the 155 mm (6 inches) turret fired sporadically at the crossroads at Azannes to the north.

The "Bismarck tunnel" at Mort-Homme. Hundreds of tunnels were dug to act as shelters, storage places, and accommodation for the troops fighting.

German flame-thrower in action.

Infantry of the Twenty-fourth Brandenburg Regiment was ordered around 16:00 on February 25 to dig in ready for an attack the following day. The fort lay like a large threat before them and the assault troops expected a bitter and difficult battle. Meanwhile several officers had gone to reconnoiter the situation independently of each other. They reached the fort unseen and succeeded in getting inside the moat. To their great surprise there was no resistance offered. They surprised the sixty French occupants at work and took them prisoner. They quickly called for reinforcements so that Fort Douaumont, then regarded as the most impregnable fort in the world, had fallen to the Germans without a shot fired. German press reported jubilantly that: "German troops have conquered the armored Fort Douaumont, the cornerstone of the French defense lines at Verdun, after heavy fighting." The church bells rang throughout Germany and the population rejoiced.

The fall of the fort came as a hammer-blow to the French. Counter offensives were tried to no avail. For the time being the fort remained in German hands.

French trenches come under fire. Shellfire destroyed the forward positions and killed the occupants.

German artillerymen prepare new positions.

Right: German cavalry at Verdun. The horses also wear
gas masks.

German field artillery in action near Douaumont.

CAPTURE OF THE VILLAGE OF DOUAUMONT

Immediately after the somewhat fortunate capture of Fort Douaumont the Germans realized that its capture did not achieve much for them since it was almost surrounded by French troops. They also needed to take the village of the same name with a population of just 280 and clear it of French infantry. It was defended by remnants of the First, Second, and Third Battalions of the 95th Regiment reinforced by Algerian skirmishers and a battalion of Zouaves. These were ordered to hold the village to the last man. Weather conditions were bad with the trenches filled with icy water from melting snow and there was a shortage of food and drinking water.

German artillery shelled the village throughout the night of the 25–26th and the barrage continued the following day. When the Germans started the attack they were fired on by French artillery with heavy casualties. Attack followed attack with the French defending doggedly but the village only fell to the Germans on March 3 after the use of cunning. They fired on the village for hours on end and then suddenly stopped. The French, assuming the attack was about to commence, left their shelters to man the trenches and at that point the German shelling began once again but this time targeting the French front line, killing many French soldiers. After an hour the shelling

One of the millions of soldiers who were killed at the Western Front.

German flame-throwers quelling last resistance during an attack on French positions.

A dead French soldier at Froidterre.

A group of severely-injured soldiers who waited several days for help but died gruesomely from shellfire.

General von Mudra inspecting his troops during his assumption of command of the newly formed eastern attack group for the Battle of Verdun.

The French made wide use of colonial troops. Here Senegalese soldiers arrive to take part in the Battle of Verdun, June 22, 1916.

Spahi soldiers during training at St. Goudrin, June 16, 1916.

Soldiers created accommodation as comfortable and as safe as possible behind the lines.

One of the many buildings in Verdun destroyed by shellfire.

French infantry next to unexploded German shells at Fort Souville.

stopped and once more the French occupied their trenches and the same was repeated and many more French were killed. This was repeated a third time but now the French decided to stay in their shelters but the Germans immediately overran the French in their dug-outs and captured the village, leaving the road to Fort Vaux open to them. The fighting around the village of Douaumont was one of the bloodiest actions of the Battle of Verdun. About 4,000 French died and a similar number of Germans over the possession of this small village,

THE GREAT BATTLES OF 1915 AND 1916

Shells often failed to explode and were left sticking out of the mud. An unexploded German 220 mm shell at Verdun.

which delayed the German advance and gave General Pétain the time to send reinforcements to the front. The defenders made an important contribution to the eventual failure of the German plan to bleed the French to death at Verdun, causing them in the end to halt their offensive. That stage had not been reached yet though and the bloody Battle of Verdun would not end until 1918.

THE BATTLE FOR FORT VAUX

The armored Fort Vaux was also included in the decision to disarm fortifications made in August 1915 but this had not yet been implemented and hence the fort was fully occupied and armed. The fort came under heavy German artillery fire in early March with two of its three observation posts being severely damaged. A direct hit destroyed the moat and caused the tunnel to the 75 mm (3 inches) gun to cave in so that it was no longer accessible. On March 8 German infantry managed to get close to the fort. When they reported this

Left: French infantry at the front in the village of Negre, February 1916.

A French army surgeon with field hospital orderlies at a sandbag-shielded first aid post near Fort Souville. This fort marks the farthest point of the German advance.

French medical orderlies with wounded at a bandage station at Buxerelles.

The fighting around Mort-Homme was ferocious and bloody. Here wounded are being moved behind the lines by ambulance.

down the line the message was misunderstood, leading to the German army's information service the next day to report that Fort Vaux had also fallen to the Germans. General Guretsky who was ostensibly in command of this apparent conquest was highly decorated for this heroic deed. This was a painful mistake which quickly became apparent. Fort Vaux was still in French hands and would remain so for the time being.

On May 24 the fort got a new commander, the 49-year-old invalid, Major Raynal, who was to prove a formidable opponent for the attacking Germans whose efforts were increasingly more ferocious. Artillery fired on the fort night and day and Raynal reported that "on a quiet day" some 8,000 hits had been counted.

Inside the fort, in addition to its garrison of 280 men were many soldiers who had escaped from the immediate surroundings so that there were now 600 men within its walls. Food and water were therefore scarce and were strictly rationed. The Germans attacked once more on June 1 after a furious barrage that caused great slaughter to French troops on either side of the fort. The Germans succeeded in capturing

British volunteers of the medical unit SSA-10 that was attached to the French 31st Division ready to collect wounded from Verdun.

There was a huge demand for artificial limbs for the hundreds of thousands of wounded soldiers. A new medical industry arose like this workshop for artificial limbs.

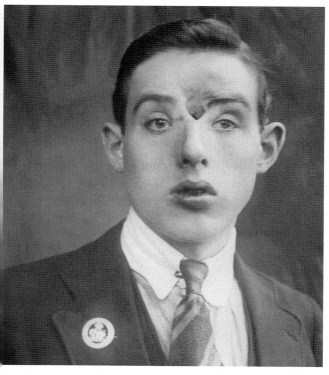

A soldier hit and disfigured in the forehead...

...gets a new face – not with the help of plastic surgery but from an artificial mask.

Left: British voluntary ambulance men wait at Tannois near Bar-le-Duc close to Verdun for a new stream of wounded.

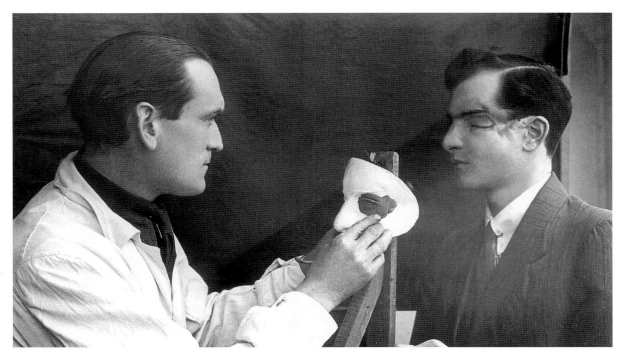

A mask is made for a soldier severely injured by shrapnel.

The German pilot Manfred Albrecht Freiherr von Richthofen (1892–1918) became famous with the squadron that bore his name. He shot down eighty enemy aircraft and was finally shot down himself on April 21, 1918.

the renowned Vaux dam and came within range of Raynal's machine-guns. These fired so furiously that trenches in which the Germans were filled with dead and injured so that the attackers were forced to climb over their casualties to gain access to the open in order to advance. The sight of the battlefield was appalling. Those who had just died lay amid others whose bodies were already decaying and parts of bodies from earlier casualties. The stench was unbearable. The cries of the wounded were heart rending and many died through lack of first aid or care. Others lay there still when the French launched a counteroffensive the following week and unfortunately burnt to death when the French fired phosphor shells.

Fort Vaux was now surrounded and on the night of June 2 twelve German battalions supported by a unit of pioneers attacked again. The fort had been seriously damaged through all the artillery fire but its defenders did not yield

The bright red Fokker DR-1 Triplane of von Richthofen became infamous among the Allies and gained him the nickname "the Red Baron."

Von Richthofen's squadron. His aircraft is second from right.

Von Richthofen during his time in hospital after suffering a severe head injury during a dogfight on June 6, 1917.

and lay down murderous fire against the advancing attackers. The Germans managed to reach the upper level of the fort and to gain access to the entrance tunnels. They had removed the nails from their boots so they would not be heard but the French had thrown away empty cans which caused the Germans to betray themselves. There were obstacles in the tunnel and a machine-gun which now opened fire but the Germans managed to overpower these after suffering heavy losses. The Germans sent reinforcements that afternoon and an officer to take command. Bizarrely, the fort now had two commanders: a French one in the main body of the fort and a German officer in the upper part of the complex.

The air vents had to be closed because Germans now threw hand grenades into the fort through them but this made the situation unbearable. Smoke and gas now filled the fort from flame-throwers used by the Germans and the air was so bad the defenders had to put their gas masks on. Oil lamps would not work

The German air force ruled the skies in 1916.

The Red Baron gets ready to fly over enemy territory.

because of the shortage of oxygen and various soldiers fainted from the poisonous atmosphere. The water supplies were also exhausted after several days and things became so desperate that men began to drink their own urine. Others tried licking the moisture from the walls. The numbers of injured increased but supplies of bandages and medicine had run out.

The attackers in the top of the fort also suffered. French artillery laid down merciless fire and there was almost no cover so losses were high. This situation continued until June 6 when French infantry attempted to relieve the fort but their efforts were beaten off, leaving most of the French assault troops dead or dying on the battlefield.

Oberleutnant Goering, commander of von Richthofen's squadron.

The remains of von Richthofen's Fokker after its was shot down by the Canadian Captain Roy Brown on April 21, 1918.

Right: Von Richthofen is buried by the British with full military honors on April 22, 1918.

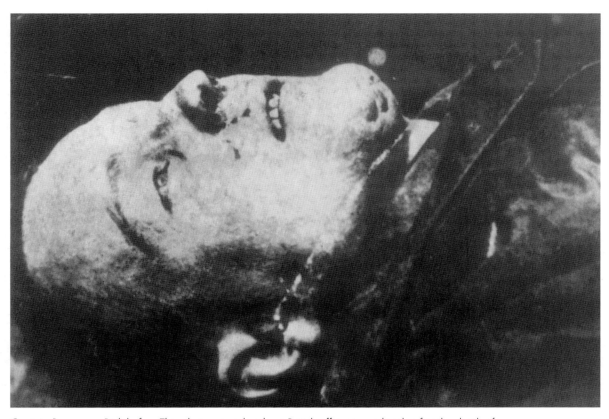

Captain Baron von Richthofen. This photo was taken by a British officer immediately after the death of the "Red Baron."

That night Major Raynal made a dramatic decision. Early the next morning he gathered the survivors together and informed them that he intended to capitulate to the Germans. Some cried at the news but others were beyond caring. An officer was sent outside with a white flag and the official surrender followed. This brought an end to the battle for Fort Vaux which had cost around 5,000 men dead or injured but in which both sides had fought bravely, tenaciously, and with considerable sacrifice. Fort Vaux was back in French hands by November when the Germans evacuated it of their own free will for tactical reasons.

THE BATTLE OF MORTE-HOMME AND HILL 304

In early March the Germans realized it had been a mistake to ignore the left bank of the Meuse. The French were given time to bring in reinforcements and artillery with which they mercilessly pounded the German troops on the right bank. Therefore a decision was made on March 6 to extend the offensive to the left bank.

Representatives of British squadrons lay wreaths on the grave of Baron von Richthofen.

The other side of the picture: one of the eighty victims of von Richthofen.

During a heavy snow storm and after a preparatory artillery barrage units of the Sixth Reserve Corps attacked at the Bois de Forges and other German troops simultaneously crossed the Meuse at Samogneux where they came under heavy French fire. Many of the French shells failed to explode in the mud so casualties were not too severe and on March 7 the Germans captured Regneville, the Bois de Corbeaux, and Bois de Cumières, taking about 3,000 prisoners of war. The village of Forges also fell that evening. The French mounted a counter attack the next morning and won back the Bois de Corbeaux. On March 8 the Germans attacked the famous hill of Morte-Homme but were beaten off. On March 14 the German's Twelfth Reserve Division succeeded in reaching the northern summit of the hill and drove off the French defenders in fierce combat. The attack had been preceded by heavy artillery fire that turn the hill into a smoking column of fire in which nothing lived. The hill looked more like Dante's inferno with fire and dead or severely injured everywhere and mutilated corpses littering the ground. There was no hope of medical care or burial and the stench of rotting flesh was unbearable. While the exhausted attackers tried to get some rest in the former French trenches they came under fire from the French on the other summit and fighting resumed. Storming the northern summit had cost the Germans 3,000 men and this now appeared to be for nothing so long as they did not take the other summit as well. Every effort to do so was repulsed and the situation became increasingly desperate.

A German fighter during a dogfight above the Western Front.

The fighting for Mort-Homme lasted throughout March and April and ended with the French succeeding in driving the Germans from the hill. They decided now to attack first the nearby hill 304.

CAPTURE OF BOTH HILLS

On May 3 thirty-six artillery batteries began the battle for hill 304. The bombardment lasted continuously for two days and two nights. After the war it was estimated that around 10,000 French soldiers lost their lives defending the hill but it still took the Germans three days before they captured the strategic high point.

The same methods were now used as at Mort-Homme which was also back in German hands by May 20. The battle was very fierce and losses were severe on both sides.

CONTINUING BATTLE

The Battle of Verdun had lasted one hundred days and by late May German losses were about 174,000 men. It was obvious that the Falkenhayn plan to bleed the French army to its death at Verdun had failed. Indeed it seemed as though it was the German army that was bleeding to death but the high command did not see it this way and prepared for further offensives.

GAS GRENADE ATTACK ON FORT SOUVILLE

The battle had meanwhile also continued on the eastern bank of the Meuse. Heavy fighting took place around Thiaumont, Froide Terre, and the village of Fleury that changed hands seventeen times and was razed to the ground. The Germans now planned an attack on Fort Souville, the final fort of the outer defensive ring around Verdun.

The attack was to take place over a front of just 600 meters but the weather worsened and a heavy rainstorm transformed the ground into a sea of mud and the attack was postponed. The attack troops who were already in position for the offensive were ordered to stay where they were in order to maintain the element of surprise. This meant that they had to remain for day after day without shelter and food in soaking wet clothing and exposed to constant French artillery fire and losses were considerable before fighting even began. Morale sank to an all-time low.

Finally, German artillery opened up on the morning of July 10, firing around 63,000 poison gas shells. French troops wore gas masks though so the effect of the gas was limited and when German infantry attacked they ran straight into a terrible barrage and suffered appalling losses. A further attempt to take the fort on July 12 also failed with the attackers being driven back with bloody losses.

A German navy Zeppelin, the L-12, on its way to bomb Britain.

Frigate Captain Strasser, head of the German navy's air section. His Zeppelin, the L-70 was shot down over Britain, crashing in flames, killing Strasser.

The Germans did not manage to penetrate beyond Fort Souville. General Falkenhayn realized that his plan had failed, albeit too late for 600,000 French and German soldiers who had sacrificed their lives for this pointless battle. Falkenhayn decided to halt all further offensives for the time being and to restrict action to consolidation and defense. Operation Gericht had been of no value with no tangible results. On August 27 Falkenhayn was relieved of his command and transferred to Romania. He was replaced by the heroes of Tannenberg – the pairing of Hindenburg and Ludendorff.

THE BLOODY BATTLE OF THE SOMME

The bad situation for the Allies caused General Joffre to call a conference of the senior Allied commanders in a quest for plans for 1916 that would give them the initiative.

The shot-down L-70's wreckage.

The top men of the Allies: (left to right) Marshal Joffre, President Poincaré, King George IV, General Foch, and General Haig.

Following the German offensive at Verdun in which the French had suffered heavy losses he wanted a joint Franco-British offensive on the Somme to relieve pressure on the Verdun front. Joffre personally visited the British commander in chief Haig and they agreed the British would be ready before July 1. The offensive would start on July 1 with the French mounting a second offensive several days later to the south that would probably take the Germans by surprise. Haig was not so certain about this latter point for he feared the French would renege on this promise leaving the British to bear the brunt with the French then joining in later to claim victory. Both did agree though about the

General Haig on horseback during a tour of inspection at the front.

Generals Haig and Foch with Joffre leaving Joffre's headquarters where they have discussed opening a second front on the Somme.

General Rawlinson, commander of the new British Fourth Army deployed to link up on the Somme with the French Sixth Army.

General Rawlinson with several staff officers familiarizing themselves on the Somme.

A French 400 mm (16 inches) gun was used on the Somme. The battle started on June 25, 1916 with an artillery barrage that lasted seven days.

A British battery of howitzers during the initial barrage. British artillery fired more than one million shells at German positions.

A British "kite" or observation balloon with two artillery spotters at the Somme.

British munitions store at the Somme.

Artillerymen move a heavy 15 inch howitzer shell.

timing and objective of the offensive: to reach the line of Bapaume–Péronne–Han with the French attacking Péronne and the British at Rancourt-Combles.

The opening of the Somme offensive was vital for Joffre to relieve pressure on the French at Verdun that was increasingly great with the heavy losses. It was extremely important to relieve the pressure on that front. Haig's lack of trust was not entirely misplaced since Joffre

The British assembled an impressive force of troops for the Battle of the Somme.

Indian cycle troops at Mametz road, July 1916.

Left: Trench grenades in readiness.

later informed him that the twenty-two to twenty-six French divisions agreed were no longer available following heavy casualties at Verdun and that the French contribution would be limited to twelve divisions.

Meanwhile, in addition to the Third Army, the British had formed a new Fourth Army under General Rawlinson (seventeen divisions and three in reserve) that were deployed along a front of approximately nineteen miles from the Somme in the south where it linked up with the French Sixth Army to Commecourt in the north where the British Third Army was positioned.

French reinforcements on their way to the Somme front.

British troops wait in their trenches for the signal to attack.

Left: British pioneers on their way to the front line to position barbed wire.

The French too were ready for the signal to attack.

British observation post in a well-constructed trench.

Ten minutes to zero: a mine explodes beneath
the Hawthorn redoubt. The Battle of the Somme
is about to begin.

The British explode a mine beneath a German position at
Beaumont-Hamel on July 1, 1916.

Australian troops in the front line just before the attack.

Over the top at the Somme 1916. Only a few returned.

British preparations were impressive. In contrast to the manner of the Gallipoli fiasco the logistics for the Battle of the Somme left nothing to chance. Haig had enormous supplies stockpiled in the area around Albert and Arras and ensured there were good lines of communications. Some 1,000 field guns, 180 heavy artillery pieces, and 245 heavy howitzers were deployed with an impressive three million shells. Launching off positions were prepared for the troops who would take part in the battle. The 29th

Division that had been decimated at Gallipoli had now been fully manned again and re-equipped and was in the line. The so-called "Pals" battalions" of Kitchener's army were also among the assault troops. For many of them this would be their first experience of warfare.

Haig's plan was to break through the enemy lines on July 1 after an artillery barrage that was to last for at least seven days. It was thought that the powerful artillery barrage would make matchwood of the Germans and hence no resistance was anticipated. The attacking troops were to take the German trenches, occupy them, and then press on the

Some never made it out of their trench.

The first wave left their trenches quietly as if for a walk, to an almost certain death.

The British and French left their trenches at precisely 7:30 to attack the German line.

A second attack wave, still confidant of victory.

Right: ...without cover and in closed order as if on an exercise.

Wave after wave left their trenches to be mercilessly mown down by the German machine-guns.

Reserves awaiting the order to move to the front line.

The few survivors tried hopelessly to find a gap in the German barbed wire entanglements that were clearly still undamaged despite seven days of heavy shelling.

...they died too. The Germans had an unobstructed field of fire across no-man's-land.

six miles to Bapaume. Haig and his staff were convinced that it would be more or less a "walk over" for the infantry and ordered the attack waves to go forward in closed order. The intention was for the field guns to deal with the barbed wire entanglements and German trenches while the heavy artillery would deal with the enemy artillery and certain reinforcements. The infantry attack was to be preceded by a creeping barrage with the attack troops following the artillery fire while the enemy took cover.

It all seemed so simple but Haig had failed to find out what had happened with a similar barrage at the start of the German's Verdun offensive. Had he done so he might have been less optimistic and

The Germans quickly sent reinforcements to the Somme after the first British attack. Troops from Verdun en route to the Somme.

German reinforcements on their way to the Somme. These soldiers are still wearing the old-style helmets.

Right: The British barrage had little effect on the German's deep concrete bunkers.

thousands of young men would not have died needlessly in the bloom of their youth or suffered mutilation. The chosen territory near the Somme was not ideal ground for an offensive. The Germans held favorable positions and had dug themselves into the chalk hills. Once again the British failed to gather sufficient intelligence. During the artillery barrage before the attack precious little consideration was given to reports from reconnaissance patrols that the Germans were still in their shelters and that the barb wire did not appear to be damaged. General Hunter Weston, commanding the Eighth Corps made the same error as at Gallipoli. He was far too optimistic and did

German dug-outs at the Somme front.

German 210 mm (8 inches) howitzer at the Somme.

A German communication trench leading to a battery of howitzers.

German soldiers tried to make their accommodation at the front as comfortable as possible using wood and corrugated iron.

Right: A heavy shell explodes among the attacking British troops.

By the end of June 1 there were 21,392 British troops dead and 36,000 injured.

German field artillery patiently await the attackers.

German artillery fires on the front line British trenches and the area behind.

Wounded British soldiers try to crawl back to their own lines.

Germans use a flame-thrower in a counter-offensive.

Killed by a shell exploding nearby.

not take the trouble to check the information for himself. He reported that the German barbed wire in his sector was totally destroyed and that his troops could "walk right in" while in reality the barbed wire remained and would cause the death of many men. The fact is that Haig assumed the barbed wire was dealt with and noted this in his diary for June 30.

The British preparations had not passed the Germans by of course. The area of the Somme had been fairly quiet until then and the Germans had taken advantage of this to organize and build thorough defensive positions. Strategic positions had machine-gun posts and there were deep communication trenches with concrete bunkers for the men ten meters below ground to protect them

Left: One of the 21,392 soldiers who did not return.

Dead soldiers in no-man's-land.

He reached the German lines but could find no way through and was killed.

A hastily formed grave for a fallen comrade.

Dead British soldiers on the Somme near Arras.

The battle continues: British orderlies bring in wounded during a gas attack.

Just a hand remains, almost imploringly held aloft.

One dead and one injured soldier waiting to be taken away.

Right: Ambulances come to and fro to convey the wounded.

from shellfire. Finally the trenches were heavily protected by barbed wire obstacles. In short, the German defenses were well-prepared and excellently suited for defense against the coming attack.

Haig gave his final instructions to his officers commanding the Third and Fourth Armies on June 16 and set out the objectives once more. The artillery bombardment of the German positions began on

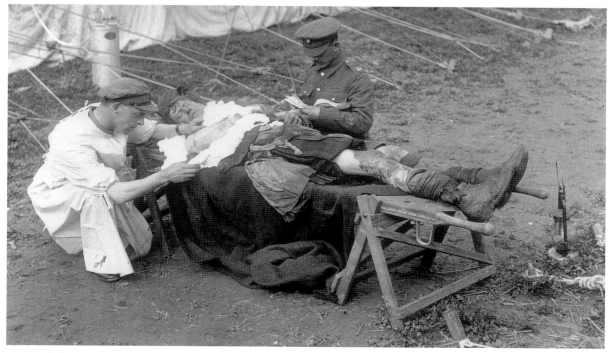

A wounded soldier gets first aid from a dressing station near the front.

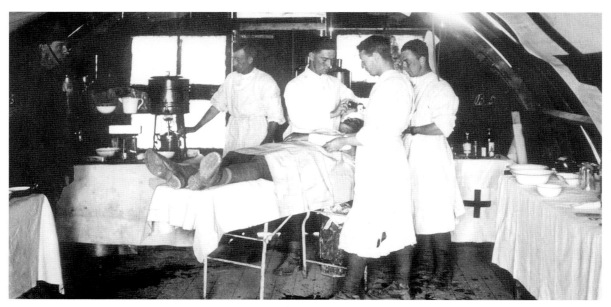

Operating tent of a field hospital on the Somme.

German humor at the Somme: "Don't get worked up about it."

Right: The destroyed cathedral of Péronne.

Dry British humor in adversity.

A French trench on the Somme.

Yet another attack: British troops prepare for the advancing Germans.

A British officer briefs his men just before the attack.

British soldiers place canisters in specially constructed cylinders under the eye of their officer as they prepare to launch a gas attack.

The British attack again under cover of a smoke screen.

A new invention first used at the Somme: a British flame-thrower, July 1, 1916.

June 25. More than one million shells of every caliber were fired continuously for seven days. The entire area was a mass of smoke and flames and it seemed impossible that anyone could survive. Finally July 1 dawned, the day that is now written in British military history as the greatest disaster of all time. It was the day on which British self-confidence was lost and never restored. The day on which 20,000 young men would never see the sun set.

THE FIRST OF JULY

The first of July dawned with blue skies and a bright sun. At 7:30 precisely the men were ordered to attack. They left their trenches and

A German gas attack on the Somme in 1916.

Mud also caused transport difficulties on the Somme.

Only a few returned.

Nothing but death, destruction, stench, and endless mud.

set off towards the enemy's trenches under cover of smoke and behind a creeping artillery barrage. The French Sixth Army under General Remile Fayolle to the south of the Somme fared well but on the British side where conscripted soldiers were fighting for the first time (Britain introduced conscription on January 12, 1916) everything seemed to go wrong. The creeping barrage of which Haig had such expectations and which formed such an important part of his plan moved too rapidly and reached the German lines much too far ahead of the infantry. The Germans were therefore able to reoccupy their trenches and had sufficient time to direct their machine-guns towards specific sectors. The British soldiers therefore came at the Germans wholly unprotected in the open in great swathes and were mown down in their thousands. New lines followed and were equally decimated and yet these too were followed by new lines. Of the seventeen attacking British divisions only five reached the first line of German trenches. The remaining twelve got no further than no-man's-land and many were dead even before they had left their own trenches. German soldiers later declared themselves dismayed at the wholly senseless manner in which the British attacked them. It was not even necessary for the Germans to aim to hit their victims and when the British finally did fall back the Germans ceased firing to prevent further casualties.

When the British attacks that day ended 21,392 young British soldiers had died with another 35,000 more or less seriously wounded

Left: A cheerless and disfigured landscape in which men had to live, fight, and finally almost certainly die.

British troops during a lull in the fighting, April 1917 at Tilloy.

Trenches filled with water, mud, and graves.

Mine craters filled with water at Mametz.

What remained of Beaumont-Hamel after the battle.

Soldiers at the front tried to create a feeling of home between the fighting. Australian soldiers brew tea in their trench.

soldiers remaining on the battlefield. Their cries for help could be heard from no-man's-land for days without any help coming. Finally it fell silent as they died through loss of blood, exhaustion, or lack of water.

If Haig had made a closer study of the Battle of Verdun then he would have been aware that a heavy artillery barrage, regardless of how severe, did not have the effect upon well prepared defensive positions that had been anticipated. At Verdun the French had withstood heavy bombardment and surprised the Germans afterwards by their presence. The Germans had also expected a "walk over" and were the dupe for it.

French Prime Minister Clemenceau during a visit to the front.

Conditions at the front became more unbearable as winter came.

Expecting an attack.

Soup is taken to the front line by donkey.

French barbed wire appeared not only not to have been damaged but to be made more difficult to penetrate through the shelling. Lessons could have been learned from this but no one gave it any thought.

Communications during the attack failed completely. Haig thought the Eight Corps were still in their trenches on July 2 while 14,000 had died. Even on July 3 Haig still had no full overview of the battle and ordered the fighting to continue. As a result of this 3,000 men attacked that morning towards Ovillers. One hour later 2,400 of them died. General Rawlinson in charge of the battle only then began to think that perhaps a disaster had taken place.

The terrible casualty figures were no reason to stop fighting for Haig and hence the Somme became a repetition of Verdun. Increasingly more futile attacks with ever increasing losses were made with attacks through to late October while the weather worsened and the ground became impassable. It stopped when the supply of men was almost entirely "used up." When this finally happened the British losses amounted to 400,000, dead, wounded, and missing. The French lost 200,000 and German losses were estimated at 600,000: a total of 1,200,000 men. The British advanced just 10 kilometers (6.2 miles) at a cost of 40,000 men per kilometer.

Pack horses at Méricourt, 1916.

Jammed roads, troops, ambulances, and mud: the Somme 1916.

Many seriously wounded men were left in the open for lack of space. Many died from the cold or lack of medical help.

An injured British officer is carried by German prisoners of war.

A German trench hit by British shellfire near Avillers.

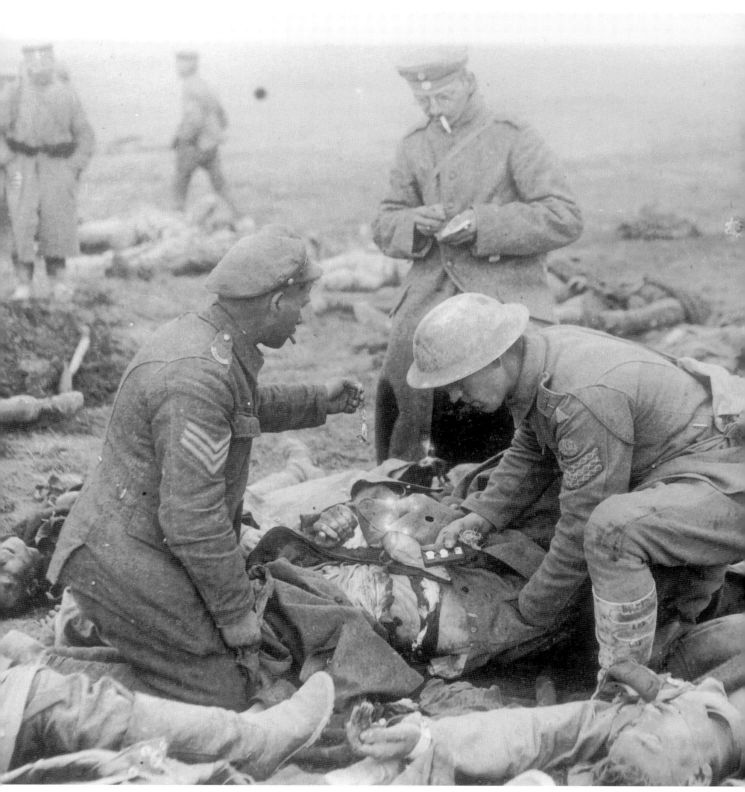

British prisoners of war help a severely wounded German soldier amid his dead comrades.

German prisoners of war are moved to the rear. The hell of the Somme is over for them.

A Tommy wounded in the neck is given a light by a German soldier.

The Battle of the Somme was not yet done though. The Germans retreated during the winter to a new defense line, the Hindenburg line. The area vacated by them was occupied by the Allies without a struggle in March 1917 but during the German's March offensive in 1918 they drove the Allies back out of these positions in a single day and in the course of two weeks drove them back more than thirty miles. Once again tens of thousands of soldiers died on the battlefield of the Somme and a final end only came in November 1918.

THE BRITISH BREED

Haig came under tremendous and continual criticism. Even today the debate about his leadership has not fallen silent. In his own diaries he wrote that the fighting on the Somme was worthwhile because the Germans were forced to take troops and artillery away from Verdun so that they were unable to continue that offensive. This is true. The Germans were forced at a critical time to move six divisions and heavy artillery from the Verdun offensive to defend their lines on the Somme. It is dubious though if this was the reason

The sad end to a sad battle: a German cemetery with 500 graves of those who never returned.

The famous Russian General Brusilov, who opened an offensive on June 4, 1916 with four armies across a front of more than 200 miles. At first the offensive was very successful.

why the Verdun offensive was halted in November.

Haig gave a second rationale that the Germans were forced to suffer heavy casualties. This too is true but was at the cost of equivalent losses that were difficult to replace, making the involvement of America essential. It is virtually certain that the British and French could not have continued the war without American help and admitted this in their plea to the US President. Finally Haig declared that it was essential to demonstrate to the world that the Allies were capable of mounting and continuing with a great offensive in order to demonstrate to everyone the fighting spirit of the British race. That British race was hellbent on self-destruction in 1916 and entirely dependent on American help.

THE BRUSILOV OFFENSIVES

THE JUNE OFFENSIVE

During the talks in 1915 between General Joffre and the Allied commanders about military plans for 1916 the Russians and Italians had agreed to go on the offensive so that the Germans would be pressed heavily on all fronts at the same time.

In accordance with those agreements and following an urgent request from the Italians to relieve pressure on their front by a Russian offensive, the Russians started a major offensive on March 18, 1916 at Lake Naroc but this went disastrously with the loss of 100,000 men and a further 10,000 taken prisoner. This was due to poor coordination between the artillery and the infantry which resulted in the infantry being shelled by their own side. Because the attack was made on a small front it resulted in the Russians being shelled from three sides by German artillery. The Russians lost 15,000 men in the first eight hours of the offensive and the slaughter continued when reinforcements were sent to face the same conditions. By the end of that month the Russians had to halt their offensive. The conditions in which the battle was fought were horrendous and some 11,000 died from the bitter cold. Several days later the Germans mounted a counter attack in which they regained all the ground they had lost.

Russian troops triumphantly enter a conquered town.

Austro-Hungarian officers with Russian prisoners of war.

Food shortage in a town occupied by the Russians.

NEW EFFORTS

The Russians tried again in June. Under the command of General Brusilov they mounted a major offensive against the Austro-Hungarian troops over a front of 323 kilometers (201 miles) from the marshes at Pripet to Bukovina. Brusilov launched two simultaneous attacks with four armies, the Eighth at Luzk (15 divisions), the Eleventh in the south (9 divisions) which established a bridgehead over the Turya river at Sopanov, the Seventh (10_ divisions) in East Galicia to the west of the River Tarnopol, and the Ninth Army (14 divisions) between the River Dnjestr and the Romanian border. Facing these forty-eight Russian divisions were thirty-eight Austro-Hungarian divisions of respectively the Fourth, First, Second, and Seventh Austro-Hungarian armies and the German southern army.

The Russian offensive was preceded on May 31 by a diversionary action followed by an artillery barrage with 1,938 guns firing on the Austro-Hungarian lines. This lasted a full day and destroyed much of

Right: Austro-Hungarian Arch-Duke Frederick visits the Dolomites front.

Emperor Charles of Austria inspecting German troops in Tyrol.

the Austro-Hungarian positions with the soldiers in the front line suffering considerable losses. The Russians overran the first three lines of defense and took 55,000 prisoners and captured many guns. Panic took hold among the Austro-Hungarians and their Fourth Army, that faced the Russian Eighth Army, turned heel and ran but was captured intact. The Russian Eleventh Army was also successful, breaking through at Sapanov and capturing 15,000 prisoners and occupying the town of Dubno.

The Russian Ninth Army opposed the Austro-Hungarian Seventh Army consisting of elite troops under the renowned General Pflantzer which was tasked with defending the line between the Dnjestr and the Carpathians. Despite inferior artillery (150 medium-heavy and heavy guns to 47 Russian heavy guns) the Austro-Hungarians were decisively beaten by the Russians. They broke right through the Seventh Army and took almost 100,000 prisoners of war. Misunderstanding of orders caused further panic and the rest of the Seventh Army fled in disarray on June 7 with all their artillery.

On July 8 the Russians reached Dalatyn about thirty-two miles from the Hungarian border and at the end of July the town of Brody in East Galicia fell and 40,000 were taken captive. On August 7 the town of Stanislau fell to the Russian Seventh Army who captured 7,000 Austro-Hungarian and 3,500 German soldiers. The Austro-Hungarian front over some 260 miles fell apart.

After a short rest in which Brusilov re-supplied his troops and renewed their strengths he began his campaign once more and took Bukovina and reached the Carpathian mountains. In the meantime the Germans had rushed to the aid of the Austro-Hungarians while supplies became a problem for the Russians because of the ever longer supply lines. His troops grew weary and reserves were exhausted. When Brusilov asked for reinforcements there were none available and in late October he was forced to halt his offensive.

The Russian losses were enormous, amounting to some one million dead, wounded, or missing. The Austro-Hungarian losses were also huge, amounting to 600,000 with a further 400,000 ending up in Russian camps as prisoners of war. In their efforts to help the Austro-Hungarians, the Germans lost 350,000 men. Brusilov had broken the backbone of the Austro-Hungarian armed forces and from then on the dual monarchy was dependent on its German ally which now had a great say in the decision-making process and forced the Austro-Hungarians to listen. Hindenburg was appointed commander in chief of the entire eastern front to Tarnopol. The Archduke Karl remained in charge of the southern front but with the German General von Seeckt as his chief of staff and the Germans in reality having the leadership.

The Brusilov offensives had a further political consequence. After difficulty making up their minds the Romanians decided to abandon their neutrality. The Russian successes contributed to this decision together with the Franco-Russo promise of important gains for Romania after the war, including Transsylvania, Bukovina, South Galicia, and Benat, in the southern corner of Bulgaria. Both the great

Headquarters at the front of the Austro-Hungarian army.

Soldiers celebrate the first of May after the Russian revolution in 1917.

powers had secret discussions with each other that decided not to keep this promise.

The Brusilov offensive was the most successful of the entire war but did not bring peace any closer.

ITALY ENTERS THE WAR AT THE BATTLE OF ISONZO

When the war broke out in 1914 Italy had declared its neutrality in accordance with expectations. As we have seen earlier, Italy had made a secret agreement with France in 1902 that it would remain neutral in the event of a war between Germany and France. Italy had stipulated certain conditions against which it would decide whether to honor this treaty or not. The reality is that Italy looked to its own interests and the side that offered most to Italy would gain its favor. This eventually proved to be the Allies. They offered the Italians the Brenner Pass as a natural border, Trentine, Trieste, Istria, and the

Emperor Franz-Joseph of Austria-Hungary died on November 21, 1916, aged 86 after ruling for sixty-eight years.

The Emperor was buried with great ceremony on November 30, 1916.

Coronation of Emperor Charles.

Emperor Charles and Empress Zita during the coronation.

Kaiser Wilhelm II and Emperor Charles of Austria-Hungary in 1917.

harbors in Dalmatia and also Turkish territory in Asia Minor and parts of the German colonies. The people in Italy were very keen on war and pressed the king and government to take part. Italy finally broke its links with Germany and Austria–Hungary and left the Tripartite alliance in order to take the side of the Allies on May 24, 1915.

Emperor Charles inspects German troops about to leave for the front.

German troops used flame-throwers in the Battle of Isonzo.

General Otto von Below visits the Isonzo front.

Austro-Hungarian soldiers at the Italian front.

Austrian ski-troops in the war against Italy.

Austrian positions high in the mountains.

Left: an Austro-Hungarian cannon on the Isonzo front.

367

Austro-Hungarian mule train at Asiago, May 1916.

The Austro-Hungarians brought materials and munitions rapidly to the front.

Austro-Hungarian wounded taken prisoner by the Italians.

Austro-Hungarian positions in the Italian Alps.

One of the theaters of war in which the Italian and Austro-Hungarian troops fought each other in twelve bloody battles at a cost of hundreds of thousands of dead and injured was the Isonzo river.

This river ran at that time on Austro-Hungarian territory along the border with Italy from the Gulf of Venice in the south to around Piezo in the north. The Italians hoped to gain the large port of Trieste and to then push ahead to Ljubljana.

The Italians entered the war on June 23 with an offensive of some 250,000 men in the first Battle of Isonzo. This came to a close on

Emperor Charles visits the front at Bukovina.

July 7 with losses of 25,000 men on both sides without any breakthrough by the Italians. The Italians made a further three attempts that year at a cost of around 240,000 men without success. Further attempts at a breakthrough were made in 1916 and 1917 with massive attacks at the cost of many lives but again without results. On the other hand the Germans sent a large force to support the Austro–Hungarian offensive. After an artillery barrage lasting four hours in which gas was widely used the Italians were routed and retreated some twelve miles with the Germans taking the Italian town of Caporetto and capturing 260,000 prisoners of war. It was here that the German *Oberleutenant* Erwin Rommel, who become renowned as a general in World War II, stormed a hill-top and took 3,000 prisoners

Die Offensive am Isonzo: Trommelfeuer auf die feindl. Linien vor dem Sturm. 4984

An Austro-Hungarian artillery barrage on the Isonzo front.

Their families wave goodbye as Austro-Hungarian reserves leave for the front.

Many did not return.

Austro-Hungarian soldiers examine a shot-down Italian bomber.

of war, and the following day during his advance captured a further 9,000 men.

On October 27 the Italians were forced to relinquish their positions on the Isonzo. The battle had cost about 200,000 Italians and Austro-Hungarians their lives with a further 200,000 Italian soldiers deserting. This bad ending caused a major crisis in Italy.

Support from their British and French allies eventually halted the Austro-Hungarian advance and the fighting ceased on June 18 resulting in quieter times. It was not until the almost the end of the war in October 1918 that a united force of Italians, British, and French drove the Austro-Hungarians back to the Isonzo with the capture of 300,000 prisoners of war and a great deal of artillery. When the war was over the Italian casualties amounted to 615,000 dead and almost one million wounded. This was a sad ending to what had begun with such enthusiasm in response to the will of the Italian people.

The soldiers became dirty and lice and rats were a plague. Here men are deloused at the Italian front.

THE NAVAL WAR

The Grand Fleet and the Hochsee Flotte come to blows

THE GERMAN NAVY'S PLANS

Germany was a nation in the ascendancy in the nineteenth century. With more than one third of its population under the age of fifteen and population growth from forty-one million in 1871 to sixty-eight million at the end of 1914, Germany had rapidly developed as a highly industrialized exporter that was finding the provision of raw materials increasingly troublesome. The growth of German exports was enormous and exceeded those of the USA, Great Britain, and France.

This development was of great concern to some in Britain, especially when the German chemical industry started to win business that had previously gone to British companies. Germany took a primary position in markets previously dominated by the British such as those for electrical equipment and textiles and also become a fierce competitor to the British in shipbuilding. In some cases Germany exported more goods to previously purely British markets than the British did.

A U-boat approaches the German submarine base at Zeebrugge.

German U-boats at Zeebrugge.

It is obvious that this rapid growth caused an increased demand for raw materials. Germany became increasingly dependent upon foreign countries and on the British merchant navy.

It was logical from a business point of view that Germany needed its own means of shipping. The first step was to start building their own merchant fleet which resulted in further growth for the German shipbuilding industry and of German ports leading to increasing competition with other countries and Great Britain in particular. Economic policy lay at the heart of German foreign policy. With its rapid population growth Germany could no longer restrict itself to Europe and felt it essential to develop a "world" policy. This was not greatly appreciated by everyone, indeed efforts were made to obstruct or oppose this policy as in the case of a lease of Kiow Chow in 1897, and German efforts in 1898 to establish themselves on the Solomon Islands, the opening of a trading mission in the Philippines, the founding of a bunkering stations at Aden, along the Persian Gulf, for the route to India etc. Everywhere the Germans found Russia, Japan, and Great Britain opposing it and it became virtually

Torpedoes being loaded at Zeebrugge.

impossible to achieve the necessary economic expansion by peaceful means.

It is therefore not surprising that Germany felt the need for its own colonies and its own navy to protect the trading routes to and from those colonies. Foreign policy without the backing of a powerful navy in those days was deemed impossible and every country of note had its own navy.

The desire for its own navy suddenly came to the fore when two German merchant ships were detained off the coast of South Africa by two British warships at the end of December in 1899 and escorted to Durban. This news burst upon Germany like a bomb and the press protested strongly. When a third German merchant ship was detained several days later the German government delivered a formal protest of what it described as "piracy on the high seas." The British subsequently made their excuses and released the ships in early January but the harm had been done. The German public was wholly behind Admiral von Tirpitz who wrote in a memorandum that it was clearly impossible to conduct foreign trade and operate colonies without a powerful navy.

A U-boat being supplied at sea.

A rendezvous at sea in heavy weather.

The Danish sailing ship *Marie*.

Tirpitz had already put forward plans for a fleet in 1897 and this had been approved by the Reichstag the following year. In 1900 he put forward his second proposed navy law. The fundamental point of this was that the German fleet should be big enough to deter an attack by another power. Simultaneously he insisted that while the fleet was being built nothing should be done to harm British interests. The relationship with Britain needed to be carefully maintained and Germany should not excessively arm itself and not provoke aggression.

Tirpitz's naval law envisaged a ratio of two German warships to three British. The German fleet did not need to be superior but it would be risky to attack the German fleet. That fleet would therefore be a factor that had to be reckoned with and was precisely what was required to implement the new "world policy" as a great power.

Enemy in sight! The crew man the gun.

U-boat firing at a merchant ship.

In Britain though the admiral's plans were regarded as a threat to British naval supremacy and the British were not prepared to let that happen. In 1908 the British decided to introduce the "Two Power Standard" by which the Royal Navy was to be a strong as the combined fleets of the two strongest navies of other countries. From this moment and arms race began between the two countries that was to end to Germany's disadvantage.

In 1912 it looked as though some agreement between the two was possible. Germany took the initiative over talks to try to bring an end

Right: Shells fall around the ship that was later hit.

In the engine room of a U-boat under way.

to or reduction in the costly fleet building program. Although these talks went well initially and the British delegated minister, Haldane, sent hopeful reports of promising progress, nothing came of them, largely because of the resistance to them by the Foreign Secretary, Edward Grey, who saw his policy of *entente* with the French being at risk and had deep-rooted distrust of Germany.

Admiral Tirpitz's plans for the navy were eventually doomed to failure. Once construction got underway it became apparent Germany could not find the money. Then Britain launched the *Dreadnought* in 1906 that was an entirely new concept in warships. The *Dreadnought* was not only much faster but also more heavily armed than any warship existing at that time, meaning that the new German ships were greatly inferior to the British ships. Tirpitz's prestige fell and he eventually had to admit that the British and French navies combined would be a formidable opponent for the German fleet.

It is quite evident that the British strongly exaggerated the threat posed by the German fleet building program and this is supported by a document written by Churchill in which he pours scorn on the falseness and exaggeration of a British Admiralty report comparing the Royal Navy and German fleet in which it was claimed the Germans would possess twenty-one "dreadnoughts" in 1912. He describes the report as part of an aggressive policy by the Conservatives that had caused panic in the Royal Navy. He concluded that Britain's national security was in no way threatened by Germany's expansion of its navy and that the suggestions that it was were made for party political reasons. The Admiralty report was indeed wrong. In 1912 Germany only had twelve "dreadnoughts" rather than the twenty-one the British Admiralty had suggested.

The British did not consider though that Germany had need of a large fleet and its building could therefore only be aggressive and directed at Great Britain. At first view this appears to be quite logical but it does not concur with the reality. According to the British, expansion of the German navy disturbed the existing balance of power but in reality there was no balance for the British had by far the strongest navy in the world and intended to keep it that way at any cost. No single country could be allowed to become too powerful, that is sufficiently strong to put Britain's extensive colonial expansion in jeopardy. A powerful German navy was entirely at odds with such British thinking.

Officers' mess on board a U-boat mother ship.

One of the hundreds of merchant ships sank by German U-boats.

TOTAL WAR BY SUBMARINES

When war broke out in 1914 the Royal Navy turned to a plan that had been accepted by the British Imperial War Committee as official strategy in 1909. This plan envisaged a complete economic blockade of Germany in the event of war with that country.

On November 3, 1914, when the war was merely a few months old, the British put the plan into operation. They declared the North Sea/English Channel as a war zone and subjected neutral shipping to stringent checks. Neutral ships were required to report to the Royal

Survivors leave their sinking ship.

Navy once they entered this area in order to be searched. All goods destined for Germany were to be seized. Several countries, including the USA, Norway, and Sweden protested against these measures that were in contravention of international law but the British took no notice of them.

The blockade was illegal in international law and immoral. It was the first time that the civilian population of a country were declared as war targets (many thousands of Germans were to die of hunger as a result). The British recognized this but pointed to the war which made the blockade essential.

In response to this British measure Germany declared all waters around the British Isles, in addition to the English Channel, a war zone forbidden for all enemy merchant shipping that would without exception be torpedoed by German submarines. The Germans added that the international agreement known as "Cruiser Rules", whereby the crew would first be allowed to man their life boats would no longer be observed as this posed a great threat to the submarine itself.

Ship abandoned after being torpedoed.

Left: A U-boat fires at a merchant ship.

TORPEDO ATTACK ON THE LUSITANIA (1)

Unfortunately this decision meant that neutral shipping was often hit. The first example was a Norwegian merchant ship, then an American tanker, and a week later on May 7, 1915 the British liner *Lusitania*, with a large number of American passengers on board on her way from New York to Liverpool. The torpedo attack on this ship in which 1,198 passengers lost their lives, including 128 Americans, made a powerful impression on the US government that demanded that Germany cease forthwith with its unrestricted submarine war.

In Germany there was also shock and an offer of compensation was made for the victims but attacks were continued on enemy merchant shipping. On August 19, the British liner *Arabic* was torpedoed and on March 24, 1916 the British liner *Sussex* in which there were again some American victims.

The US government delivered an ultimatum in which it demanded the use of Cruiser Rules before the use of torpedoes or it would break off diplomatic relations. This time the Germans yielded to the pressure and ordered their submarine captains not to attack any more passenger ships.

At the end of 1916 though following the appalling Verdun and Somme offensives things turned against Germany at the front and the German high command pressed to resume all out submarine warfare. Bethmann Hollweg, the German Chancellor, was strongly opposed to its resumption. He was convinced that this would bring the Americans into the war and refused to grant his approval. This was a reason for Admiral Tirpitz to resign. He was replaced by Admiral von Capelle.

The crew of a merchant ship are taken on board *U-35*.

The German commander in chief continued to press the necessity of resuming the all out submarine war. The German Admiral Henning von Holtzendorff, head of the German naval staff, had calculated that if the Germans could sink 600,000 tons capacity of British shipping per month, Britain would be forced to discontinue the war after five months for lack of food and materials. He declared that the risk that this would bring the USA into the war was minimal since before the Americans could be ready the war would be over. On October 7 Germany decided to resume the submarine war with commanders instructed to adhere strictly to the Cruiser Rules. The results were such that Bethmann Hollweg could no longer oppose them and on February 1, 1917 he realized that Germany no longer stood any chance of winning the war on land and that a rapid fall of Great Britain could only be achieved by submarines. Germany therefore officially advised of the resumption of all out submarine war. The results were quickly apparent. One out of four ships on its way to Britain was sunk and the situation did indeed start to look critical for the United Kingdom.

Left: A British merchant ship torpedoed by the *U-35*.

The resumption of the submarine war though had another consequence. The US government broke off diplomatic relations with Germany and on April 6, 1917 USA declared war against Germany.

From the outset of the war until November 1918 the Germans torpedoed more than two thousand merchant ships and warships with twelve thousand crewmen losing their lives. More than two

Meeting at sea: the *U-35* passes the *U-42*.

hundred U-boats were damaged or destroyed or failed to return. The Germans had miscalculated though when they estimated Britain could be brought to its knees. Just in time the Allies switched to a convoy system and the number of torpedo incidents reduced dramatically. The hope that the war would end in Germany's favor before American troops reached Europe was not realized. American involvement in the war eventually sealed Germany's fate in a dramatic way.

THE BATTLE OF JUTLAND

THE GERMAN HOCHSEE FLOTTE SETS SAIL

On May 31, 1916 the German *Hochsee Flotte* or deep-sea fleet set sail into the North Sea under its new commander, Admiral Scheer to join battle with the British at what was to later become known as the Battle of Jutland. Opinion remains divided on the outcome of this maritime battle. Some historians record it as a strategic victory for the British and others as a triumph for German tactics. What is the truth?

GERMAN TACTICS

The Germans recognized that their relatively small fleet would not be able to break the British blockade and therefore German naval policy was to avoid a direct confrontation with the "Grand Fleet" but to make surprise attacks that would damage the fleet and reduce its size until it was closer in size to the German fleet. Only then could a direct action be envisaged.

Admiral Scheer followed this policy closely and added an element of his own. He wanted to blockade the British by means of submarines, cutting Great Britain off from supplies of food and materials desperately needed for war. The ending of the all out submarine war as a result of American pressure ran contrary to this and he was therefore forced to use his surface ships. On May 31, 1916 he took his fleet to sea with the intention of making a strike against the British coast in order to draw out the British cruisers under Admiral Beatty that lay at anchor at Rosyth. Scheer split his force in two: a reconnaissance group led by

The German Admiral of the Fleet, von Scheer, who dealt the British a sensitive tactical victory at the Battle of Jutland.

Admiral Hipper commanded the German vanguard which decimated the cruiser fleet of Britain's Admiral Beatty in a matter of hours.

Admiral Hipper taking the point about fifty miles ahead of the main German strength. If the British were enticed out Hipper was to attack them and lure them in the direction of the main German force so that Scheer could finish off the British fleet with the German's superior numbers.

The British, who had access to the German naval code, were entirely aware that the *Hochsee Flotte* had put to sea and planned a trap of their own. Admiral Beatty had his ships weigh anchor and head towards the Germans. At the same time the main British force under Admiral Jellicoe left its base at Scapa Flow. Their intention was identical to the German plan, with Beatty's ships ordered to drop back towards the main fleet once they made contact with the Germans, which would then destroy the vanguard of the German fleet. Following this the Royal Navy would engage the German *Hochsee Flotte* and given its superior numbers almost certainly destroy it.

A great drama, that was to keep the world fascinated for many years to come, was about to unfold. About 250 ships, including the largest and most modern of the age, manned by about 100,000 sailors who had been trained for just such a confrontation, closed with each other at full speed.

At 14:30 hours the advance ships in both vanguards sighted each other and Admiral Beatty attempted to maneuver so that he blocked Hipper's path back to the main fleet but Hipper turned in accordance with his orders towards the approaching main body of the German fleet and the two fleets sailed alongside each other for a time on a convergent course. About three hours later the ships were within range of each other and the *Lützow* opened fire first, immediately answered by *HMS Lion*. It was at this moment that the British naval supremacy ended for although the Royal Navy's ships were faster, carried heavier guns that were aimed by more modern fire control systems, they proved not to be a match for the German naval guns which were more accurate, possessed better range-finding

Right: When Jellicoe was promoted out of harms way he was replaced by Beatty.

equipment, and had better communications. The German armor proved superior and British armor no match for German shells.

Within half an hour of the first shots in which both the *Lützow* and *Lion* were hit, *HMS Indefatigable* that came under concentrated fire from the *Von der Tann* was sunk with the unfortunate loss of more than one thousand men. A half hour later the flagship of Admiral Beatty, *HMS Lion* was hit and immediately after this *HMS Queen Mary* exploded and sank, taking 1,200 men with her to the bottom. *HMS Princess Royal* was also badly damaged and forced to break off action.

Within a short time the Germans had put one third of Beatty's force out of action and the main German force now drew near at high speed to finish the job. Admiral Beatty realized that he was now in danger of falling into the trap himself and gave orders for a change of course towards the Grand Fleet that was also approaching at high speed. Poor communications though

Admiral Jellicoe commanded the Grand Fleet at the Battle of Jutland. His hesitant leadership and fear of torpedo boat attacks cost him the victory.

APPROACH OF RIVAL FLEETS

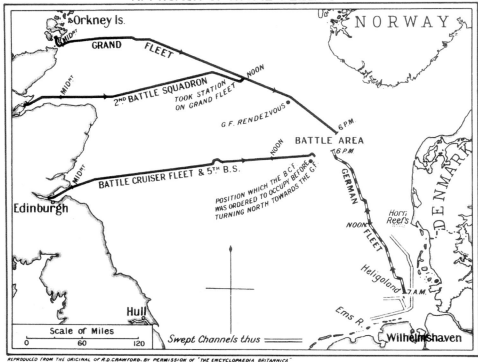

REPRODUCED FROM THE ORIGINAL OF R.D.CRAWFORD, BY PERMISSION OF "THE ENCYCLOPAEDIA BRITANNICA"

Sketch map of the Battle of Jutland in which the might Grand Fleet failed to put the German Hochsee Flotte out of action.

The Grand Fleet leaves its base at Scapa Flow on its way to Jutland.

The German Hochsee Flotte heads to sea. Around 250 warships are headed towards each other.

HMS Superb opens fire.

HMS Lion returns fire from *SMS Lützow* at the start of the battle on May 31, 1916.

meant that his order was misunderstood. The four ships of the fifth squadron which had just come to his aid missed the signal and continued straight on towards the Germans who opened fire and quickly hit *HMS Warspite* which had to break off and the other three ships were also damaged.

At 18:30 the Germans began a torpedo attack but this was beaten off with the *V-27* and *V-29* being hit and sunk. The British lost three torpedo boats in this action with two of them sinking immediately.

Meanwhile Hipper ships now came with range of the Grand Fleet. The Germans succeeded in setting fire to *HMS Chester* but soon after this the *Wiesbaden* was hit and set on fire. The *Pillau* and the *Frankfurt* were also hit by British fire and severely damaged. When *HMS Defence* moved in to finish the *Wiesbaden* off, Admiral Scheer came to the rescue and *Defence* was destroyed and *HMS Warrior* set on fire.

Scheer, who knew that his much smaller force had no chance of defeating the might of the Grand Fleet, ordered his ships to disengage and alter course away from the action. In a remarkable maneuver the entire German fleet turned so that the vanguard suddenly became the rearguard. Minutes before this maneuver the Germans succeeded in hitting the flagship of Admiral Hood, *HMS Invincible*, and sinking the third battle cruiser of the day, once again with the regrettable lost of around one thousand men.

Scheer was surprised to discover that he was not being pursued by the faster ships of the Grand Fleet and once again turned his fleet back to the attack with his cruisers and destroyers. This brought him though right into the heart of the British fleet so that the German fleet came under heavy fire. The *Seydlitz* immediately caught fire and the *Lützow* was also hit and Scheer had to transfer his command to the *Von Moltke*. At the same time the *S-35* was hit and sunk. Scheer realized the British were about to eliminate his fleet and gave orders for a torpedo attack and while this took place he repeated his complete change of direction of the German fleet again and disappeared once more with his ships towards the west. As before, he was surprised that Admiral Jellicoe did nothing to prevent him and he chose the shortest course back to port and gave an order by radio to break directly through the British fleet to safety. Once more

German cruiser *SMS Von der Tann* destroyed *HMS Indefatigable*, costing 1,000 British lives.

HMS Indefatigable just before she was hit.

HMS Indefatigable sinking.

Jellicoe did not mount a counter attack. It was Admiral Beatty who maintained contact with the Germans and asked permission to attack them. Albeit somewhat reluctantly Jellicoe gave his permission and during the firing that ensued the severely damaged *Seydlitz* and *Lützow* were hit again and the second turret of the *Derflinger* was put out of action but the Germans managed to disengage from the action and disappeared into the dark.

During the night there was contact once more with the British Second Light Cruiser Squadron in which *HMS Southampton* and

Shortly afterwards the *HMS Queen Mary* exploded after being hit by a German shell. The ship took 1,200 men with her to the bottom.

The British cruiser *HMS Princess Royal* received similar medicine and was forced to quit the battle.

A similar fate befell *HMS Warspite* of Beatty's Fifth Cruiser Squadron.

HMS Chester was set ablaze by German shellfire.

In the ensuing chaos one gun kept firing at the Germans, manned by ship's boy Jack Cornwall (16) who kept on firing although wounded until he died. He was posthumously awarded the highest British decoration for valor, the Victoria Cross.

Dublin were damaged and the German light cruiser, the *Frauenlob* was sunk.

Meanwhile Scheer's radio order to return to base had been received and decoded. His course and position were handed to Jellicoe who only needed to take a parallel course to cut them off at day break. Jellicoe though did not trust the information he received and remained on his south western course. Later that night there was further action when Scheer found his ships in the midst of the Royal Navy's Fourth Flotilla in which the destroyers *HMS Tipperary* and *Broke* were put out of action and the confusion was so great that *HMS Spitfire* collided with *HMS Nassau* and the *Sparrowhawk* rammed the severely damaged *HMS Broke*. The German cruiser *Elbing* received heavy hits and the *Rostock* was torpedoed.

Several hours later the two fleets engaged each other once more when the destroyers *HMS Ardent* and *Fortune* were

The boy sailor, Jack Cornwall at his gun on board *HMS Chester*.

HMS Chester in dock for repairs after the battle.

sunk, soon followed by the armored cruiser *HMS Black Prince* with 750 men disappearing beneath the waves. The Germans were engaged again early that next morning and sank the destroyer *HMS Turbulent*. Two hours later the British in turn succeeded in sinking the German cruiser Pommern and the *V-4* torpedo boat, closing the final chapter in the Battle of Jutland.

The damage on board *HMS Chester*.

In the battle that involved 246 ships and some 100,000 men, the Germans lost one battle cruiser *(Lützow)*, one armored cruiser *(Pommern)*, four light cruisers *(Wiesbaden, Frauenlob, Elbing,* and *Rostock)*, five torpedo boats, and 2,551 men killed or wounded.

The British lost 6,097 men killed, 510 wounded, and 177 were rescued by the Germans and taken captive as prisoners of war. They also lost three battle cruisers *(HMS Indefatigable, Queen Mary,* and

Right: A German shell pierced the armor of *HMS Chester* setting her ablaze and forcing her to disengage.

HMS Defence opened fire on *SMS Wiesbaden* and was then destroyed by the *SMS Lützow*.

HMS Warrior was also set on fire.

The flagship of Admiral Hood, *HMS Invincible*, was destroyed with the loss of 1,025 British sailors. She was the third battle cruiser to be lost by the Royal Navy that day.

HMS Invincible sinks at 18:34 in a mass of fire and smoke.

HMS Invincible explodes and sinks to the bottom at 18:34 on May 31, 1916.

HMS Invincible split in two parts during sinking, which jut out of the water.

SMS Derfflinger that took part in the Battle of Jutland, seen here when she fired on Scarborough and Whitby on the English coat on December 16, 1914.

Invincible), three armored cruisers *(HMS Black Prince, Warrior,* and *Defence)*, and eight destroyers *(HMS Ardent, Fortune, Nestor, Nomad, Shark, Sparrowhawk, Tipperary*, and *Turbulent)*.

THE RESULTS

Who actually won the Battle of Jutland? The Germans claimed victory and the British maintained that the Germans had failed to lift the British naval blockade, so that they had failed in their objective. It is clear from the evidence that the German *Hochsee Flotte* inflicted considerable damage to the Royal Navy's Grand Fleet while the resistance of the German ships appeared to be greater than that of their British opponents. The British lost fourteen ships in the battle (around 115,000 tons) compared with

The *SMS Derfflinger* suffered heavy damage during the Battle of Jutland.

After Admiral Scheer had turned his ships about they found themselves in the midst of the Grand Fleet
and the *SMS Seyditz* was hit and set ablaze.

The *SMS Lützow* was also hit forcing Scheer to transfer his flag to the *SMS Moltke* (shown here).

HMS Revenge and *HMS Hercules* took part in the Battle of Jutland.

eleven German ships (61,000 tons). The British lost almost twice as many men killed or injured as the Germans (6,784 compared with 3,058) or about 11.6 percent of her men compared with 4.5 percent for the Germans.

Scheer succeeded in penetrating the British lines twice, sinking a number of their ships, and disappearing again into the darkness without the British managing to stop him or cut off his retreat despite the British having the superior number of ships that were also faster. Instead of vigorously pursuing the Germans in order to destroy them, Admiral Jellicoe ordered his ships to put about in order to remove them from the risk of a German torpedo attack. This gave the German fleet the opportunity to return to the safety of its home port, and a unique chance to finish off the enemy's fleet at one go was frittered away.

In fairness it should be noted that Jellicoe's decision not to pursue the German fleet and to protect his fleet against torpedo attack was not a spur of the moment decision. He had already written to the Admiralty on October 14, 1914 that the German supremacy in torpedo warfare was so great that in the event of a confrontation with them he might well choose to avoid battle to prevent his ships coming off worst. In his opinion the loss of the Grand Fleet equated to loss of the war and his principal task was to prevent this. With hindsight his fears of torpedo attacks were groundless but he had

The British light cruiser *HMS Galatio* at Jutland.

HMS Iron Duke.

HMS Canada that had earlier seen action at Gallipoli.

given the Admiralty plenty of warning of his point of view. Churchill had agreed entirely with this opinion, based on the then numerical relationship between the two navies.

In 1916 the relationship was entirely different. The British had thirty-seven "dreadnoughts" to the German's twenty-one and possessed twice as much firepower as the Germans. Despite this the Germans achieved a great tactical victory which the Royal Navy just had to accept.

The shock of this hit hard in Britain and was difficult to come to terms with. Various historians have attempted to paint the outcome of the Battle of Jutland in a rosier hue for Britain. The Germans, they maintain, had admittedly achieved the tactical victory but the battle should be regarded as a strategic success for the British because the German fleet never ventured into the North Sea again and left this entirely under British control.

Those historians who maintain this appear to be partial in their history and distort the facts. Why was it therefore when the Royal Navy reported itself once more ready for action four days after the battle that it did not attack the German coast, aware that the German fleet was repairing and only reported itself ready for action in August that year. It is also not correct to suggest that the German fleet no longer ventured into the North Sea after Jutland. Scheer took his ships out various times. On August 18 he attacked Sunderland in the hope of enticing the Grand Fleet into open water. The Royal Navy's intelligence service drew attention to the

HMS Indomitable and *HMS Inflexible* during the Battle of Jutland.

German fleet movement and created great alarm. The Royal Navy did respond and action between the vanguards of the two led to the *Westfalen* being damaged and forced to return to base. When *HMS Nottingham* was then sunk by a U-boat it was once again Admiral Jellicoe who beat a hasty retreat, steaming northwards for two hours before returning to his original course. Scheer, who had meanwhile been advised that the entire Grand Fleet was on its way towards him, turned his ships back to home base, leaving Jellicoe once more in the lurch. Once again Jellicoe missed an

HMS Tiger

opportunity to destroy the German fleet because of his fear of torpedo attack. There were further actions in November 1917 close to Heligoland and in April 1918 Scheer made a further raid in Norwegian waters.

The suggestion therefore that the Germans no longer dared show their faces in the North Sea is entirely incorrect. If anything the opposite was the case. It was the British who after their experiences at Jutland decided to stay clear of the North Sea. Admiral Beatty declared at a naval conference held in January 1917 that the German battle cruiser squadron needed to be regarded as entirely superior to the Royal Navy's battle cruiser squadron so that engagement with it was to be avoided for the time being. He wrote a report in November 1916 in which he considered it unwise to challenge the German fleet and recommended avoidance of engagement with it for the time being because there was apparently something "very wrong" with the ships under his command. He pointed to poor communications, poor sighting and range finding equipment, poor munitions, and inadequate armor and insisted that these be improved before a new challenge was made.

The Battle of Jutland was in reality a defeat for the Royal Navy. It never completely recovered from the blow it was given by the German navy, even though it is true that the blockade was not lifted. Admiral Scheer himself recognized this reality when he recommended to the Kaiser a resumption of the all out unrestricted submarine warfare because the *Hochsee Flotte* could not force the British to end the war on its own. The myth of the invincible Royal Navy had been broken but this unfortunately did not bring peace any nearer.

SCUTTLING OF THE GERMAN FLEET AT SCAPA FLOW

The end of the war found the German *Hochsee Flotte* in a state of chaos at Wilhelmshaven. Mutiny had broken out and led to a general uprising and revolution. The mutiny left deep traces and "revolutionary councils" had taken command from the officers. Discipline had vanished and no maintenance was carried out. On some ships the officers were held captive while on others they were submissive but in every case it was the crews who had command.

This was the situation at the end of the war when the Allies demanded that the entire German fleet was to be interned as part of the Armistice. The German submarine fleet, comprising some 200 vessels, was required to sail to Harwich where the crews would become prisoners of war.

The British light cruiser *HMS Mirningham* is hit by German fire.

Scheer launches one of his torpedoes, so feared by Jellicoe.

The Allies could not agree though about what to do with the *Hochsee Flotte* and it was decided that German fleet should be interned in neutral harbors but it soon became apparent that there were no neutral harbors with adequate facilities and so without advising the Germans it was decided to gather the German's ships at the British naval base at Scapa Flow to intern them.

The German government had no other choice, faced with a resumption of hostilities, to accept the Allied decision to intern the *Hochsee Flotte* and ordered Rear Admiral Herman Ludwig Reuter, who had commanded the *SMS Stettin* at the Battle of Jutland, to comply and to deliver his ships into internment. Reuter accepted the order even though he knew his task would be difficult given the open mutiny aboard his ships. He deemed it his duty to accept the request because he knew that the terms of the Armistice must be met to the letter to prevent further hostilities against Germany by the Allies.

Because the German ships would continue to remain in German possession during the internment, Reuter hoped that the fleet could be a bargaining point in the peace talks and that part of it could be preserved for Germany.

On November 18, 1918 Reuter had talks with the Admiralty and with the revolutionary committee of sailors and workers who were in reality in possession of the fleet. He insisted that the officers rather than the crews were to be responsible for navigation and that these officers were to be given the freedom to prepare for this in whatever manner they saw fit. He demanded that the revolutionary council ensure that the sailors cooperate with the officers to get the ships ready to sail and not refuse orders from officers nominated by

Reuter. Because it was also not in the mutineers interests for the ships to come directly under Allied command they accepted this, which meant that Reuter could count on a certain level of discipline on board the fleet he had to lead. In the afternoon of November 18 he formally accepted the request from the Admiralty to take the *Hochsee Flotte* to its place of internment.

Before the fleet could set sail it first had to be disarmed. The mutineers undertook this task with apparent glee. Valuable sighting equipment, munitions, weapons, etc. were ripped from their places and unceremoniously dumped on the dock. Supplying the ships was chaotic and some of the designated officers did not reach their ships on time and a flotilla of torpedo boats put to see without any officers.

Finally the time came on November 19 for the once proud German fleet to depart, with Reuter on board his flagship, the *SMS Friedrich der Grosse*, in the vanguard, on way to their rendezvous indicated by the British. On departure, Reuter had warned the mutineers that if they continued to fly the Red Flag there was a possibility that the Allies would regard them as pirate ships and therefore fire at them. Once at sea the mutineers accepted this and one by one lowered their red flags and replaced them to the great joy of their officers with the Imperial German flag.

The fleet that steamed from port consisted of seventy-one ships in all, comprising five battle cruisers in the vanguard, followed by nine battleships, seven light cruisers, and five groups of ten destroyers. During the departure from port the *V-30* hit a mine and sank so that only seventy ships steamed to the meeting place designated by the Allies.

Early on the morning of the 20th the Germans lookouts saw to their astonishment that almost the entire Grand Fleet awaited them. They were formed up in two long lines between which the German fleet was as it were made to run the gauntlet.

About 250 Allied ships, almost the entire Grand Fleet, a number of US, and French Navy and other Allied warships formed the reception party that now set sail under the command of Admiral Beatty on board *HMS Queen Elizabeth* for the Firth of Forth where the Germans were ordered to drop anchor.

Commander Marsden, the only survivor from one of the British destroyers sunk at Jutland.

The warships *SMS Von der Tann, Hindenburg,* and *Derfflinger* anchor at the British base of Scapa Flow.

This was followed immediately by orders given by radio that all the German warships were to drop the Imperial Ensign and that this was not to be flown again. Despite a furious protest from Reuter, Beatty refused to rescind this order and threatened to carry it out by

The flagship of Rear Admiral Reuter departing to the place of the fleet's internment.

force by sending his marines if the ensigns were not immediately lowered.

Several hours after dropping anchor, Reuter received his instructions for the interned fleet. Signals between ships were forbidden. Radio installations were to be dismantled and no one was allowed to leave any ship without permission of the Allies. In reality all the Germans were treated as prisoners of war aboard their own ships. Until that time Reuter had believed that the fleet was assembled at the Firth of Forth to enable the Allies to confirm that all the requirements of the truce were being complied with and that the ships would then be directed to various neutral harbors as had been agreed. But the British no longer had any intention to stick to this part of the Armistice agreement. This soon became apparent when the German fleet was ordered, under the pretext that they were exposed to the strong easterly wind, to steam to Scapa Flow. Only then did Reuter realize that this would be their final anchorage and that departure to neutral harbors was no longer the intention. Reuter protested of course but had no other choice than to make the 280 mile voyage to Scapa Flow and imprisonment. The fleet of seventy warships hoisted anchors on November 22 with some 20,000 men on board to steam to Scapa Flow. Four days later, on November 26, they reached their final anchorage. The ships would never, except as salvage, leave Scapa Flow again.

At the beginning of the internment the British had demanded that the Germans themselves ensure the provisioning of the ships with food, fuel and maintenance supplies. There were therefore regular visits by supply ships from Germany with the necessary provisions and materials. The British quickly demanded that the level of crewing be reduced and hence there was a regular ferry service with Wilhelmshaven which took some 15,000 men back to their homeland. Initially five thousand men remained in order to maintain the ships.

SMS Emden leaves a German port for the last time. Reuter later made this ship as his flagship because of better order and discipline.

Meanwhile the official direct contact between Reuter and the German admiralty was broken off. All messages were now routed through the British flagship and all news about the progress of the Armistice talks were withheld from him. The British censored all letters and only permitted English newspapers that were four days old. Reuter got some news of course from time to time from the supply ships and learned that the peace talks were not going well.

On December 13 Reuter went home on leave to Germany. The situation on board the ships had deteriorated badly and morale was extremely poor. The relationship with the "revolutionary' council" was so bad that Reuter speculated that he could no longer function effectively. Every trivial matter had to be deliberated over and his officers had to put up with contemptuous behavior and the ships were no longer being maintained and had quickly become dirty and rusty. Reuter was ashamed at their sight.

Reuter returned to his post on January 25, in order – as he later wrote – to carry out his duty of attempting to have some say about the future of the fleet. This was made easier for him by a decree of the new German government which significantly reduced the power of the revolutionary councils, although they could not be entirely ignored. Reuter moved to the *SMS Emden* aboard which the revolutionary council was more realistic and less demanding so that the situation was closer to normality.

In May 1919 though the final news about the peace talks reached Scapa Flow and it became known that the Allies intended to reduce the German fleet to an absolute minimum. This caused great unrest on board the German ships and Reuter heard that the revolutionary councils had decided in secret to have a general strike throughout the fleet. This would give the British an excuse to intervene and to occupy the ships which Reuter wanted to prevent at all costs. He therefore agreed to a British

German flotilla of destroyers on passage to Rosyth, the first anchorage on their way to Scapa Flow.

SMS Seydlitz on passage to internment, followed by the *Moltke* and the *Hindenburg*.

proposal to further reduce the crews to an absolute minimum and a further 2,500 returned to Germany on June 17. Eventually, just 1,750 men remained on board to carry out the most essential duties. It was at this time that Reuter gave up hope that his ships would ever be returned to the fatherland. He feared that his government would hand the ships over to the Allies in order to reduce other demands for compensation. Although as an officer of the old school this was abhorrent, Reuter could follow this logic.

Meanwhile there were rumors that the British would not wait for the outcome of the peace talks but would take control of the German fleet before these were completed on May 31, in memory of the first day of the Battle of Jutland, which had been declared a national holiday in Germany.

SMS Kaiser, immediately after leaving Germany.

The flagship of Admiral Beatty, *HMS King George*, and *HMS Ajax, Centurion,* and *Erin* wait on November 21 to escort the German fleet to Scapa Flow.

One of the most important standard orders for commanders in the Germany navy was that they must not allow their ships to fall into enemy hands. If this happened the officer could be tried for treachery at a court martial. This order remained in force and Reuter instructed his officers to be alert to any attempt to board by the British and at the first signs of such to scuttle their ships. May 31 came and went though without any action by the British.

That same day Reuter received news of a cabinet meeting held by the German Chancellor, Scheidemann at the Reichstag the previous day in which he rejected the terms proposed by the Allies. The risk was now acute that the British would take action. The British did in fact have detailed plans to take possession of the German ships once an agreement was signed, before it could be ratified by the various governments, in order to prevent their crews from scuttling them.

Reuter foresaw this and was determined at any cost that the British should not carry out their plan. He confirmed his previous order and instructed his officers that the ships be prepared for scuttling but added that the crews were not to be informed, to prevent the news leaking out.

German officers from the scuttled ships being taken away as prisoners.

He was convinced after Schediemann's cabinet meeting that hostilities would resume and that in that event his duty was to prevent his ships falling into British hands.

On June 17 a supply ship brought the latest news. Reuter learned that the Allies had given an ultimatum for Germany to accept the Allied terms by June 21. He now decided to scuttle his ships before that date and wrote detailed instruction for his commanders that same day. Following the hoisting of two signal flags on the mast of his ship the other ships were to open their valves to flood and therefore scuttle them on the morning of May 21.

What Reuter did not know, because the British kept news from him, was that Scheidemann resigned on June 20 and that the Reichstag accepted the Allied terms by 237 votes to 138. Nor did he know that the Allies had extended their ultimatum to June 23.

In his order to the German *Hochsee Flotte* Reuter wrote that the ships were only to be sunk if the British made an attempt to take them without permission of the German government. If the German government agreed to the ships being handed over under the terms of a peace agreement then the ships were to be handed over undamaged to the Allies. He was certain though, following Scheidemann's decision, that his government would not accept the terms and his duty lay in not allowing the ships to fall into enemy hands.

Hence the final day dawned on the once proud German *Hochsee Flotte* on which it would bring about its own self-destruction to maintain the honor of the German navy. Reuter appeared on the bridge of his flagship early that morning. He was surprised not to see any sign of the Royal Navy. The British admiral had chosen that very day to take his ships on exercise in order to return on the 23rd (when the ultimatum expired) in order to occupy the German ships.

Reuter gave the order on the morning of June 21 to scuttle the German fleet. The "attack" signal was flown from the mastheads while the sea cocks were opened. This is the SMS Hindenburg.

The cruiser Frankfurt also sank quickly.

Reuter now order the hoisting of signal flags "D" and "G" which ordered his officers to their posts to await further orders. Half an hour later he had the signal "confirm paragraph eleven" flown, referring to that paragraph in his written orders which ordered his commanders to open the sea cocks. Ship after ship hoisted a confirmation signal while officers below decks opened the sea cocks.

What happened next is somewhat of an anticlimax. It was as though nothing was happening and as if the orders had not been carried out but an hour later at 12:10 the crew of the SMS Friedrich der Grosse suddenly took to their boats and exactly six minutes later the ship capsized and sank. At this same time many ships hoisted the signal "Z" for attack. Now, as if by appointment, ship after ship capsized and sank or sank

The *SMS Bayern* capsized and slid beneath the surface.

immediately without capsizing. The German *Hochsee Flotte* had performed its final engagement and would never leave Scapa Flow. The ships did not fall into enemy hands and the honor of the German navy was upheld.

Meanwhile the British ships still in Scapa Flow saw what was happening and radioed Admiral Freemantle to return immediately at full speed. Between 14:00 and 16:00 hours his ships returned to find only some ten ships remaining of the seventy. The other ships were on the bottom but the masts and funnels could still be seen of some of them. The water was full of lifeboats with German crews.

Once more the *Hochsee Flotte* had caused panic among the British. There was wild firing of machine guns and some destroyers opened fire on the lifeboats killing nine and wounding sixteen. The British managed to beach three German destroyers that had not yet completely sunk but at precisely 17:00 hours the last of the German ships, *SMS Hindenburg* sank to the bottom with just her masts and funnels visible above the surface of Scapa Flow.

The British took the approximately 1,700 German crew and officers prisoner, including Admiral Reuter. He was accused of breaking the truce but he responded by saying his standard orders prevented him from allowing his ships falling into enemy hands. When they were being taken away to prisoner of war camps Admiral Freemantle accused the Germans of bad faith and treachery but Admiral Reuter responded by saying this was unfair and that every single British officer in the same position would have done the same. These words concluded the drama of Scapa Flow, and the existence of the *Hochsee Flotte*, that had once been the pride and hope of the German people. The peace treaty was finally signed and a definitive end was brought to four years of severe struggle that cost tens of millions of lives. The creation of Admiral Tirpitz and the dream of the Kaiser lay as just so much scrap on the sea bed of Scapa Flow.

AMERICA ENTERS THE WAR

The USA seals Germany's fate

NEUTRAL USA ?

Much has been spoken about the position of the USA at the outbreak of World War I and during the early years of that war when America remained neutral and formally wished to remain outside the conflict. Although the majority of the American people supported this point of view it must be recognized that the general sympathies were with the Allies, against an autocratic Germany that was seen as the country that had started the war in order to force its will on the democratic countries in a bid for greater power.

It was the President, Woodrow Wilson, who took a pacifist stance and declared that the USA must stay out of the conflict. He was severely criticized by the Republicans, and in particular by their leading statesman, Theodore Roosevelt, who was a fervent advocate of conscription and an American intervention.

As time passed, sympathy for the Allied cause grew, not least because of the enormous trade in weapons, munitions, and other war material ordered from American industry.

It was entirely legitimate at that time for companies to supply armaments to countries at war but the trade appeared to be entirely one-sided. The Allies profited greatly from this while Germany and its allies were excluded. To avoid the state becoming involved in any way in these supplies by private companies and thereby compromising the neutral status, the US government had banned war loans for the purpose of financing weapons purchases. There were quickly huge sums of money involved and new factories were built, new industries were born, and there was full employment. The US government feared the Allies would not be able to meet their obligations for these huge orders and felt obliged to finance the supplies with huge loans rather than face severe downturn or at least reduction in economic growth with the consequences for employment and the unrest that might be caused. The US Secretary of State, Lansing, advised President Wilson to permit war loans in favor of the Allies on economic grounds alone. Wilson accepted this proposal, whereupon he said goodbye in reality to the principal of neutrality, not least because it became apparent that the Germans and their allies would not be eligible for these loans.

The powerful American industry had been pressing for some time for war loans and got the press behind them. The British had gained considerable influence in the American press with the British press baron Northcliffe playing a key role. Because US interests were so great the American press increasingly took the side of the Allies, leading to anti-German sentiment increasing among the American people.

A second breach in neutrality was the toleration by the Americans of armed merchant ships in US ports. International law and custom required armed merchant ships to be regarded as warships which should therefore be interned. Although the German ambassador protested a number of times to the US

It later became apparent that the Lusitania was carrying armaments for the British, including 5,000 shells, munitions, and other explosives. The ship was regarded by the Germans as helping the British war effort and the German Embassy placed advertisements immediately before her departure warning that the ship ran a risk of being torpedoed.

REMEMBER THE LUSITANIA!

One mother lost all her three young children, one six years, one aged four, and the third a babe in arms, six months old. She herself lives, and held up the three of them in the water, all the time shrieking for help. When rescued by a boat party the two eldest were dead. Their room was required on the boat, and the mother was brave enough to realise it. "Give them to me," she cried. "Give them to me, my bonnie wee things. I will bury them. They are mine to bury as they were mine to keep."

With her hair streaming down her back and her form shaking with sorrow, she took hold of each little one from the rescuers and reverently placed it into the water again, and the people in the boat wept with her as she murmured a little sobbing prayer to the great God above.

But her cup of sorrow was not yet completed. For just as they were landing, her third and only child died in her arms.

BERLIN, MAY 8.

Hundreds of telegrams have been sent to Admiral von Tirpitz congratulating him.

✳ ✳ ✳

ARTICLE IN **COLOGNE GAZETTE.**

The news will be received by the German people with unanimous satisfaction, since it proves to England and the whole world that Germany is quite in earnest in regard to her submarine warfare.

✳ ✳ ✳

ARTICLE IN **KOLNISCHE VOLKSZEITUNG.**

With joyful pride we contemplate the latest deed of our Navy and it will not be the last.

✳ ✳ ✳

NEW YORK, MAY 8.

Riotous scenes of jubilation took place last evening amongst Germans in the German clubs and restaurants. Many Germans got drunk as the result of toasting "Der Tag."

ENLIST TO-DAY.

British recruiting poster after the *Lusitania* disaster.

government at the presence of these armed ships a blind eye was turned. The US government did formally warn the British about the practice but took no steps to bring it to an end. This was clearly in breach of US neutrality. The same is also true of the entirely illegal use by British ships of the US flag. Here too there were official protests but nothing more.

Far more important though was the acceptance by the US government of the economic blockade of Germany invoked and maintained by the British. This was in direct conflict with the Declaration of London of 1909 to which the British had been a party. Although this attempt to establish international maritime law was not ratified by the British House of Lords it had been agreed that all countries should regard the declaration as "customary law." The British blockade was directly contrary to these principles and American merchant ships were also widely checked to the anger of the US State Department. The US government had to meekly note that ships with cargoes the British regarded as contraband – and that quickly became anything – were arrested and their cargoes confiscated. This caused great annoyance for the Americans who considered halting arms shipments to Britain. When several of his departmental secretaries proposed this in a cabinet meeting President Wilson was vehemently opposed to the idea. He insisted the Allies had their backs to the wall in a battle with "savage beasts" and he did not want to be a party to anything that made things more difficult for them to win the war.

This was clear language that showed the Germans that President Wilson was not neutral in his thoughts. Although Germany protested strongly to the US government about the illegal blockade that was directed at the civilian population – it aimed to halt supplies of food and other staples of life – the US government remained one-sided in its neutrality and took little account of the protests. In order to release the stranglehold of the blockade the German government decided to introduce a counter-blockade of the North Sea and English Channel by declaring this a war zone and the start of all out submarine warfare. Germany advised neutral governments not to allow their shipping within this zone because it might not always be possible for German U-boats to recognize that a vessel was neutral.

It is an interesting conjecture what might have been if the USA had not tolerated the British blockade and the abuse of the rights of neutral countries. It is probable that the blockade would have taken a different form and perhaps the Germans would not have moved to all out submarine warfare. In response to a question from the US Secretary of State, Lansing, asking if Germany adhered to international maritime law according to the Declaration of London of 1909, the German government answered positively. Great Britain on the other hand stated that it reserved the right to make changes to it. Those changes were

The British liner *Lusitania* on her final voyage en route for Britain where she was torpedoed on May 7, 1915 by the German submarine *U-20*. Almost 1,200 passengers lost their lives in the waves.

The elderly British warship *HMS Juno* that was unexpectedly recalled to port after sailing to escort the *Lusitania* through the mines.

chiefly in respect of items considered as contraband, to which it added food and medicines, cotton, copper and other items, making the import of these from neutral countries impossible.

Meanwhile President Wilson made his statement that he felt that the USA should remain out of the war. Even though he was heavily criticized for this stance, particularly by Republicans, many Americans shared his attitude. When Wilson ran for re-election in 1916 he did so under the banner of "He kept us out of war" and the president did not miss opportunities to make speeches throughout the country defending his stance that made a great impression.

Despite this it is questionable to what extent Wilson genuinely believed his own stance because closer examination suggest that in reality he thought otherwise. In 1915 he appears to have already concluded that America ought to side with the Allies and join in the war.

So what is the truth? During 1915, Wilson sent his personal emissary, Colonel House, to Britain to meet with the British Foreign Secretary, Edward Grey. During that visit, House asked Grey to tell him what the British wanted the Americans to do to help the Allies win the war. This is a surprising question that shows the USA was not really neutral.

After House's return to the USA he wrote to Grey with the president's approval on October 17, 1915. The letter clearly offers to join the war on the side of the Allies under certain conditions. In this letter House wrote that he was coming to Europe to discuss the Allied wishes. He would then visit Germany and suggest that he expected the Allies to reject his proposal of a peace conference. He was almost certain the Germans would accept such a proposal but if not this would be a reason for the USA to side with the Allies and drop ideas of peace talks. If Germany did come to the talks then the USA would support the Allied demands and if these demands were rejected, the USA would leave the talks as one of the Allies.

In January 1916, House traveled to Britain again. He repeated the agreement for the USA to join in the war in London. From London he went on to Paris where he met with the French Prime Minister Briand and Ambassador Cambon during which he told them that the USA would soon – probably that year – take part in the war on the side of the Allies. The Frenchmen could hardly believe their ears and asked him to repeat what he had said. Following this they wrote it down but House wrote in his diary that he had merely promised that if the Allies were losing the war, America would intervene. He wisely left his definition of "intervene" in the air. In February, House returned to London and met once more with Foreign Secretary Grey who asked him what he precisely meant by "intervene." House repeated the details and the two set this down

US recruiting poster based on the famous British poster that featured Kitchener.

in a memorandum of February 17, 1916 that established the US proposals. With care, the wording established that President Wilson would call for peace talks at a moment the Allies deemed favorable. If Germany refused then America would probably join the Allies in the war. The memorandum continued to record that Colonel House had declared that the US government would make proposals during the talks that were favorable to the Allies. If the Germans rejected these and acted unreasonably and peace could not be achieved then America would leave the talks one of the Allies.

The snake in the grass of this Grey-House memorandum that appear at first sight to be so favorable for the Allies, lay in the fact that it would be the Americans who would dictate the peace terms and this caused enormous resistance among the French. The plan therefore ran into a dead end to Wilson's great regret.

This entire affair though does clearly demonstrate that Wilson was already intending in 1915 to force a peace by taking the side of the Allies and thereby pressing the Germans to accept. At this same time he was mounting his re-election campaign under the banner of "He kept us out of the war." It is obvious from what we have just seen that he privately had other plans. These plans were translated into deeds following his re-election.

There was something entirely ambivalent in the position of the US President. While he was certainly no warmonger and made

Further Americans were killed following the *Lusitania* when the *Arabic* and *Sussex* were torpedoed.

The US Navy prepares for war. The *USS New Mexico* leaves harbor for exercises.

efforts to the last to achieve a just peace his motives are unclear and historians are consequently divided in their judgments of him. Wilson was clearly pro-British and saw a German victory as intolerable. Once the USA became increasingly financially and economically linked with the Allied cause, pressure from industry – and hence also the press – became ever greater. This had a huge influence on the American people and the sinking of the *Lusitania* – with tremendous loss of American lives – followed by the *Arabic* and *Sussex swung* the mood of the people in the Allies favor. Meanwhile Wilson had become convinced that his plans for a "just peace, a peace without victors, and without punishment" could not be achieved without America taking sides in the conflict. His ideal was to restore world peace with America playing a leading role. He was supported in this by Secretary of State Lansing and the president's own personal advisor, Colonel House, who had been of the opinion from the outset that America could not stay out of the war and should take the Allied side. Wilson then decided to take his country into the war when the American people permitted this. This happened when the Germans announced a resumption of the all out U-boat war, following which the US government had to break off diplomatic relations in view of earlier exchanges and shortly afterwards declared war against Germany. This decision is understandable in

President Wilson decided on May 1, 1916 to prepare America for the eventual calamity. A "preparedness parade" in New York on May 13, 1916.

view of the fact that the US government in reality had never been neutral. The resumption of the U-boat war was just the excuse rather than the reason why America decided to enter the war.

TORPEDO ATTACK ON THE *LUSITANIA* (2)

A BLEAK DAY

It was a bleak day on May 7, 1915. The former holder of the blue ribbon *SS Lusitania* with her decks filled with passengers approached the British Isles following a calm crossing from the USA. There were about 1,700 British and American passengers on board who wanted to catch a first glimpse of the approaching coast. Of these, 1,198

Large-scale recruitment was begun in America. Here a newly-formed infantry division in formation.

would never reach that coast and would be dead within hours, drowned in the cold, inhospitable sea. Men, women, and children, including 128 Americans, wholly unaware that their deaths would be one of the reasons for the US government deciding to go to war against Germany.

The drama of the *Lusitania* has evoked emotions ever since and historians still have different opinions all these years later and the debate continues.

What was the truth? The voyage of the *SS Lusitania* had gone without a hitch. Under what were known as the "Cruiser rules", according to which submarines were expected by international custom first to enable passengers and crew to abandon ship in their lifeboats before sinking the vessel, the passengers felt fairly safe. The coast was in sight and the old British cruiser *HMS Juno* joined them to escort them through the mines to a safe harbor. Suddenly there was the cry of "Torpedo in sight." This was almost immediately followed by a huge explosion between the third and fourth funnels. Shortly afterwards there was a second explosion, bigger than the first. The ship listed rapidly and disappeared beneath the waves in less than twenty minutes. Only a few hundred of the people on board survived and almost 1,200 went down with her to their grave.

The world was shocked. The arguments about the drama started right then with Britain and Germany on clearly delineated different sides. There are two accounts of events, both of which are given below.

THE BRITISH ACCOUNT

The British were furious of course. Yet another act of barbarity by the Germans, murdering almost 1,200 innocent people, including many women and children, slain by a furtive assassin without any warning, or any chance. It was in contravention of international laws respected by every civilized nation. The entire world found this deed abhorrent and this abhorrence increased when the British press reported that the German government had issued a commemorative medal to glorify this "victory" against the enemy. The killing of innocents by this furtive stroke by the submarine *U-20* and the celebration of this act in Germany clearly caused shock and revulsion for the Germans throughout the world. Any remaining goodwill towards Germany vanished completely.

Submarines being built at an American shipyard.

There was an official inquiry into the disaster of course and the commission of inquiry's conclusion was unanimously anti-German. It established that the *Lusitania* had been torpedoed without any prior warning, that there was evidence of a second torpedo, and that the ship sank within twenty minutes. The inquiry pronounced against this "act of piracy" which proved the "Hun's" barbaric acts such as the poisoning of wells, use of poison gas, and appalling slaughter of civilians in Belgium were far from over. Now Germany had extended its crimes with the cold-blooded and calculated murder of innocent passengers, a crime the like of which had never been seen on the high seas, that was a blot on the German character that could never be forgotten.

Following this use of emotional language there was a factual summary of the facts in which it was recorded that the *Lusitania* was an unarmed passenger ship that did not form part of the Royal Navy and which did not convey troops or weapons. Since Germany was not justified under the Cruiser Rules to torpedo the ship without warning, Germany was clearly guilty of breaching international maritime law and the murder of 1,198 passengers.

Anna Olenda, who broke the world record for filling shells, with 10,600 in one day.

Germany completely refuted this judgment but the German arguments were unconvincing and attitudes changed towards her in the USA. The torpedoing of the *Lusitania* caught the public's imagination and public opinion swung completely against a nation that could perform such barbaric acts.

THE GERMAN ACCOUNT

The German government was shocked by the strong reaction, particularly that of the Americans. In a note to the US government they declared that it was no longer possible to employ Cruiser Rules for submarines because these put the crews in danger. The British decision to arm merchant ships and order to them to try to ram German submarines if confronted by one made it possible, they argued, to adhere to the convention. The all out submarine war was a direct result of the illegal British blockade and the decision of the British to arm merchant ships.

Right: Mass production of shells by an American armaments factory. Empty shells were then filled with explosives by women workers.

President Wilson asked Congress for permission to declare war against Germany on April 2, 1917.
The first American soldiers left for France shortly after this. Here troops of the 142nd Infantry Regiment
embark on the troop ship *MS Charles*.

They declared that the *Lusitania* was an armed British auxiliary
conveying contraband in the form of weapons and munitions and
that the use of torpedoes was therefore justified. They added that
they had explicitly warned of this danger through advertisements in
American newspapers and by declaring the waters around the

Ship after ship left American ports filled with troops on their way to fight in France. On average 200,000 to 250,000 departed each month for Europe.

British Isles as a war zone where any British or allied ship was at risk of being torpedoed and that traveling on board such a ship as a passenger had its attendant risks. Finally the German government referred to its note to all neutral countries in which it announced a policy of all out submarine war and gave the reasons for it.

THE AMERICAN POSITION

The position of the USA as a neutral country following the *Lusitania* disaster was extremely difficult because of the American victims. The government had never issued any warning to its people that travel on British ships might be dangerous, nor had they taken any measures to reduce these risks. Passengers thought that the Cruiser Rules were still valid and that they were therefore running a negligible risk. After all a submarine would have to warn them before firing a torpedo.

The note from the German government was difficult for the US government, for if they accepted the German assertions they would have to take responsibility for their failure to prevent US citizens from entering a war zone. There was an exchange of notes between the two governments that were futile. The US government demanded that the Germans take the full responsibility and acknowledge that the use of torpedoes in the circumstances was wrong and unlawful. The German government refused to do this, although were prepared as a gesture of goodwill, and to prevent relations with the USA deteriorating, to pay

American troop ship at Le Havre. By the end of 1918 two million US soldiers had landed in France.

Arrival of the US commander, General Pershing, and his staff at Boulogne on June 13, 1917.

compensation, but this was refused. Because of further cases of torpedo attacks the discussions concerning the *Lusitania* ran aground and the government decided to postpone further reactions or measures until after the Presidential election of 1916.

So which of these accounts of this drama, that gripped the world's imagination for so long, and almost caused the US government to break off diplomatic relations, is the truth? The answer is not straightforward. The debate still continues to this day and may never be finalized. There are answers of course. Generally the following facts have been established.

THE FACTS

It is quite logical that the Germans regarded the SS *Lusitania* as a British auxiliary. Her silhouette was recorded in *Jane's Fighting Ships*, an international publication that carries details of all the

world's warships. The first indication that the *Lusitania* was a naval auxiliary was given when the American shipping magnate J. P. Morgan tried to take over the Cunard Line in 1902 but ran into a ban by the British government which declared that the passenger ships of the Cunard Line were essential to the navy and therefore must not be removed from the British register of shipping. The decision to build the *Lusitania* was made that same year. The British government provided large subsidies but made a number of

US troops come ashore at Le Havre.

conditions. The ship must be capable of a speed of 24 knots and be suitable for mounting several guns. Cunard was also required to crew the ship with a certain proportion of officers from the Royal Navy Reserves. This agreement, which was signed on July 30, 1903, also required the *Lusitania*, in common with most passenger ships, to be available as a naval auxiliary in time of war. The Germans were aware of all of this.

On February 19, 1903, the shipping company was ordered to put the ship into dry dock so that a number of modifications could be made to make the ship a more suitable naval auxiliary. Six of the twenty-five boilers were removed and the forward hold was enlarged by removing some steerage accommodation. This area was entirely intended for carrying cargoes for the admiralty. Rumors that the ships also had six guns fitted at this time appear to have been unfounded. On September 24, 1914, the shipping company was advised that the ship was not to be used as an auxiliary but would be required to carry goods for the admiralty between the USA and Britain, and one assumes this means the conveyance of armaments and other military items or in other words, contraband. The Chairman of the Cunard Line, Alfred Booth wrote of this: "In

Welcoming party for General Pershing on the quay at Boulogne.

The American ambassador Page, British parliamentarian Lord Darling, and British General French during the welcome for Pershing.

essence, I was ordered to be a high grade contrabandist in the national interest."

This supports a conclusion that the German's assertion the *Lusitania* was not merely an innocent passenger ship but a British auxiliary, in the service of the Royal Navy is not wholly unfounded. The assertion she was armed appears to be based on the fact that the Royal Navy had ordered twelve six-inch guns for the *Lusitania* but these were never fitted because it was decided at the last moment not to use the ship as an auxiliary.

The Germans were correct though in their assertion that the ship carried contraband, or in other words goods to wage war against Germany. It has been established that the ship was carrying 1,248 cases (US Customs later gave this as 1,250) each containing four shrapnel shells for British thirteen-pounder rapid fire guns used by the Horse Artillery. This made a total of 5,000 shells with a total weight of explosives of 6,260 lb. The shells were fitted with a timing fuse filled with fulminate of mercury that is highly explosive.

In addition to these 5,000 shells, the *Lusitania* was also carrying further cases of munitions, parts for munitions, and explosives intended for the British army. From a German standpoint this was an enemy (British) ship, forming part of the Royal Navy, that was conveying weapons and munitions from a neutral country to Britain for use in the war against Germany. This is why the Germans felt justified in sinking such a ship.

In the matter that the German U-boat commander had not acted in accordance with Cruiser Rules, the German government insisted this had become necessary following the British decision to arm merchant ships and they also pointed to the fact that the US government allowed those armed merchant ships access to their neutral ports and had not condemned the illegal British blockade.

The first contingent of US troops march through Paris on July 5, 1917.

It is true that Churchill had given orders for the merchant ships to be armed and that their captains were to ignore orders from German U-boats to stop. They were to steam at full power towards the U-boat in an attempt to ram it or destroy it with their guns. Churchill also emphasized that captains who yielded their ships to the enemy would be court-martialed and regarded as *franc-tireurs*. The Germans were well aware of this order. A copy of it had fallen into their hands when they stopped the *Ben Chruachan* on January 30, 1915 before sinking her. Awareness of these instructions led to the Germans no longer observing the Cruiser Rules.

The Germans also had a point too when they claimed the British economic blockade was against international law. It is true that the British had not ratified the Declaration of London of 1909 in which the international rules for conducting blockades were established but

US Marines ready to leave for the front, March 18, 1918.

they had signed the Treaty of Paris in 1856 in which the rules of such blockades were established and internationally recognized. The US government was also of the opinion that the British were contravening international law by arresting neutral ships and confiscating their cargoes, and also in the matter of the broad remit of what the British deemed to be contraband. Of course the abandonment of the Cruiser Rules by Germany was also in contravention of international law.

The US government suggested to both parties that in return for the re-introduction of Cruiser Rules by the Germans, the British should permit neutral ships to carry food destined for the civilian population of Germany. Germany accepted this proposal but it was rejected by the British and so the situation remained unchanged. Although the US government did protest, they carried out little or no action, mainly because with an eye to the future they did not want to harm their relationship with the Allies.

Although Germany possibly had the strongest argument, its act of torpedoing a passenger ship turned American public opinion against it. Once again President Wilson did not break off diplomatic relations despite strong pressure to do so from the press and the Republicans. Even so the torpedo attack must be seen as a turning point and was one of the reasons why America chose to enter the war on the side of the Allies in April 1917. America's involvement set the seal on Germany's fate. The death of 128 American citizens was eventually to be the downfall of the German Reich.

The two MacDonald brothers during training.

THE ZIMMERMANN TELEGRAM, THE FINAL STRAW

The torpedo attack on the SS *Lusitania* changed the mood in the USA towards Germany but did not immediately bring America into the war. The resumption of the all out submarine war and an attempt to get Mexico to act against the USA caused a major fuss though and were directly responsible for the President's decision to enter the war on the side of the *entente countries*.

Why was this? There was a struggle within the German government about whether to resume the unrestricted submarine war. The German Chancellor, Bethmann Hollweg, was adamantly opposed because he was convinced it would bring the Americans into the war. Zimmerman, who replaced Jagow as foreign minister on November 22, 1916, had an entirely different opinion. He agreed with Hindenburg and Ludendorff and the German admiralty that an all out war with submarines could bring the war to an end in 1917. They dismissed the USA as an insignificant factor, which is not as strange as it might seem because the US Army at that time was small and they did not believe that a major force could be mounted,

Before going to the Front the inexperienced US soldiers first received a further two months of training in France.

trained, and brought to Europe. By the time this could be achieved they were certain Germany would have already won a U-boat war and therefore its resumption was regarded as a responsible choice to quickly finish the war.

It was the announcement on February 1 that Germany was to resume the unrestricted submarine war though that brought the USA to the brink of war. On February 3 President Wilson announced that the US government had broken off diplomatic relations with Germany but the decision to declare war had not yet been taken. A simple telegram pushed him over that brink and made him take the final decision to join the Allies. On November 12, Zimmermann sent a telegram to the his ambassador Eckhardt in Mexico with a request to discover whether Mexico would be interested in an Alliance with Germany. The answer that he received was sufficiently positive for him to send the following telegram to Eckhardt on January 19, 1917:

"We intend to begin unrestricted submarine warfare on the first of February. We shall endeavor in spite of this to keep the United States of America neutral. In the event of this not succeeding, we make

The US 307th Regiment marches towards Farnechon to music of a British military band.

Mexico a proposal or alliance on the following basis: make war together, make peace together, generous financial support and an understanding on our part that Mexico is to reconquer the lost territory in Texas, New Mexico, and Arizona. The settlement in detail is left to you. You will inform the President of the above most secretly as soon as the outbreak of war with the USA is certain and add the suggestion that he should, on his own initiative, invite Japan to immediate adherence and at the same time mediate between Japan and ourselves. Please call the President's attention to the fact that the ruthless employment of our submarines now offers the prospect of compelling England in a few months to make peace." Signed, Zimmermann.

What Zimmermann did not know is that the British Intelligence Service had been successfully intercepting and decoding German diplomatic telegrams for some time. On February 24, they handed a copy of the Zimmermann telegram to Walter Page, the US Ambassador in London, who immediately sent it on to Washington. This was the straw which broke the camel's back and on March 20, 1917, the US President decided to take his country to war. The declaration of war was made on April 2. Germany's chances for winning the war were now gone.

THE FINAL DEED: THE USA DECLARES WAR

American public opinion turned increasingly anti–German following the torpedoing of the *SS Lusitania, Arabic,* and *Sussex.* The Zimmerman telegram was the final straw that broke the camel's back and convinced President Wilson that the moment had arrived when the American public would no longer resist their participation in the war on the side of the Allies. He now took the decision to take the USA into the war.

On April 2, 1917, the President addressed Congress, proposing a declaration of war against Germany. The President spoke with the following words: "With a profound sense of the solemn and even tragical character of the step I am taking and of the grave responsibilities which it involves, but in unhesitating obedience to what I deem my constitutional duty, I advise that the Congress declare the recent course of the Imperial German Government to be in fact nothing less than war against the Government and people of the United States; that it formally accept the status of belligerent which has thus been thrust upon it, and that it take immediate steps not only to put the country in a more thorough state of defense but also to exert all its power and employ all its resources to bring the

American soldiers in their tent during training in France.

Government of the German Empire to terms and end the war." The President declared that the USA would immediately mobilize all resources in order to force Germany to bring an end to the war and to make peace.

The US Congress unanimously supported the President when he formally declared war against Germany on April 2. The tremendous potential of American manpower and industrial capacity was now brought to bear behind the Allies and against Germany, sealing their fate for the future. Within twenty months of Wilson's address Germany was forced to sue for peace and the war ended. This did not bring an end though to the suffering of the German people. The Treaty of Versailles which enshrined that "peace" did not deliver the peace that the world sought and contained the seeds of a second and more terrible World War in which millions of people lost their lives. *"L'Histoire se répète."* History has a habit of repeating itself and World War II will not be an end to war.

American soldiers practice bayonet drill. The photograph was taken on August 3, 1918.

THE END
"Peace without victors" is an illusion

THE RUSSIAN REVOLUTION

The war created increasing levels of unrest in Russia. The huge losses, increasing hunger, and lack of leadership at home and at the front made the people more rebellious. The Czar, who had taken command of the Russian forces but was not suited to the task, was increasingly overcome by bouts of depression. The Czarina increasingly came under the influence of her confidante, the monk known as Rasputin who advised her and used her to attempt to destroy his enemies. Confidence in the court ebbed and the Czar gave in to almost everything his wife demanded. Rasputin was slain by two aristocrats, Prince Romanov and Archduke Dimitri Pavlowitch at Christmas 1916 in accordance with one of Rasputin's own prophecies, in which he also foresaw the fall of the monarchy. The second part of Rasputin's prophecy also came true only ten weeks later when the Czar abdicated and the land was gripped by a revolution.

The German government had kept in touch since the start of the war in 1914 with Russian communists who lived in exile, mainly in Switzerland. These included Lenin, the most important communist leader, who prepared himself for a return to Russia when the time was right.

THE CZAR ABDICATES

In the spring of 1917, the situation in Russia became increasingly serious. The chairman of the Russian duma or parliament, Michael Rodschanko, warned the Czar that his presence was urgently required and that things were in danger of getting out of control but the Czar entirely ignored this urgent plea and remained

Russian poster calling for people to take out 5 ½ % war loans.

The Czar with the Russian commander in chief, Archduke Nicholas, from whom he assumed command of his troops in 1917.

General Suchomlinov, former Russian war minister, who was later tried for corruption.

where he was. In early February there were large-scale riots in St. Petersburg with the people demanding food and they stormed and looted the shops. The local commander sent Cossacks in to deal with the crowds but they refused to act and in some cases even joined in the looting. The unrest repeated itself several weeks later and 250 rioters were shot dead when the police opened fire. Once again the army refused to help the police. Two guards regiments that were brought in to help also refused to obey orders and this was the moment when the people of St. Petersburg grasped power for themselves and revolution took hold. Prisons were stormed and political prisoners were set free. The fortress of Peter and Paul was set ablaze and looting took place on an unprecedented scale. The revolution quickly spread and the minister of war informed the Czar that many regiments and army units had mutinied. On February 27 the Chairman of the duma sent an urgent message to the Czar in which he informed him that the monarchy would be lost unless he returned at once to St. Petersburg to take command. The Czar did not even bother to reply. Even further reports of the growing mutiny in other regiments could not jolt him out of his apathetic state. He ignored all these cries of help, as if they had not existed. The situation was explosive. The army did not take action, on the contrary, the troops no longer obeyed orders of the superiors and joined in the looting and sided with the revolutionaries. A revolution had happened and it spread through the country at lightning speed. The Czar, who finally grasped that things were more serious than he had thought, now asked the chairman of the duma for advice. The only advice he could give the Czar was to abdicate. The people were in revolt, the army mutinied, workers and sol-

Russian hero Sgt. Chibenko of the Fifth Siberian Army, four-times holder of the Cross of St. George, the highest decoration awarded to non-commissioned officers of the Russian army.

Right: After the Russian Revolution broke out there were mass desertions from the front. Here wounded soldiers have hijacked a train to take them home in their retreat from Galicia.

A train loaded with Leninist agitators sent to the front arrives in Kiev, where most of them were executed.

Bolshevik troops at Kronstadt in 1917. A Captain of the 56th Regiment speaks to the soldiers.

diers' councils were being formed everywhere who held power, and there was nothing else the Czar could do but abdicate. On March 16 he signed the act of abdication in favor of his brother Michael and was taken prisoner.

His successor also relinquished his right to the throne that same day and the minister of labor, Kerensky became head of the interim revolutionary government. Kerensky decided to continue the war on the side of the Allies and it seemed as if order was being restored. In reality things were to be entirely different. The Czar joined his wife and children at the palace at Czarskoya Selo where the royal family was held prisoner and subjected to considerable humiliation.

Some time later they were transferred to Ekaterinburg where they were brutally murdered in the night of July 16–17, 1918. The centuries old dynasty of the Romanovs had finally come to an end.

RUSSIA PULLS OUT OF THE WAR

The Germans watched events in Russia with great interest. There was a thought that an agreement could be made with the provisional Russian government but when it became clear that Kerensky wanted to continue the war, they decided to give the revolution a helping hand. They granted permission for Lenin to travel to Russia in order to strengthen the radical groups. On April 9, 1917, Lenin and his party of thirty loyal persons left on a special train from Zurich for St. Petersburg, where they arrived on the sixteenth. He was

The Revolution began in St. Petersburg with fire and destruction. Here victims are buried on May 3, 1917.

Soldiers councils were formed during the Revolution. Here one meets at St. Petersburg.

A time of great unrest. A soldier reads one of the many proclamations to the troops.

welcomed enthusiastically and from the following year until his death in 1924 was to take the leadership of the new Soviet state.

But this lay in the future. Kerensky became minister of war in the new government. In this role he ordered General Brusilov to open a new offensive. This was to be the beginning of the end. On June 1, 1917, Brusilov attacked the German and Austro-Hungarian troops in the Carpathian mountains with forty-five divisions. Within a week his troops had advanced almost nineteen miles and the action promised great success but the Russians were then held and the offensive totally ran out of steam. His soldiers refused to follow orders, many deserted and simply went home, and the Germans quickly recovered the ground they had lost. Brusilov was recalled and a new provisional

The Russian Prime Minister Kerensky who had been minister of war visited the front on September 12, 1917 following the Czar's abdication on March 27 and Lenin's assumption of power in April. Kerensky is center with finger pointing.

government was formed, again under Kerensky. The St. Petersburg garrison lost confidence in the provisional government and Lenin took power. He formed a council of people's commissars and declared that he wanted an end to the war, even if that caused a loss of Russian territory.

Leon Trotsky, who had been exiled in America while the Czar was in power but returned to Russia that February, was put in charge of foreign affairs by Lenin. He made contact with the Germans and offered a separate peace. Talks to this end were held in Brest-Litovsk but the German demands were deemed unacceptable by Trotsky. He now unilaterally declared the war with the Central Powers ended and anticipated the acceptance of this by Germany but the German commander in chief now ordered a continuation of the Russian campaign and German troops rapidly penetrated deeper into Russia.

Right: Kerensky ordered General Brusilov on June 1, 1917 to open a new offensive against the Germans. Russian troops are seen here ready for the last great attack. The offensive was initially very successful, advancing almost nineteen miles but the soldiers then refused to continue and the offensive ground to a halt.

In their advance towards Tarnopol the Russian soldiers moved from shell-hole to shell-hole under fire from six and eight inch shrapnel shells, which killed many.

A Russian negotiator is taken blindfolded to the German headquarters.

...and received there to discuss a truce.

The end is near. Trotsky arrives in Brest-Litovsk to hold peace talks with the Germans.

The room at Ekaterinburg in which the Czarina spent her last days in captivity before she and her family were brutally slain.

A fence was placed around the Ekaterinburg villa by the Bolsheviks to prevent any contact with the outside world.

The room in which the Czar's daughters were held until they were brutally killed in the night of July 16–17.

Lenin now intervened and ordered that the war be brought to an end at any cost and so finally the war between Germany and Russia was officially ended on March 3, 1918. Russia lost a third of its territory to Germany. About ninety percent of all the Russian coal mines were now in German hands together with one third of agricultural land and almost half of Russian industry.

Germany was jubilant and rapidly moved troops from the Eastern to the Western front in a hope this would turn the tide. We now know of course that this proved fruitless. The soldiers who were transferred appeared to be infected by the Russian Revolution which spread among the troops. A new opponent in the form of the USA had also now appeared at the front. Germany's chances of winning the war were now definitely at an end.

THE GERMAN MARCH OFFENSIVE OF 1918

ONE FINAL EFFORT

In March 1918 the war continued on every front except the Eastern front with Russia where the Russian Revolution had brought an end to hostilities between Russia and Germany. In the west the Allies were exhausted and sought to avoid any large-scale battles, waiting for the time when the Americans, who had now entered the war, would be present in sufficient strength to make a positive turn in the struggle. It was anticipated that the war would continue into 1919 and events had not yet been decided in the Allies favor.

On the German side several futile attempts were made to get talks with the Allies. The Pope also made an effort at mediation, again without result. In December 1916, the first attempt at peace talks had been taken by President Wilson but these were rejected by the Allies.

This made it clear that Germany quite understandably could not count on any benevolence towards it from the Allies. America's decision to enter the war would swing the odds in favor of the Allies so this was not the moment to talk about peace. The German commander in chief also understood this and decided to stake all on one final decisive battle before the massed ranks of American troops were available, when they would shift the balance and make a favorable peace for Germany impossible.

The motivation therefore behind the great March offensive, that was intended to give Germany a quick victory, were largely these reasons. The German staff argued that:

It was anticipated that the US troops would not be available in great strength before the summer of 1918.

There were more German soldiers on the Western front than Allied troops.

It was expected that one million soldiers

Waging war was beyond Germany's means in 1918 and the government tried to raise the necessary money to continue the fight through war loans.

Germany decided on a final big offensive in March 1918 to seize the advantage. German troops on their way to the front in March 1918.

German troop concentration near Templeux, March 1918.

Another final inspection by Field Marshal Hindenburg.

Operation Michael begins: specially-trained stormtroopers of the German Eighteenth Army start the attack.

from the Eastern front could be transferred to the Western front to achieve an even greater supremacy. These were sound military reasons for an offensive and were also supported by the political rational that there was growing unrest in Germany at food shortages that might lead to demands to end the war.

OPERATION MICHAEL BEGINS

The offensive, code-named Operation Michael, was not a surprise to the Allies, like thunder from a clear-blue sky, but they were surprised by its scale.

Hundreds of thousands of men had been trained, supplies brought in, and troops transported to the front for many months and positions, trenches, and shelters had been prepared and an enormous quantity of munitions made ready without the enemy being greatly aware. All movements were made at night. During daylight everything appeared calm and the new troops hid as much as possible in the woods. Sometimes, if there was a risk of discovery, they even marched for a time away from the front before returning when darkness fell.

Storm troops attack the enemy.

German 77 mm (3 inches) field artillery is moved forward to attack near Ypres.

Right: Retreating British troops in Picardy.

British infantry retreating near Avelay.

The training of the special stormtroops was extremely thorough with nothing overlooked. Finally everything was ready for the battle on March 21, 1918 and the signal to begin could be given once General Ludendorff had moved his headquarters to Avesnes. Three armies were set in motion: the Second under General von Marnitz, the Seventeenth commanded by von Below, and the Eighteenth under General Hutier, making seventy-one divisions in all.

Thousands of guns and three thousand mortars opened fire at five in the morning and fired at the area between La Fêrre and Arras for four hours before the infantry left their trenches and began the

A munitions depot captured from the British.

Not everything fell into German hands. British soldiers move a munitions dump before retreating.

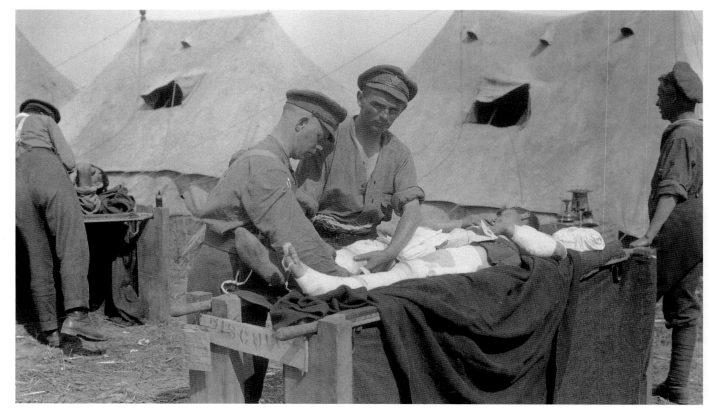

The Allies losses were appalling and it was impossible to cope with the wounded. A field hospital.

British wounded awaiting collection.

The British threw everything into the defense. An eighteen-pound field gun defending St. Albert on March 28, 1918.

The German advance found heavy-going across difficult terrain.

The Battlefield at Armentières between April 9 and 11. The Germans attack the town from this position.

Wounded of the 51st Highland Division on their way to a field post behind the front.

Wounded British soldiers at a dressing station at Merville that fell into German hands that day (April 8, 1918).

attack. The plan was for the Seventeenth Army to advance towards Bapaume before swinging north to Arras. The Second Army had Péronne as its target. After investing this place it was to swing north towards Doullens, while the chief task of the Eighteenth Army was to press towards the Somme in order to protect the right flank of the Seventeenth and Second Armies against French counter attacks. Ludendorff intended in this manner to force a breakthrough before then rolling up the front, forcing the British towards the Channel coast while threatening Paris on the other side, splitting the two Allied forces before then destroying them.

British troops defending the canal at Merville, April 8, 1916.

British field gun at the bridge at Vermont.

Horses pulling a munitions wagon killed by shellfire.

A six-inch Mark VII gun at Goesteren on April 23, 1918.

German transport column on its way to the front passes seated British prisoners of war waiting to be taken to the rear.

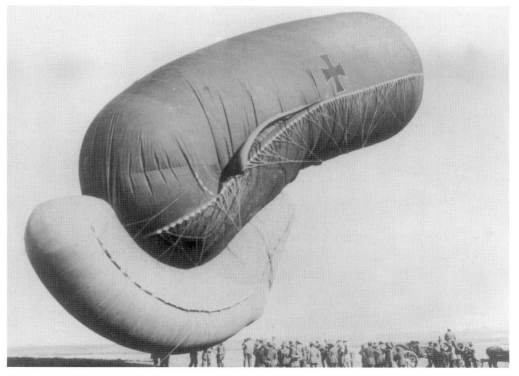

A German artillery spotting balloon is raised.

Left: The number of wounded increased.

German troops ride to the front on a narrow gauge railway.

The British were weak at the point chosen. The northern sector was held by the British Third Army under General Byng (14 divisions), while the British positions to the south were in the hands of General Gough's Fifth Army. To the south of the British lay the Sixth French army under General Duchêne.

The Eighteenth Army quickly made the most rapid progress after the German attack was launched. The British Third Army offered fierce resistance but the forward British lines to the south were captured around noon and the second line fell by the evening. Ludendorff now modified his plan and moved the main thrust of his attack to the south. By the third day General Gough had to withdraw his troops behind the Somme. Hutier was now ordered to advance along both sides of the Somme, attacking both the British and French in an effort to create the required split. The German troops swung towards Arras in the north and Amiens in the center while the

Right: British machine-gun posts await the enemy.

German infantry attacks the Aisne canal in May 1918.

German infantry crosses a road under British fire.

German troops press forward. German infantry attacks near Fisnes on May 27, 1918.

A fresh glass of milk during a break from fighting at Soissons, May 1918.

Eighteenth Army advanced towards Paris. The rapid breakthrough quickly ground to a halt though. Rapidly deployed reserves succeeded in halting the Germans near Amiens and the Eighteenth Army attempting to break through at Noyon was forced to halt because its troops were exhausted and needed rest. On April 4 a further effort to break through at Arras was made but this attack lacked the necessary strength and on April 5, Ludendorff was forced to halt the offensive.

OPERATION GEORGE IS A SECOND ATTEMPT

Ludendorff was already making plans for a second offensive on April 7. The troops were to attempt to break through to the north and south of Armentières. Nine German divisions attacked on April 9 at Armentières. This area was defended by four Portuguese divisions which crumbled under German pressure and ran away in panic. A gap almost four miles wide was created through which the Germans rapidly moved their troops. The attack to the north of the town was also successful and on April 11, the two armies tried to link up.

The following day it appeared as if the breakthrough would succeed. Haig sent in reserves but these were unable to change

The Germans captured Kemmel near Ypres from the French.

A German soldier throws a hand grenade during fighting near Soissons.

German soldiers in a trench captured from the French on Kemmel hill.

German rail troops prepare to lay a narrow gauge railway towards the British trenches at Ypres...

... which were soon captured.

the situation. Entreaties to Foch to come the their aid were ignored. Haig's orders of the day now stressed the importance of defending at all cost because a German breakthrough would prove fatal. He charged General Plumer with the defense on this front and he had the good sense to reduce the width of the front even though this meant ceding ground that had been fought over at the cost of thousands of British lives but this worked. The German advance through difficult terrain was delayed and eventually ground to a halt on April 29 when Ludendorff called a halt to this offensive. The Germans had lost 350,000 men, the British 305,000.

A THIRD EFFORT WITH THE HAGEN PLAN
Once again Ludendorff directed his effort at the British sector. He was certain the British were severely weakened and that a large-scale attack would succeed. This operation was named the Hagen

Paris was brought under artillery fire. One of the long-range German guns that fired on Paris.

Plan. In order to divert as many British and French troops from the northern sector he first planned a feint at Chemin des Dames. In addition to this there would be an attack by the Eighteenth Army of Hutier, the Seventh Army of General Boehn, and the First Army of von Mudra comprising forty-one divisions across a front of more than 22 miles between Anizy and Berry-au-Bac. This area was defended by four British and seven French divisions of the Sixth Army of General Duchêne. Ludendorff's aim was to break through here to the Soissons–Reims line and the attack was thoroughly prepared.

The Germans opened fire on May 27 with about four thousand guns that fired at the French and British positions continuously for four hours. After this there was a rolling artillery barrage behind which stormtroops advanced. The attack was a tremendous success, in part due to the poor defensive positions of the French Sixth Army. The attackers punched straight through the French lines and on May 30 had already taken 45,000 prisoners of war, captured some 400 guns and thousands of machine-guns. Reinforcements were rushed to the gap and managed to delay the German thrust. After taking

German artillerymen fasten the caps to shells for the guns firing on Paris.

Assembled British prisoners of war wait to be taken away.

Chateau Thierry, American troops succeeded in holding the Germans. Paris was now directly threatened and panic was great among the Allies. On June 1 the Germans held positions some forty miles from Paris and had taken 65,000 prisoners of war. Reims was also threatened but supplies were now more difficult and their soldiers were exhausted. The advance was further delayed because German troops diverted to looting Allied stores that were captured and gorged themselves on food and drink and did not respond to orders. Ludendorff could no longer supply sufficient reserves either and on June 3 he decided to halt the offensive and gave his men a rest.

Dogs were also used at the front. Here one brings food to the front line.

A German field wireless telegraph station powered by a dynamo driven by two "cyclists."

FOURTH ATTEMPT WITH OPERATION GNEISENAU

Ludendorff ordered a new offensive on June 9, once again with Hutier's Eighteenth Army, eleven front line divisions and seven reserve divisions supported by five hundred aircraft and 625 artillery batteries. The divisions were no longer at full strength though following the losses in previous attacks, often being no more than half strength and with many inexperienced recruits. The food situation was also critical. There was no fodder for the horses and food supplies for the troops were minimal. Many soldiers suffered hunger leading to wide-scale looting and also desertion.

The attack took place with nine divisions along a front of some twenty-two miles between Montdidier and Noyen and within hours reached the Oise where the troops broke through between Rollot and Thiescourt across a six mile sector to the west of Méry. The French sent reinforcements and managed to hold the attackers. On June 11 they mounted a counter attack and halted the German offensive at a cost of 40,000 men. The Germans lost 25,000 men in this offensive. The German offensives had gained them a lot of ground and some 212,000 prisoners of war but failed in parting the French and British armies.

FIFTH EFFORT, OPERATION MARNESCHUTZ AND THE BATTLE OF REIMS

Ludendorff decided to make a final attempt at a decisive offensive. In spite of warnings to wait until his troops were strong enough and had rested he decided to take the risk of a new attack. He believed the war had to be finished in 1918 before the Allies became much stronger with the arrival of US troops while his own troops became progressively weaker and could not fight much longer. He had forty-nine divisions available and gave General Boehn's Seventh Army orders to cross the Marne to the east of Château Thierry in order to take Tére-Chamenois. The First and Third Armies of von Mudra and von Einem were to attack east of Reims in order to occupy Châlons sur Marne.

Ludendorff was remarkably optimistic and completely certain the attack would succeed. This attack he declared would be the absolute defeat for the Allies and would bring Germany the victory it had been fighting for so long. This optimism is difficult to understand given the severe weakening of his forces. The four offensives had lost him almost half a million men (95,000 dead) and he lacked reserves. The reserves that had come from the east front brought many problems with them. Their discipline was very poor and they lacked any enthusiasm. The numbers of deserters increased alarmingly.

A British look-out post near Ypres.

British collection point for bandages that were washed and re-used.

German troops moved once more though on July 15. The attack was preceded by mustard gas that had no effect because the wind was in the wrong direction. The First and Third Armies immediately ran into heavy resistance and made little progress, not least because of the lack of artillery support. The Seventh Army did make progress and advanced over four miles across the Marne to take French positions. Because of the lack of progress by the First and Third Armies the link between them and the Seventh Army put them in danger and General Boehn asked permission to withdraw. Ludendorff, seeing yet another offensive failure in which he had pinned so much hope hesitated to agree and by the time he did it was already too late. Meanwhile he decided to give the go-ahead for the original Hagen Plan for which he had already positioned troops in Flanders. This never happened because the French mounted a counter attack on July 18 and Ludendorff was forced to drop the Hagen Plan and move the troops intended for it to Soissons.

ALLIED COUNTER-OFFENSIVE

Although severely weakened, the French opened their long-planned counter attack on July 18 with 1,600 guns. The French Tenth Army under General Mangin (10 divisions including 2 US in the first wave and 6 infantry divisions and a cavalry corps in the second together with 2 British divisions in reserve) and the Sixth Army under General Degoutte (7 divisions including 2 US divisions and 1 reserve division in the second wave) against the German Seventh Army (5 divisions and 6 reserve divisions), and the Ninth Army (6 divisions and 2 reserve divisions). American troops were present in large numbers for the first time (about 85,000 men). Three other US divisions (each US division comprised of 17,000 men and was much larger than Allied or German divisions) were on their way to the front. This supremacy in the numbers of the Allies slowly but surely forced the Germans back and Ludendorff was now advised by his staff to withdraw to the Siegfried Line. Fearing the political consequences of this for his fatherland and the morale of his troops, he rejected the advice. He did not have any reserves available to halt the Allied offensive and the pressure became stronger.

Dead French soldiers in a trench captured by the Germans.

Marshal Joffre visits the front, October 1918.

Luck was on his side this time for the French had also suffered heavy losses (about 160,000 men) and they were also no longer able to find replacements. The Allied offensive ground to a halt therefore on July 22. The Germans lost 110,000 men and had no prospect of replacing them.

Ludendorff, who still planned to get the Seventh Army to hold its position, was forced by Hindenburg to abandon this idea and to withdraw his troops behind the Marne. He was very depressed and made a nervous and forlorn impression on his staff and commanders. This is not surprising for the great reverse had started and the German commander in chief had lost the initiative to the Allies.

AUGUST THE EIGHTH: A BLACK DAY FOR THE GERMAN ARMY

There was a period of relative calm following the counter-offensive which enabled the Allies to reinforce their positions and to give exhausted troops some rest.

Meanwhile they planned to push the Germans back further. This time the British Fourth Army under General Rawlinson (who succeeded General Gough who was fired in March) and the French First Army under General Debeney were to jointly mount an

Britain's King George and King Albert of Belgium also visited the front.

German troops march to new positions further back in September 1918...

...leaving devastation behind them.

Right: Barely a brick left standing as part of a strategic withdrawal to hinder the Allied pursuit.

Retreating German troops blow up a railway yard.

The Germans managed to save most of their guns. A battery of 210 mm (8 inches) howitzers prepares to withdraw, October 1918.

German soldiers shelter in a shell crater, October 1918.

German troops during the withdrawal to the Hindenburg line.

Retreating German troops come under heavy Allied shellfire.

A large French howitzer shell explodes in the center of German positions.

It was bitterly cold in November. A German sentry surveys the snowy landscape.

offensive against the German Second Army of General Marwitz and the Eighteenth Army of General Hutiers between the River Avre and St. Albert.

Two thousand Allied guns laid down furious fire early in the morning of August 8 along a front of about six miles followed by a tank attack with 450 tanks that were followed by infantry. By that

A German machine-gun captured by the Allies at Landreville, November 7, 1918.

A German 85 mm (3.3 inches) trench mortar ready to fire. This type of mortar bomb is still found on the old battlefield in France.

Left: The Germans placed anti-tank obstacles everywhere.

A German 210 mm (8 inches) howitzer captured by American troops.

German Schneider howitzer.

Camouflaged US gun, July 27, 1918.

US troops ready to attack behind a smoke screen.

German mortar bunker at Varneville captured by US troops on October 22, 1918.

German trenches in the Bois des Esparges where the US 261st Regiment led the attack on September 19, 1918.

Left: Dead German soldier at Hamel.

Rail-mounted 14 inch gun fires at German positions in the Argonne woods.

There was great chaos during the American advance. A huge traffic jam near St. Michiel.

evening the British troops had penetrated nearly ten miles into the German line, taken 16,000 prisoners of war, and captured hundreds of guns.

The French were less successful and made slower progress. They did capture about five thousand Germans though and 160 guns but rapid German reinforcements managed to slow and then halt the Allied offensive. This was a reason for General Rawlinson to seek Haig's - permission to end the offensive. Haig agreed but Marshal Foch demanded that the British first take Péronne and Ham in order to push the Germans back behind the Somme. The British Fourth Army made an attempt to do this the following day without success and this time Haig dug his toes in and ended the attack. The losses were heavy

American soldiers study a German warning of air raids after their capture of Bayonville.

once more. Of the 450 tanks only sixty-seven survived while the French and British lost 45,000 men to the German's 75,000. The Franco–British counter attack did not succeed in forcing a breakthrough although it was clear the Allies had now taken the initiative.

Although the German troops had halted the Allied offensive their commander in chief regarded it as a disaster. Although they had succeeded in halting the advance, the breakthrough had come as a shock. For the first time it was apparent the will to win was absent from the German troops. Entire units had surrendered to the enemy, soldiers no longer obeyed their officers, and hundreds of thousands deserted. Ludendorff realized for the first time that it was over for the German army and that victory was no longer possible. In his memoirs he later

The German government tried to get money to pay for the war right to the end. A poster that tried to interest the public in new war loans.

American first aid post in a ruined church at Neuville, September 26, 1918.

Wounded American soldiers at a hospital in Paris.

Left: Supplying troops in the front line. American soldiers carry bread to the front.

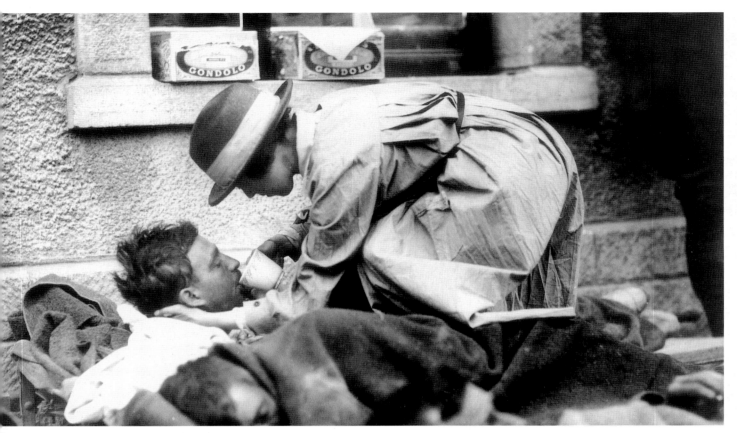

A Red Cross nurse gives a drink to a badly wounded man.

The clothing of soldiers affected by a mustard gas attack is collected and burnt.

Right: An American hospital train takes wounded to Paris.

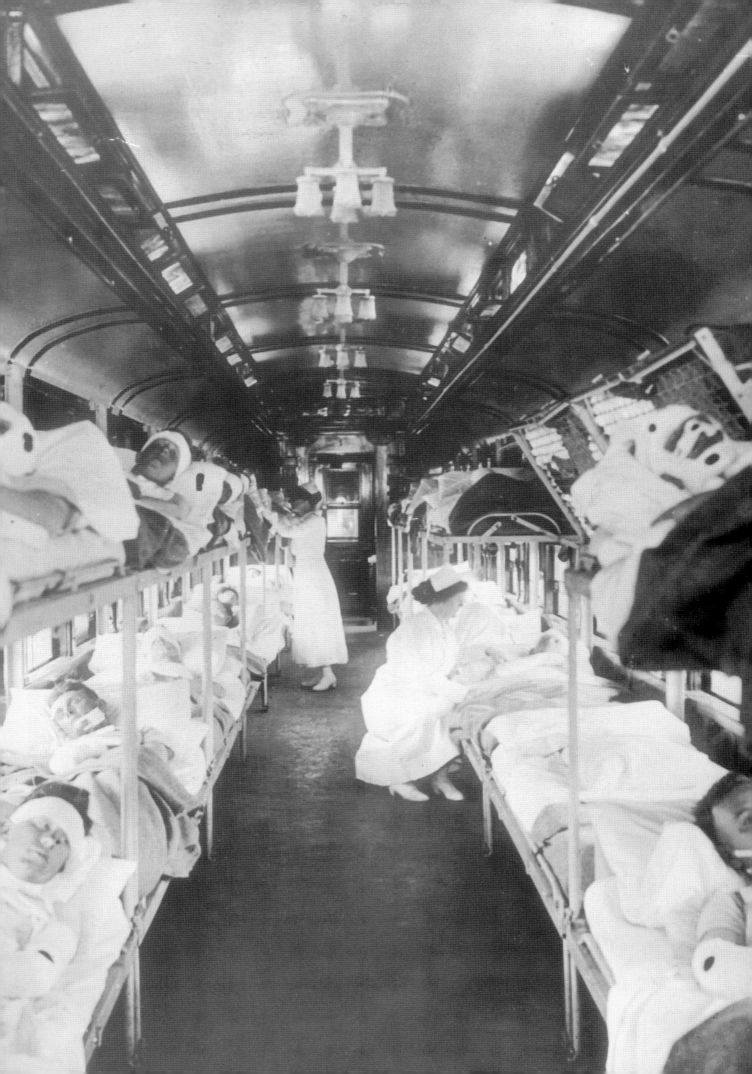

An US Army chaplain holds a field service.

The 39th Regiment of the US 93rd Division comprised African American soldiers under French command. They held positions and fought near Maffrecourt in May 1918. They fought well and many were awarded French decorations.

The US 326th Infantry Regiment attacks on August 1, 1918.

The American troops often suffered unnecessary losses through their inexperience.

US troops during their march to the important German railhead of Soissons.

wrote he felt betrayed by his own troops, that it was no longer sensible to continue the war, which should now be ended. From henceforth Germany would have to limit itself to defense and continued fighting could only serve to win time for peace talks with the enemy. Once again he refused to withdraw his troops. The troops should hold where they were and were needed to defend the forward defense line. To achieve this he sent as many reinforcements as possible but this of course significantly weakened other fronts.

That same day he informed Hindenburg and the Kaiser of the situation and explained that he no longer considered victory possible. Wilhelm II listened in a deathly hush and then called a meeting with the Chancellor and minister of foreign affairs at the headquarters at Spa. The meeting took place on August 13. Ludendorff brought them up to date on the situation and stated that victory was no longer possible. He added that the Allies were also at the end of their tether and that his new strategy was for a strong and rugged defense of the territory currently occupied. He was

The US 308th Regiment after capturing the German second line in the Argonne woods north of Four de Paris.

Communication was still primitive. Tanks were not equipped with radios. A homing pigeon is released from a tank with a message for the command post.

French tanks made a big contribution to the advance by US troops at Soissons in 1918.

Allied tanks in the attack at Soissons.

American troops dig in near Nanteuil on June 29, 1918.

US troops attack near St. Barbe on August 13.

American casualties were heavy during this attack.

Left: US 326th Regiment attacks at Choloy on August 1.

American troops again in action on October 8. The 30th Division attacks at Fremont.

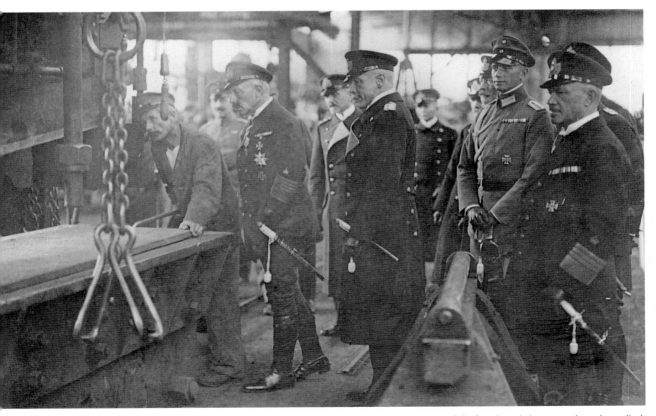

Kaiser Wilhelm II visits an arms factory in October 1918, a month before his abdication where he called on the workers to stop work.

convinced this would break the will of the Allies to fight on and force them to consider peace. This was a far too rosy picture of the situation at that time and devoid of reality and quite over optimistic. The Chancellor wanted to make preparations for opening peace talks but Ludendorff was strongly opposed. Peace talks could only take place he said after victory and although the situation was serious, it was not without hope. Von Hertling and minister Hinze left for Germany with heavy hearts but with their fears to some extent

Dead German soldiers during the American advance.

There was a shortage of everything in Germany. A poster begs women to collect their hair for the defense industry.

The German Kaiser talks to a worker during his visit to Keil.

American reserves pass along the Marne.

View of the American front line from "A" Company, June 14, 1918.

American field bakery. Its fifty-four bakers and eight ovens baked 54,000 loaves every day in the field.

Use of savage and heartless means of war: a mantrap.

The battle for Argonne wood. The Varenne-Four de Paris road on November 4, 1918.

German prisoners of war captured by the US 27th and 33rd Divisions.

Caught at the last moment. Four German spies in US uniforms were discovered and executed on the spot, November 1918.

An American soldier prays by a surviving crucifix at Somme Dieu in November 1918, amid death and destruction.

assuaged after Hindenburg also declared that they must not forget that German troops still occupied enemy territory and were likely to remain there.

It was quickly apparent in view of the true situation at the front that the confidence shown by the commander in chief was ill-founded and that holding their positions was not possible. The Allies were now planning a further great offensive with considerable American help for which the Germans did not have

A Canadian soldier calls for any hiding Germans to come out at a captured German dug out. Dury, September 2, 1918.

the troops and it soon became obvious to both Ludendorff and Hindenburg that they must accept that the situation was hopeless. In order to save whatever possible they now demanded the government to ask for a cease fire and warned that this must happen quickly because every day it was delayed would lead to a total disaster. This demand shocked the government. They now felt forced to call for a cease fire while holding no cards, in a position of weakness, and under the worst possible circumstances. A great drama was about to take place.

GERMANY CALLS FOR A CEASE FIRE

The German offensives of March to July had achieved tactical victories but not the strategic breakthrough intended and with this failure the possibility for the war to be won by armed conflict was ended. In March Germany still had a significantly larger force but this was considerably changed in July. The final offensive cost 700,000 men and between July and October the Germans lost a further 800,000 men. The total German casualties since the start of the war in 1914 amounted to 4.5 million dead, wounded, missing, and prisoners of war and there simply were not enough men living to replace these losses. It was not even possible to find the manpower to build positions behind the front lines. Many divisions at the front existed only in name or were only partially manned.

At the same time the Allied fighting strength was steadily growing. By the start of November 1918 the US troops landed in France amounted to 1.8 million men and a further 200,000 to 250,000 were added each month. These American troops were only partially ready for combat of course and very inexperienced.

It seems very odd that the Allies appear not to have been aware of just how serious a condition the German forces were confronted.

A British soldier stands in the "impregnable" Hindenburg line.

Although the feeling grew that the Allies had now seized the initiative from the Germans it was felt the war would continue for some time to come and certainly into 1919 in view of the stiff opposition still posed by the Germans in defense. There was concern about whether the public would continue to support the war. The Allies own losses were huge, amounting to 850,000 men between March and July. The losses between July and November were even bloodier. The French lost 530,000 men, the British 410,000, and the

Marshal Foch. The German delegation asked him for his proposals. He said he had none.

The Allies met on July 2, 1918 to establish their cease fire demands.

British Prime Minister Lloyd George during the Inter-Allied Conference of July 2, 1918.

The US representative at Allied HQ, General H. Bliss.

Americans 300,000, amounting to 2,100,000 in all. This was not all. It was not just the German divisions that had been decimated, British divisions had been reduced from twelve battalions to just nine and in May ten divisions were scrapped for lack of manpower. The offensive capacity of the French army had never been fully restored following the great mutiny of 1917 and depended entirely on British and later also American support. The Allies too had virtually exhausted their reserves. In June 1918 the Allies asked President Wilson to send four million men immediately or the war would be lost. This demand for four million men is absurd. It amounts to more than the total Allied forces in France at that time but it does indicate how bad things were for the Allies at this time and also that they had no indication of how bad things were for the Germans. The Allied generals could plan great offensives but they lacked the manpower to successfully carry them out.

There was another important matter. President Wilson had put forward peace proposals that the Allies were wholeheartedly

The new German Chancellor, Prince Max von Baden, who was given the task of initiating cease fire talks with the Allies.

Churchill at Lille immediately before the cease fire, October 24, 1918.

General von Winterfeldt, head of the German cease fire commission on November 29, 1918.

Herr Erzbrger, member of the German Reichstag and of the cease fire commission following a talk with Marshal Foch in his train.

Members of the cease fire commission on their way to Marshal Foch.

opposed to. The US government had let it be known that if the Allies rejected their peace proposals they might make a separate peace agreement with the enemy. This had to be avoided at any cost for it was not possible to win the war without the Americans. The British were of the opinion that if it appeared the war would continue much longer it would be sensible to hold peace talks quickly with the Germans from a position of strength when more favorable terms could be demanded than those put forward by President Wilson. They were keen to prevent the American position prevailing with them forcing their terms on the other allies. The increasing number of US troops on French soil made the likelihood of the US view prevailing more likely by the day.

This was the situation then when the German high command decided to ask its government to bring about a cease fire. That request came like a bolt of lightning from a clear blue sky for the German people. Up to then the high command had openly maintained that victory was possible in spite of all the sacrifices. On August 13 Hindenburg and Ludendorff had continued to claim that at the very least the Germans could hold the territory they had occupied and could force an honorable peace. They had rejected the notion of peace talks. Now, suddenly, a cease fire would be a saving

Allied members of the cease fire commission at Spa. From left to right: Lieutenant-General Sir Richard Haking (GB), Major-General Rhiodes (USA), and General Dunant (France).

grace and this news caused shock, disbelief, and a lack of confidence among the German people. It was just the signal the revolutionaries in the land needed to start a revolution and hence to bring the war to a definite end.

The German high command brought this revolution on its own heads by systematically misleading the public about the situation at the front. When the reality finally became public it had the effect of a thunderous shock wave that wiped away the last vestige of hope

Announcement of the cease fire in Le Havre.

Street scene in Winchester, England when the Armistice is announced.

There was jubilation too in Germany. Returning troops are greeted as heroes.

Left: A jubilant crowd gathers outside Buckingham Palace on November 11, 1918 to celebrate the Armistice.

A jubilant crowd outside the royal palace as German soldiers return home.

and trust among the German public, with all the consequences that stemmed from that. The cease fire request was also a great shock for the Allies and wholly unexpected. Given that it now appeared the Germans wanted to stop fighting at any cost the Allies could raise their demands for terms as high as possible. This became clearer still during the peace talks. The dice had been thrown. Germany had lost the struggle and was forced to accept armistice and later peace demands that held the seeds of the next and even more appalling war that broke out some twenty years later, when once again the USA would need to come to the rescue. History repeats itself but this lesson had not been learned with tragic consequences.

Left: German troops march into Berlin with banners waving and drums beating. There was no sense of defeat.

German troops left behind in Russia return home by train.

Hindenburg's private quarters at Spa.

Right: Lightly wounded British soldiers return home.

Ludendorff's quarters in Spa.

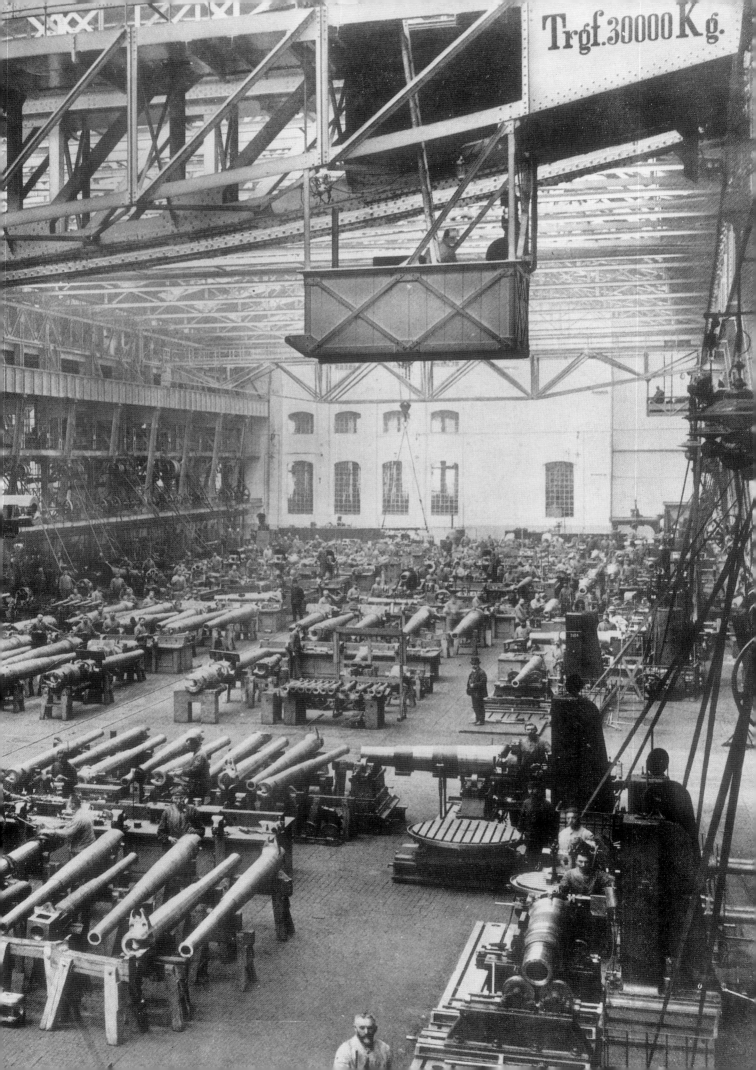

PEACE WITHOUT VICTORS

THE ARMISTICE NEGOTIATIONS

There were already German politicians in 1917 who no longer believed that a victory was possible and called for a quick peace. One of these was Erzberger, who discovered from a friend in the armed forces that the military situation for Germany was becoming increasingly difficult and that their ally, Austria-Hungary might be forced to end the war unilaterally. Erzberger formed a group of members of the Reichstag consisting of those of the center, social

The British commander in chief, General Haig with his officers on Armistice Day, November 11, 1918.

Left: The enormous armament factories of Krupp had to be dismantled.

US Sergeant Philips fires the very last shot of the war from the American sector at Meuville-sur-Meuse on November 11, 1918.

American troops cross the Luxembourg border on their way to Germany on November 20, 1918.

British troops on their way to Cologne.

The British King George V and his consort Queen Mary on their way to St. Paul's Cathedral for a commemoration service for the Armistice.

democrats, and progressives who drew up a "peace resolution" as an initiative to bring an early peace. They believed that first the constitution needed to be amended to a parliamentary system. Their plan quickly gained wide support and was eventually, if reluctantly, accepted by the Kaiser.

The Chancellor, Bethmann Hollweg, did not regard the moment opportune to implement the plan although he was largely in favor of it and therefore the peace plan ended up in a drawer and an early introduction of a parliamentary system was deferred.

There were others who worked towards peace. The way was led by President Wilson's ambition for peace which he put his strength behind. His first major effort at mediation between the warring parties took place shortly after the torpedo attack on the British ship *SS Lusitania* in 1915. Wilson summoned the German ambassador and suggested that Germany stop the submarine war in return for US pressure on the British to halt the sea blockade of Germany but this attempt got nowhere.

Somewhat later the President send his emissary Colonel House to Britain in the winter of 1915–1916 for talks with the Foreign Secretary, Edward Grey, in which he raised the possibility of peace talks.

House repeated this visit to Grey several months later when he strayed outside the principles of strict neutrality. He asked Grey what his wishes were and told him the USA would like to do everything possible to help the Allies win the war. He said: "The USA wanted the British government to do what would enable the USA to do what was necessary for the Allies to win the war."

He came more openly out behind the Allies when he then visited Paris and declared that if the Allies should lose the US government would support them. The Allies took this to mean that USA would side with the Allies but House later stated this had not been his meaning and that this conclusion was wrong, although he did not explain what he actually meant.

US President Wilson made a special visit to Britain. Shown here visiting Manchester on December 30, 1918.

House then proposed peace talks for which he would ensure the points for discussion should express the Allies' standpoint. If Germany then rejected these points the USA would then enter the war on the side of the Allies. Matters were committed to the famous House-Grey Memorandum of January 22, 1916. The "snake in the grass" of this apparently so favorable memorandum lay in the fact that the Americans were to dictate the peace terms if the proposal was accepted and this was greatly opposed in both Britain and France. For this reason this plan was not pursued and once more a peace initiative by the US President came to nothing.

At the end of 1916, following its victory against Romania, Germany approached the Americans and asked the President to make a further effort at mediation. The President was positive to this approach and sent a note to the combatants asking them under what terms they would accept a lasting peace. This note came in for severe criticism from the Allies. The Allies were annoyed that President Wilson had not yet openly sided with the Allies. Despite this, the

Crowds cheer the US President Wilson during a procession through London.

The German foreign minister, Brockdorff-Rantzau who headed the German mission to the Armistice talks in 1919. "We could feel the hatred towards us when we came in. The admission of guilt from my mouth would be a lie..."

Allies reluctantly did what he asked and presented their demands. The nub of these was that Germany was to surrender unconditionally.

Germany also responded without much enthusiasm and sent a somewhat half-hearted and ambiguous response. Those waging war were clearly not yet ready to consider peace and became increasingly more hostile towards each other. Despite this the Germans realized that their position was unlikely to get better in the long term and hence they grasped at the weapon of the unrestricted

President Wilson leaving the Armistice Conference on May 17, 1919 at which the Germans received the peace proposals.

submarine war so that the inequality between the parties could be removed.

The US President continued to pursue peace and on January 22, 1917 he gave a resounding address in which he called on the world to support his astonishing plan for peace. The main theme of this was for a "Peace without Victory" or victors. The parties were to agree peace on the basis of existing agreements concerning the freedom of the seas, the right of self determination for all peoples, ending of all secret alliances and treaties, and a withdrawal to the former own territory. This was all to be on a basis of complete equality and without any apportioning of blame.

British Prime Minister Lloyd George leaves the conference.

The palace at Versailles where the Germans signed the peace treaty under protest on June 28, 1919.

This was a noble plan but somewhat naive and everybody rejected it. There was a deathly hush surrounding Wilson and the lack of positive reactions caused Wilson to ask if he should abandon his policy of neutrality and side with the Allies. This hesitancy was strengthened by the *Lusitania* and *Arabic* incidents. The Zimmermann telegram and resumption by Germany of unrestricted submarine warfare closed the door on peace and made Wilson decide to side with the Allies. On February 3, 1917, he broke off diplomatic relations with Germany after they had announced a resumption of unrestricted submarine warfare. On April 2, 1917, America declared war against Germany.

PRESIDENT WILSON'S FOURTEEN-POINT PLAN

Although The USA was now officially on the side of the Allies this did not prevent President Wilson from pursuing his peace initiatives. On the contrary, his decision to enter the war went hand in hand with the thought that this would give him much more influence with those waging the war than when the USA was not engaged in the war. By being involved he would be able to make demands of the Allies and if necessary back these from a position of strength.

Meanwhile he worked throughout the summer and part of the winter of 1917–1918 on his "Peace without victory" plan and gave his

A wing of the palace of Versailles.

famous fourteen point address on January 8, 1918 that was greatly acclaimed in the USA.

Unfortunately people were less enthusiastic in Europe. The Allies did not agree any one of the fourteen points. The French Prime Minister Clemenceau made a caustic remark and The Times remarked that Wilson perhaps thought the Final Judgment had already been brought down to earth. Germany also reacted coolly and not very positively.

The President's plan comprised of a number of important issues such as the freedom of the seas, the removal of economic barriers, the return of Alsace-Lorraine to France, a free and fair ruling in respect of colonial agreements in which the interests of the people concerned themselves should carry equal weight, self-determination for the Balkan countries, the opening of the Dardenelles, and the creation of a League of Nations in which every nation, large and small should possess the same rights of political independence and territorial integrity.

At first glance this was a brilliant plan but to make it work in practice was a different matter. The total freedom of the seas would not be acceptable for the British whose rule over the seas lay deep in the national psyche. For Germany the return of Alsace-Lorraine was equally unpalatable and no one agreed with the proposals regarding colonies. The negative reactions did not discourage Wilson though. On the contrary he gave an address on February 11 in which he added four more or less new points (The four principles) to the earlier fourteen. This held that in so far as possible the aspirations of the leaders of territories governed by colonial powers should be acceded to and that every territorial agreement should be in the interests of the people of that territory.

This address was also widely criticized. In Britain they immediately thought about their Empire. What Wilson was proposing was a dismantling of the British Empire and the British were not prepared to accept this but once again the President took little notice of the criticism. On June 4, 1918, he added a further four points to his "manifesto." In summary they can be described as follows:

1. Impartiality and justice between peoples.
2. A definite ruling in respect of self-determination.
3. The same moral principles for all people.
4. Further detail to be worked out for a world peace organization.

This time the situation in the war worked to Wilson's advantage. The Germans had begun a major offensive in March and the Allies

The British Imperial War Cabinet.

had been forced to retreat everywhere. The Allies were now afraid they might lose the war and therefore they pleaded with Wilson to send his troops. Now that they needed him it seemed they were more ready to listen to Wilson's proposals and plans.

The President responded by adding yet new proposals of "the five particulars" to his plan. A major point was the demand that there should be complete equality for all participants in future peace talks, that all existing secret agreements between countries should be made public and that secret alliances and treaties were to be banned.

The British Prime Minister Lloyd George promised the British public he would squeeze Germany like "the pips from a lemon."

The demand that each party should be treated as equals was very important for Germany which had seen its initially successful March offensive fail and saw its strength being sapped. The German government informed President Wilson on October 4 that it accepted his fourteen point plan as a basis for entering peace talks with the Allies and asked him to initiate talks to bring about a cease fire.

The other Allies were entirely unhappy with Wilson's fourteen point plan or rather his twenty-seven point plan. Clemenceau was

The hall of mirrors in the palace of Versailles, June 8, 1919: the same place where the new German state was launched on January 18, 1871 had ended in disaster with a demeaning peace treaty.

The signatures on the Treaty of Versailles which officially ended World War I but which held the seeds of an even more terrible war twenty years later.

A French regiment at the victory parade in London on July 19, 1919.

unable to stop himself from remarking: "God himself only needed ten commandments," and immediately rejected the German request for a cease fire because he felt the Germans should have approached France and Britain rather than the USA with their request.

The British Prime Minister, Lloyd George, was more realistic towards the proposals. He was concerned that Wilson would press ahead, if necessary without their cooperation and might give too much away to Germany. The sly old fox realized that Wilson's plan was noble and lofty but was not really thought through or at all workable and its points could be significantly modified in the heat and pressure of negotiation.

Eventually the French and British responded that they were prepared under certain conditions to accept Wilson's plan as a starting point for discussion. The President found himself in a awkward predicament after receiving the German note. He knew the other Allies were not jumping at his plan enthusiastically. How would his own people, who he had just got in a mood for war, react to his peace plan? And how sure could he be of the German's true desire for a cease fire?

General Pétain, the "hero of Verdun" receives a high decoration from Britain's King George V on July 19, 1919.

On October 8 he sent the German government a note in which he said that he not only held to his fourteen point plan but that he wanted the Germans to immediately leave the territories it occupied. He also demanded that the German government should speak for the people and not for the Kaiser or commander in chief.

Germany answered positively too on October 12 to these new demands but under pressure from his Allies Wilson now made new demands. He responded on October 14 that there were also military demands to be met that would be made by the Allies. Germany was to end the submarine war immediately and to end its systematic destruction of the occupied territory.

The son of General Pershing and both daughters of General Haig were also present at the celebrations.

General Pershing (USA) and General Haig (UK).

On October 20 the German government responded that it accepted these proposals too but now Wilson demanded that the Kaiser must first abdicate before there could be talks about a cease fire. In view of the revolution that had by then broken out in Germany the Germans were forced to accept this demand too and although the Kaiser had not yet abdicated the German government once more sent a positive response. Wilson sent a draft peace treaty for Germany to study.

Under pressure from Britain and France there were a number of important changes made to Wilson's fourteen point plan. The point about the freedom of the seas vanished and an entirely new point

After the war an independence movement rose up in Belgium demanding independence for Flanders.

was added demanding considerable compensation from Germany, which meant the principle of equality between the parties and of Peace without Victory was completely lost.

Germany had accepted the Wilson plan specifically because of this point and now felt betrayed. In view of the state of anarchy in the country though the government felt obliged to agree the demands in the hope that during negotiation they could modify the peace according to the principles promised by Wilson's fourteen point plan. It was to prove an idle hope.

THE ARMISTICE

Finally by November 8, 1918 a German delegation came to the French town of Compiègne where they were received in a railway carriage by Marshal Foch on behalf of the Allies. Foch asked them the reason for their visit. The German delegate Erzberger said he would

Thousands of Flemish people demonstrated for independence but nothing came of it.

The Allies immediately started demolishing the fortifications and guns at Heligoland in accordance with the Treaty of Versailles.

be pleased to have Foch's proposals for arriving at a cease fire. Foch said he had no proposals.

"We are asking for your response from the Allies," another delegate said. This was followed by silence.

"Do you want a cease fire?" Foch now asked. "If you do then I will tell you our demands," and he then got one of his colleagues to read the demands aloud in French. The German delegation was astounded. The demands amounted to nothing less than an unconditional surrender. Foch pointed out that they could accept or reject these demands. Negotiation was not possible.

The demands included:
1. Immediate vacation of occupied territory.
2. Immediately vacation of the western bank of the Rhine.
3. Making a bridgehead to German territory available.
4. Return of all prisoners of war.
5. Immediate handing over of 5,000 guns, 25,000 machine-guns, 3,000 mortars, 1,700 aircraft, and all submarines.
6. Internment of the entire German fleet.
7. Payment of the cost of an Allied army of occupation in Germany.
8. Restoration of all damage done in the territories occupied by the Germans.

American troops mount guard along the Rhine. Sentries of the "Rainbow" Division stand watch at Nieder Briesig, December 19, 1918.

9 The handing over of 5,000 fully serviceable locomotives, 15,000 wagons, and 5,000 trucks.
10. The economic blockade was to remain in place for the time being.

It is clear the Allies were taking advantage of their knowledge of revolution within Germany. The demands were not terms for a cease fire but formed an immediate part of capitulation demands. There was no negotiation and it was quickly obvious the Allies had no intention of doing so. Germany merely had to comply and was treated as a defeated enemy.

People in Germany still clutched at the straws of Wilson's announcement that the Allies had agreed to his Fourteen Point Plan but the Germans were deceived once more. For the cease fire itself there appeared little else for the delegation to do than to sign the Armistice agreement on November 11 with a metaphoric gun to their head.

THE PEACE TREATY OF VERSAILLES, CHANGING EUROPEAN BORDERS

The Allies started the preparation of the Peace Treaty immediately after the Armistice. It took until June 28, 1919 before the Treaty could be signed under protest by Germany. This was preceded by an embarrassing moment for the Allies. The German delegation went to Versailles in early June in order to receive the definitive peace terms.

When the delegation entered the Hall of Mirrors the hubbub became silent. Clemenceau stood up together with the other two hundred delegates. The German foreign minister, Brockdorff-Rantzau walked at the head of his delegation through the silent mass to the places indicated for them, bowed slightly and sat down.

All the assembled company except Clemenceau sat down. He welcomed those present and then directed himself to the German delegation, saying: "Gentlemen delegates of Germany: we meet here to settle our account once and for all. You asked for peace, we are prepared to grant you peace. We will now give you our terms. You can have time to study them but it must be obvious to you that the Allies wish full compensation. We will await your answer within two weeks, Do you wish to say something?"

Brockdorff-Rantzau stuck up his hand to show he certainly had something to say. When he began to speak he did not stand up but to

One of the many soldiers who did not return await a burial.

A gruesome sight. The bones of hundreds of thousands of dead soldiers are collected.

the surprise of all present remained seated. It was a clear signal and regarded as a slap in the face by everyone, especially as Clemenceau had stood while addressing the Germans.

"We could feel the hatred as soon as we stepped into this room," began the German foreign minister, raising his voice. "You expect us to accept the sole guilt for the war. Such an admission from my mouth would be a lie. Germany and the German people are still steadfastly convinced that they fought a defensive war and I deny here most vehemently that Germany bears all the blame. When you start to talk shortly of compensation I ask you to recall that it took you six weeks to hand us your armistice terms and a further six months thereafter to formulate your peace terms. The hundred thousand innocent German citizens, women, and children who have died of hunger since November 11, 1918 because you continue the blockade were deliberately driven to their deaths after your victory and after you had more than ensured your own safety. I ask you to think of them when you talk of concepts such as guilt and punishment." With these words his address was finished.

There was a deathly hush for a time in the room but then a loud tumult burst forth. Clemenceau hammered the table for silence and

Right: 100,000 tons of bones, the grim harvest from just sector of the war zone.

closed the meeting. The German delegation left the room and people heard Brockdorff-Rantzau say aloud to another member of his delegation: "How dare that senile old fool Clemenceau humiliate us so. The only way I could show my disdain for him was to remain seated. We shall never forget this and this scandal will be erased!" These were prophetic words that were soon fulfilled. The treaty was to have disastrous consequences for the world.

Germany lost thirteen percent of its former territory and ten percent of its population, all its colonies, including all German private possessions in them, almost their entire merchant fleet, and most of its railway equipment which broke the back of the country's economy for a long time.

Worse still, the British blockade continued well into 1919 through which many more Germans, especially women and children, died of hunger. The British wanted to ensure the Germans would not re-establish their trade links too quickly before the British themselves had recovered. Without a merchant fleet the Germans had little chance of that but Germany was also obliged to build at least 200,000 tons of shipping per year for five years for the Allies. Germany was also

forced to ignore its coal deposits in Saarland for thirty-five years. These held more coal than in the whole of France. On top of this Germany was required to pay compensation to the Allies of around 1,000 billion gold Marks while everybody knew the country could not possibly afford this money.

The greatest insult though was the finding of the peace conference that Germany was solely responsible for causing the war and should therefore bear the entire damages. These were not assessed by a neutral commission but by the enemy.

The famous economist Keynes, who was a British delegate at the conference, described the treaty as "immoral and incompetent" and resigned in protest. He was not the only one who protested. Even Lloyd George at the eleventh hour tried to get changes in the treaty

Death for king and country.

but Clemenceau blocked every attempt and strangely enough he was supported by President Wilson. It was the South African statesman General Smuts who later remarked that instead of creating peace they had decided to continue the war in order to turn Europe into a ruin. "The peace treaty will eventually lead to a revolution or a new war," he suggested.

Germany's will to resist had vanished and the country was forced to yield to superior force on pain of occupation by the Allies. There was nothing else that could be done than to accept the scandal and to declare: "Bowing to the overwhelming supremacy but without revising our position concerning the ignored injustice of the peace terms, the government of the German Republic declares itself prepared to accept the peace terms as laid down by the Allies and their countries and to sign them."

And so it was done. A new drama that would become known as World War II was gestated through the Treaty of Versailles of 1919. Preparations for German revenge were soon to get underway.

It was not until 1950 when a group of international politicians and historians met at Verdun that it was officially recognized that no one country or its people was solely responsible for the guilt of World War I but rather a complex chain of events and reactions to them.

Unfortunately once again millions of people had become victims and this recognition came to late for them.

The German delegation leaves the former German HQ at Spa in which the Allied Armistice Commission was located. Note the German sentry.

BIBLIOGRAPHY

Albertini, L., *The Origins of the War 1914* (London 1965)

Anderson, E. N., *The First Moroccan Crisis, 1904–1906* (Chicago 1930)

Andrew, C. M. & Kanya Forstner, A. S., Gabriel Hanataux, 'The Colonial Party and the Fashoda Strategy' in *Journal of Imperial and Commonwealth History* (1975)

Andriessen, J. H. J., *De Andere Waarheid,* (2nd Impression, Amsterdam 1999)

Andriessen, J. H. J. & Dagniaux, S. F. J., *Verdun 1916* (2nd Impression, Amsterdam 1999)

Asprey, R. B., *The German High Command at War* (London 1993)

Asquith, H. H., *The Genesis of War* (London 1923)

Baernreiter, J., *Fragmenten eines Politisches Tagesbuches* (Vienna 1928)

Bailey, T. A. & Ryan, P. B., *The Lusitania Disaster* (New York 1975)

Ballard, R. D., *Op het spoor van de Lusitania* (Amsterdam 1995)

Bainville, M., *Italy at War* (Toronto 1916)

Barlos, I., *The Agadir Crisis* (London, Chapel Hill 1940)

Barth, *Aus der Werkstatt der Deutschen Revolutions Almanach für 1919*

Bennett, G., *Naval Battles of the First World War* (London 1983)

Enver Pasha

Kaiser Wilhelm II

Bentley-Moth, Col. T., *The Memoirs of Marshal Joffre* (London 1932)

Berghahn, Volker R., *Der Tirpitz Plan* (Düsseldorf 1971)

Bethmann Hollweg, T., *Betrachtungen zum Weltkriege* (Berlin 1921)

Bernstein, E., von, *Dokumente zum Weltkrieg 1914* (in color, Berlin 1921)

Beumelburg, W., *Bismarck gründet das Reich* (Berlin, no year)

Birdwoood, Field–Marshal Lord, *Khaki and Gown* (Canberra 1941)

Bismarck, Count Otto von, *Gedanken und Erinnerungen* (Berlin 1911)

Bitten, L., *Österreich-Ungarns Aussenpolitik von der Bosnischen Krise 1908 bis zum Kriegausbruch 1914,* Diplomatic archives of the Austro–Hungarian Foreign Ministry (Vienna 1930)

Blake, R., (Ed.) *The private papers of Douglas Haig 1914–1919* (London 1952)

Bled, J. P., *Franz-Joseph* (Oxford 1992)

Blond, G., *Verdun* (Hamburg 1962)

Bogitchevich, M., *An examination into the causes of the European War.*

Bordeaux, H., *The last days of Fort Vaux,* (London 1917)

Brandis, C. von, *Die Stürmer von Douaumont* (Berlin 1917)

Brook Shepherd, C., *November 1918* (Boston 1981)

Edward Grey

Delcassé

Bruun, G., *Clemenceau* (Connecticut 1968)

Buchan, J., *The Battle of the Somme* (London, no year)

Bucholz, A., *Moltke, Schlieffen and Prussian War Planning* (Oxford 1993)

Buffetout, Y., *Verdun, Images de L'enfer* (Paris 1995)

Bülow, B. von, Count, *Denkwürdigkeiten* (Berlin 1931)

Cain, P. & Hopkins, A. G., *The Political Economy of British expansion overseas* (1980)

Callwell, C. E., Maj–Gen., *Field Marshal Sir Henry Wilson* (London 1927)

Churchill, Winston, *The World Crisis* (London 1923)

Clemenceau, G., *Grandeur and Misery of Victory* (London 1930)

Collin, H., *La Côte 304 et le Mort Homme* (Paris 1934)

Hötzendorff, Conrad von., Feldmarschall, *Aus meiner Dienstzeit* (Munich 1922)

Poincaré

Haldane

Cranon, A, von, *Deutschlands Schicksalbund mit Österreich-Ungarn* (Berlin 1932)

Dalton, Hugh, *With British Guns in Italy* (London, no year)

Dokumente zu den englisch-russischen Verhandlungen über ein Marineabkommen aus dem Jahre 1914 (Berlin 1922)

Documents diplomatiques. Les accords franco-italiens de 1900–1902 (Paris 1920)

Dollinger, H., & Hiltermann, G. B. J., *Geschiedenis van de Eerste Wereldoorlog in foto's en documenten* (Baarn 1969)

Enthoven, H. E., *De dal van Delcassé* (Utrecht 1930)

Erbelding, E., *Vor Verdun* (Stuttgart 1917)

Ettighofer, P. C. *Verdun, das Grosze Gericht* (Gütersloh 1936)

Falls, C., *Caporetto 1917* (London 1966)

Farrar-Hockley, A. H., *The Somme* (London 1983)

Fay, S. B., *The Origins of the World War* (New York 1932)

Ferguson, N., *Virtual History* (London 1997)

Fischer, F., Griff nach der Weltmacht (Düsseldorf 1984)

Fischer, F., *Wir sind nicht hineingeschlittert* (Reinbak 1983)

Fischer, F., *War of Illusions* (New York 1975)

Fischer, K., *Die Kämpfe um die I-Werke* (1982)

Suchomlinov

Fischer, K., & Klink, S., *Spurensuch bei Verdun* (Bonn 2000)

Foch, Marshal, *The Memoirs of Marshal Foch* (London, Gulford 1932)

Frémont (Ed.), *Geschichte der Kampfereignisse über das fort Vaux*

Freud, Sigmund & Bullitt, W., *Thomas Woodrow Wilson* (London 1967)

Geiss, I., *Das Deutsche Reich und die Vergeschichte des Ersten Weltkrieges* (Munich 1985)

Gelfand, L. E., *Britain and the Paris Peace Conferences 1919–1923* (Yale 1963)

Gelfand, L. E., *The Inquiry, American Preparations for Peace 1917–1919* (London 1963)

Gilbert, M., *First World War* (London 1994)

Giles, J., *The Ypres Salient* (London 1979)

Gliddon, G., *The Battle of the Somme* (Sutton 1998)

Admiral Tirpitz

Goodspeed, D. J., *Ludendorff* (Gütersloh 1968)

Gorbett, J., *Naval Operations* (London 1921)

Gras, G., *Douaumont* (Verdun 1949)

Grey of Falloden, E., *Twenty Five Years* (London 1926)

Grupp, P., *Deutschland, Frankreich und die Kolonien* (Tübingen 1980)

Guin, P., *British Strategy and Politics 1914–1918* (Oxford 1965)

Haffner, S., *Eine deutsche Revolution* (Munich 1979)

Haldane, Lord, *Before the War* (London 1920)

Hallauer, Dr., *Die Explosionscatastrophe im Fort Douaumont* (Berlin 1916)

Hamilton, I., *Gallipoli Diary* (London 1920)

Harper, Rear Admiral J. E. T., *The Truth about Jutland* (London 1927)

Hayne, M. B., *The French Foreign Office and the Origins of the First World War* (Princeton 1996)

Headlan, J. W., *The History of Twelve Days* (London 1915)

Heckscher, A., *Woodrow Wilson* (New York 1993)

Heller, A., *Zo waren mijn frontjaren* (manuscript 1919)

Hellmut, D., *Seemacht Politik in 20. Jahrhundert* (Munich 1924)

Henig, R., *Versailles and after* (New York 1995)

Heresch, E., *Verraad, lafheid en bedrog* (Amsterdam 1993)

General Von Hindenburg

Herre, F., *Kaiser Franz-Joseph von Österreich, senie Zeit* (Cologne 1978)

Heijster, R., *Ieper* (Tielt 1998)

Heijster, R., *Verdun, Breuklijn der beschaving* (Rijswijk 1996)

Hillgruber, A., *Deutschlands Rolle in der Vorgeschichte der beiden Weltkriege* (Göttingen 1986)

Hobbing, R., (Ed.), *Der Friedensvertrag von Versailles und das Rheinlandstatut* Berlin 1925)

Horn, D., *War, Mutiny and Revolution in the German Navy* (Brunswick 1967)

Admiral De Robeck

General Hunter Weston

Horne, A., *The Price of Glory* (New York 1963)

Hosse, *Die englisch-belgische Aufmarschpläne gegen Deutschland* (1930)

Hough, R., *The Great War at Sea 1914–1918* (Oxford 1986)

Hughes, C., *Mametz* (London 1985)

Hurst, M., (Ed.) *Key Treaties for the Great Powers* (London 1972)

Japiske, N., *Europa en Bismarcks vredespolitiek* (Leiden 1925)

Jeffery, K., (Ed.) *The Military Correspondence of Field Marshal Sir Henry Wilson* (London 1985)

Jelavich, B., *History of the Balkans* (Cambridge 1983)

Jelavich, B., *The Habsburg Empire in European Affairs 1814–1918* (Chicago 1969)

Jellicoe, Admiral Lord, *The Grand Fleet 1914–1916* (London 1919)

Johnson, J.H., *The unexpected victory* (London 1997)

Jollivet, G., *Le Colonel Driant* (Paris 1918)

Kabisch, G., *Verdun, Wendes des Krieges* (Verdun 1935)

Kann, R., *Kaiser Franz-Joseph und der Ausbruch des Weltkrieges* (Vienna 1971)

Kautsky, K., (Ed.), *Die Deutsche Dokumente zum Kriegsausbruch* (Charlottenburg 1927)

Kautsky, K., *Hoe de oorlog ontstond* (Rotterdam 1919)

Keegan, J., *The Price of Admiralty* (London 1988)

Keegan, J., *The Face of Battle* (Suffolk, Harmondsworth 1983)

Kennedy, P., (Ed.), *The War Plans of the Great Powers 1880–1914* (Boston 1985)

Kennan, G. F., *Russia leaves the War* (New Jersey 1989)

Kenworthy, J. M. & Yong, *Freedom of the Seas* (London 1927)

Kettle, M., *The Allies and the Russian Collapse* (London 1927)

Keyes, Admiral R., *Naval Memoirs* (London 1934)

Keynes, John Maynard, *The Economic Consequences of the Peace* (London 1988)

Kielmansegg, P., Count, *Deutschland und der Erste Weltkrieg* (Kempten 1968)

Liman von Sanders

592

Klüfer, K., von, *Die Seelenkrafte im Kampf um Douaumont* (Berlin 1938)

Knight Patterson, W. M., *Germany from the Defeat to Conquest 1913–1933* (London 1945)

L'Alliance franco-russe. Origines de l'Alliance 1890–1893. Convention militaire 1892–1899 et Convention navale 1912 (Paris 1918)

Laffan, R. G. D., *The Serbs, The Guardians of the Gate* (New York 1989)

Laffin, J., *Damn the Dardanelles* (London 1980)

Lambi, I. *The Navy and German Power Politics* (Boston 1984)

Von Richthofen

Lansing, R., *The Peace Negotiations, a personal narrative* (New York 1921)

Lansing Papers 1914–1920 (Washington D. C. 1940)

Lazarewitsj, D. R., *Die Schwarze Hand* (Lausanne 1917)

Lefebvre, J. H., *Die Hölle von Verdun* (Verdun no year)

Lee, D. E., (Ed.), *The outbreak of the First World War, Causes and Responsibilities* (Lexington, Massachusetts 1970)

Lentin, A., *Lloyd George, Woodrow Wilson and the guilt of Germany* (Louisiana 1985)

Lieven, D., *Nicholas II Emperor of all the Russians* (London 1993)

Lieven, D., *Russia and the origins of the First World War* (London 1993)

Linke, A. S., (Ed.), *The Papers of Woodrow Wilson* (Princeton 1966)

Lloyd George, D., *War Memoirs* (London, Long Acre 1936)

Lloyd George, D., *The Truth about Reparations* (London 1932)

Ludendorff, E., *Meine Kriegserinnerungen 1914–1918* (Berlin 1919)

Lutz, R. H., *The Causes of the German Collapse 1918* (Berlin)

Lijnar, E. W., *Deutsche Kriegsziele 1914–1918* (Frankfurt/Berlin 1964)

Macdonald, L., *Somme* (London 1983)

Mahan, Capt. A. T. *The influence of Sea Power upon history* (London 1890)

Manfred, J., *The United States and Germany* (London 1984)

Marchand, R., (Ed.) *Une Livre Noir. Diplomatie d'avant Guerre, d'apres les documents des archives russes. Novembre 1910–juillet 1914* (Paris 1922)

Marder, J. A., (Ed.), *Fear God and Dread Nought* (London 1959)

Marsden, A., *British Diplomacy and Tunis 1875–1902* (London 1972)

Marston, F. S., *The Peace Conferences of 1919, Organization and Procedures* (Oxford 1944)

Massie, R. K., *Dreadnought* (London 1992)

McMaster, J. B., *The United States in the World War* (New York 1918)

Mee, C. L., *The end of order, Versailles 1919* (New York 1980)

Middlebrook, M. & M., *The Somme Battlefields* (London 1994)

Middlebrook, M., *The Kaiser's Battle* (New York 1988)

Ministère des Affaires Etrangères,

General Monroe

Winston Churchill

Documents Diplomatiques Français 1871–1914 (Paris 1936)

Ministerie van Buitenlandse Zaken, Belgium, *Uit de Belgische archieven 1905–1914. Berichten der diplomatieke vertegenwooordigers van België to Berlijn, Londen en Parijs aan den minister van Buitenlandse Zaken te Brussel*

Moltke, H. von, *Erinnerungen, Briefe, Dokumente 1877–1916* (Stuttgart 1922)

Morel, E. D. F., *Truth and the War* (London 1916)

Morgenthau, H., *Secrets of the Bosporus* (1918)

Morris, A. J. A., *Radicalism against War 1906–1914* (London 1972)

Moulton, H. G., & McGuire, C. E., *Het betalingsvermogen van Duitsland* (Leiden 1923)

Moyer, L., *Victory must be ours* (London 1995)

Muller, J., *Engelands rol bij het uitbreken van de Eerste Wereldoorlog* (Amsterdam 1914)

Müller, Admiral G. A., *Der Kaiser, Anzeichnungen des Chefs des Marinekabinetts* (Zurich 1965)

General Falkenhayn

Neilson, K., *The Anglo-Russian Alliance 1914–1917* (London no year)

Neumann, N., *Die Kämpfe um das Fort Douaumont von 25/2–4/3 1916* (Meckenheim 1999)

Nicholson, H., *Peacemaking 1919* (London 1967)

Nitti, F. S., *Peaceless Europe* (London 1922)

Nowak, K. F., *Die Aufzeichnungen des General Major Max Hoffmann* (Berlin 1930)

Offer, A., *The First World War, An Agrarian interpretation* (Oxford 1991)

O'Keef, K. J., *A Thousand Deadlines. The New York City Press and American neutrality* (The Hague 1972)

Oncken, E., *panthersprung nach Agadir: Die Deutsche Politik während der zweiten Marokkokrise 1911* (Düsseldorf 1981)

Owen, R. L., *The Russian Imperial Conspiracy*

General Pershing

1892–1914 (New York 1926)

Owen, R. L., *Rede über die Kriegsschuldfrage* (Berlin 1924)

Paléologue, M., *La Russie des Tsars pendant la Grande Guerre* (Paris 1922)

Paschall, R., *The Defeat of Imperial Germany 1917–1918* (London, Chapel Hill 1989)

Peeters, J., *België 1914* (Utrecht 1997)

Persell, S. M., *The French Colonial Lobby 1889–1938* (Stanford 1983)

Pershing, Gen. J., *My experiences in the World War* (London 1931)

Pétain, Marshal, *La Bataille de Verdun* (Paris 1938)

Captain Strasser

Poincaré, R., *The Origins of the War* (Melbourne 1922)

Powell, E. A., *Italy at War* (New York 1918)

Radtke, E., *Die Erstürmung von Douaumont* (Leipzig 1938)

Ranke, L. von, *Serbien und die Türkei im 19 Jahrhundert* (Leipzig 1879)

Raynal, Col., *Le drame du Fort Vaux* (Paris 1919)

Renouvin, P., *La Politique extérieure de Th. Delcassé 1898–1906* (Paris 1962)

Reuter, Admiral L. von, *Scapa Flow* (London 1940)

Rhodes James, R., *Gallipoli* (London 1965)

Ritter, G., *The Schlieffenplan* (London 1958)

Robers, S. H., *History of French Colonial Policy 1870–1925* (London 1929)

Robertson, Field Marshal Sir William, *Soldaten und Staatsmänner* (Berlin 1927)

Röhm, Ernst, *Geschichte eines Höchverräters* (Berlin)

Rolo, P., *Entente Cordiale. The Origins and Negotiation of the Anglo-French Agreements* (London 1969)

Romberg, Baron G. von, *Falsifications of the Russian Orange Book* (New York 1923)

Ruge, Vice Admiral F., *Scapa Flow 1919: Das Ende der deutschen Flotte* (Oldenburg 1969)

Scheer, Admiral Reinhard, *Germany's High Seas Fleet in the World War* (London 1920)

Schulte Nordholt, J. W., *Woodrow Wilson* (Amsterdam 1990)

Schwabe, K., *Woodrow Wilson, Revolutionary Germany and Peacemaking 1918–1919* (London 1985)

Seton Watson, R. W., *Sarajevo* (London 1920)

Seymour, C. H., *The Intimate Papers of Colonel House* (Cambridge Mass. 1926)

Sharp, A., *The Versailles settlement* (London 1991)

Siccama, K. H., *De annexatie van Bosnië Herzegovina 5 Oktober 1908–19 April 1909* (Utrecht 1950)

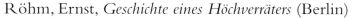

Marshal Foch

Admiral von Scheer

Admiral Jellicoe

Schilling, Baron von, *How the War began in 1914* (London 1925)

Schreiner, G. A., (Ed.), *Entente Diplomacy and the World* (London 1921)

Ambassadeur Page

Simpson, C., *The Lusitania* (Boston 1972)

Suchomlinov, W. A., *Erinnererungen* (Berlin 1924)

Stegemans, H., *Geschichte des Krieges* (Berlin 1917)

Steinberg, J., *Yesterday's Deterrent: Tirpitz and the Birth of the German Battle Fleet* (New York 1965)

Steiner, Z. S., *Britain and the Origins of the First World War* (London 1991)

Tarrant, V. E., *Jutland* (London 1999)

Taylor, A. J. P., *Germany's first bid for Colonies* (London 1938)

Taylor, A. J. P., *The struggle for Mastery in Europe 1848–1918* (Oxford 1984)

Thimmermann, H. von, *Erinnerungen* (Leipzig 1919)

Tsar Nicholas II

Toland, J., *No Man's Land* (London 1980)

Trevelyan, G. M., *Grey of Fallodon* (London 1937)

Tunstall, G. A., *Planning for War against Russia and Serbia* (New York 1983)

Trotsky

Uys, I., *Delville Wood* (Johannesburg 1983)

Vat, D. van der, *The Grand Scuttle* (London 1982)

Waller, Vice Admiral G., *The Fifth Battle Squadron at Jutland* (1935)

Warner, P., *Kitchener* (London 1985)

Watt, R. M., *The Kings Depart. The German Revolution and the Treaty of Versailles* (Suffolk 1973)

Wegener, A. von, *Die Kriegsschuldfrage* (Berlin 1926)

Wendel, H., *Die Ermordung des Erzherzogs Franz-Ferdinand* (1923)

Werth, G., *Verdun, Slacht und Mythos* (1982)

Werth, G., *1916 Schlachtfeld Verdun, Europas Trauma* (Berlin 1994)

Wesseling, H. L., *Verdeel en Heers* (Amsterdam 1991)

Wilhelm II, *Ereignisse und Gestalten 1878–1918* (Leipzig/Berlin 1922)

Wilhelm II, *Gedenkschriften van Keizer Wilhelm*

Marshal Joffre

II (Amsterdam 1922)

Williamson, S. R., *Austria-Hungary and the Origins of the First World War* (London 1994)

General Bliss

Wilson, K., *Decisions for War* (London 1995)

Winter, D., *Haig's Command* (London 1992)

Witte, Count, *Mémoires* (Paris 1923)

Wright, P., *Conflict on the Nile. The Fashoda Incident of 1898* (London 1972)

General Haig

INDEX

PHOTO ACKNOWLEDGEMENTS

All the photographs in this book, with the exception of those marked "aus", originate from The Imperial War Museum, Lambeth Road, London SE1 6HZ, UK. © The Trustees of The Imperial War Museum, London.